NATIONAL GEOGRAPHIC

TRAVELER

Barcelona

![National Geographic logo]

NATIONAL GEOGRAPHIC

TRAVELER

Barcelona

Damien Simonis

National Geographic
Washington, D.C.

Contents

How to use this guide 6–7 About the author 8
Areas of Barcelona 57–202 Excursions 203–238 Travelwise 239–264
Index 265–269 Credits 270–271

Page 1: Gaudí decoration,
Park Güell
Pages 2–3: View over
Barcelona at night
Left: Joan Miró pavement
mosaic, La Rambla

How to use this guide

See back flap for keys to text and map symbols

The *National Geographic Traveler* brings you the best of Barcelona in text, pictures, and maps. Divided into three main sections, the guide begins with an overview of history and culture. Following are eight area chapters with featured sites chosen by the author for their particular interest and treated in depth. A final chapter suggests possible excursions from Barcelona. Each chapter opens with its own contents list for easy reference.

A map introduces each area of the city, highlighting the featured sites and locating other places of interest. Walks and drives,

plotted on their own maps, suggest routes for discovering the most about an area. Features and sidebars offer intriguing detail on history, culture, or contemporary life.

The final section, Travelwise, lists essential information for the traveler—pre-trip planning, getting around, practical advice, what to do in emergencies—plus a selection of hotels and restaurants arranged by area, shops, and entertainment options.

To the best of our knowledge, all information is accurate as of the press date. However, it's always advisable to call ahead when possible.

Color coding

73

Each area of the city is color coded for easy reference. Find the area you want on the map on the front flap, and look for the color flash at the top of the pages of the relevant chapter. Hotel and restaurant listings in **Travelwise** are also color coded to each area.

Museu Frederic Marès

www.museumares.bcn.es
- **Map p. 59**
- **Plaça Sant Iu 5–6**
- **93 310 58 00**
- **Closed from 3 p.m. Sun. & Mon.**
- **$**
- **Metro: Línia 4 (Jaume I)**

Visitor information

Practical information for most sites is given in the side column (see key to symbols on back flap). The map reference gives the page number where the site is shown on the map. Other details include the site's address, telephone number, Web site (if available), days closed, entrance fee in a range from $ (under $4) to $$$$$ (over $25), and nearest metro station for sites in Barcelona. Visitor information for smaller sites is listed in italics and parentheses in the text.

TRAVELWISE

BARRI GÒTIC — Color-coded area name

⊞ COLÓN
$$$$ ★★★★ — Hotel name & price range

AVINGUDA DE LA CATEDRAL 7, 08002 — Address, telephone & fax numbers, Web site (if available)
TEL 93 301 14 04
FAX 93 317 29 15
www.hotelcolon.es

Perhaps the choice hotel in the Barri Gòtic, with views to the Catedral. — Brief description of hotel

⊡ 146 ⊞ Metro: Línia 4 (Jaume I) ⊡ ⊟ ⊠ All major cards — Hotel facilities & credit card details

⊞ CAFÈ DE L'ACADÈMIA — Restaurant name & price range
$$

CARRER DE LLEDÓ 1, 08002 — Address & telephone number
TEL 93 319 82 53

A tiny restaurant in a 13th-century house. Hearty traditional dishes dominate. — Brief description of restaurant

⊞ 50 ⊞ Metro: Línia 4 (Jaume I) ⊡ Closed weekends ⊠ AE, MC, V — Restaurant closures & credit card details

Hotel & restaurant prices

An explanation of the price bands used in entries is given in the Hotels & restaurants section (beginning on p. 247).

AREA MAPS

Point of interest

Important featured site

- A locator map accompanies each area map and shows the location of that region in the city.

WALKING TOURS

Point of interest not on walk route

Direction of walk route

Red numbered bullets link site on map to descriptions in the text

Featured site in bold on walk route

Start point

Building outline

Walk route

- An information box gives the starting and ending points, time and length of walk, and places not to be missed along the route.

EXCURSION MAP

Point of interest

Road number

Grid number

Important point of interest

Drive start point

Important featured town

- Towns and sites described in the Excursions chapter (pp. 203–238) are bolded and highlighted in yellow on the map. Other suggested places to visit are bolded and are shown with a diamond symbol.

NATIONAL GEOGRAPHIC

TRAVELER

Barcelona

About the authors

Damien Simonis, born and bred in Sydney, Australia, has had a little trouble settling down since he took a one-way flight to Cairo in 1989. In his baggage was a B.A. in modern languages from Melbourne University (itchy feet had led him away from Sydney years earlier) and seven years experience as a reporter and copy editor on some of Australia's leading dailies, including the *Australian, The Age,* and the *West Australian.*

Since landing in the Egyptian capital, Simonis has lived, studied, and worked all over Europe and the Middle East. In 1992 he started writing guidebooks and travel articles for publications in Australia, the UK, and North America. He hasn't stopped since. His wanderings have taken him from the Ukraine to the Sudan, from Syria to Morocco, from the Alps to the Strait of Gibraltar. On his two greatest passions, Spain and Italy, he has written extensively. A fluent speaker of Spanish, Italian, French, Catalan, and German (and a stutterer of Arabic), Simonis divides his time in roughly even parts between London, Barcelona, and the road. The feet remain as itchy as ever, and Simonis continues to write and shoot photographs wherever the assignment (or whim) takes him.

History & culture

Lluís Companys, little more than a figurehead leader of Catalunya during the 1936–39 Spanish Civil War

Barcelona today

SOMETIMES THERE IS SOMETHING TO THE CLICHÉS. AS THE AIRCRAFT LOSES altitude for its final approach along the Barcelona waterfront toward the airport, the panorama is stunning. Even in the depths of winter, while cities in less fortunate climes shiver under mantles of snow, sleet, and rain, Barcelona lies resplendent in precocious spring sunshine, its beaches lapped by the scintillating Mediterranean. Like a stage backdrop, a line of low mountains closes ranks behind the packed polis.

Sure, Barcelona has its off days (and in summer the place can be stifling), but the mildness of the climate is just one of the arrows in this ancient but rapidly changing city's quiver. Art, architecture, good food, nightlife, and a certain metropolitan dynamism are just some of Barcelona's trump cards. It is not all wonderful, of course. The city has never really completely shaken off a certain provincial air, a residual chip on the shoulder. It is one of the most densely populated (about 1.5 million inhabitants) and noisiest cities in Europe, and in spite of what seems like an around-the-clock campaign to clear the streets, no one will ever remember Barcelona for being squeaky clean.

In spite of the weather, the "sunny Spain" image of sea, sangria, and siesta only goes so far with Barcelona. Indeed, the more one comes to know the city, the more the sensation grows that one has little to do with the other.

Northern Europeans traveling to Spain in the 19th century, imbibing the self-indulgent ideas of the Romantics, seemed determined to find in this rough and long-neglected land a heady, exotic cocktail of dark flamenco sensuality, an almost oriental mysteriousness. Much of this was little more than a product of a collective, fevered imagination. In Barcelona, midway down the Catalan coast in northeastern Spain, it was harder still to confirm such fantasies. Said the French novelist Prosper Mérimée (1803–1870): "The Catalans seem to me a poor version of the French, a little coarse and with a great desire to make money." Not at all the hot-blooded gypsy atmosphere he had perhaps expected. By way of consolation, he added, comparing Barcelona with other parts of Spain: "If you're interested in talking to intelligent people, ask for Barcelona."

From such remarks other observers frequently go one further. That Barcelona is the "most European" of Spanish cities has by now become a household maxim. "European" means many things to many people. To the disapproving *Madrileños,* the term implies a workaday conformity with an increasingly homogeneous standard that the people of the capital profess to disdain heartily. For them, the "real Spain" is another beast altogether— nocturnal and wild at heart on the one hand, tough and weather-beaten on the other. For others, Barcelona is in the vanguard of the arts in Spain, closely linked with France and hence the rest of "cultured" Europe to the north. It signals efficiency and industriousness, and attracts comparisons with Milan or Brussels.

The Catalans' reputation for being hard working and organized has something to it. In what other town does the last metro run until just midnight from Sunday to Thursday? Got to get people home and tucked in bed early, for tomorrow is another day and another euro. This work ethic and a supposed penchant for penny-pinching doesn't impress many Spaniards from more southerly climes.

They might be surprised to see how much serious partying this city does. From Thursday night onward in particular, the city's restaurants, bars, and discos (and there are many in each category) are full to bursting. La Rambla seems as busy with traffic and pedestrians at 5 a.m. on a Saturday as at 5 p.m. on a Friday. The metro (which stays open until 2 a.m. on Friday and Saturday nights) may have to close, but it is no great problem finding bars and discos open until the small hours. It is not as frenetically hedonistic as its archrival, Madrid, but most other European cities look anemic beside the Catalan capital.

Busy virtually around the clock, La Rambla de Canaletes is the first stage of Barcelona's best known boulevard.

ALWAYS THE BRIDESMAID

It is difficult to escape the impression that Barcelona has an inferiority complex, and whereas you may not feel it in the air, you certainly read it in the press. Like a jealous older sibling whose younger sister's star shines brighter, Barcelona seems to be trying to score points, to justify itself (to itself), and seek its place in the sun. There is a long history to this.

In a sense, the city has almost always been an also-ran. In Roman times it was a self-

Catching the rays on the serpentine public benches of Gaudí's Park Güell; the ceramic design is the work of Josep Maria Jujol.

contented but not terribly important provincial town that cowered in the shadow of Tarraco, the capital of a Roman province encompassing more than half of present-day Spain. In the Middle Ages it was, until the 12th century, at the head of a relatively small principality that gradually carved out for itself

a political and cultural reality—Catalunya. But Catalunya never became a nation.

Even after the Catalan counties were joined with Aragón to create the Crown of Aragón, the count-kings who were its rulers were kings of Aragón but *counts* of Barcelona. The 13th and 14th centuries were the glory days of a city that headed up a considerable merchant empire. But although it prospered, it never enjoyed the prestige and glory of, say, Venice.

The absorption of the Crown of Aragón into a united Spain under the Catholic Monarchs (Ferdinand and Isabella) in the 15th century tied the fate of Barcelona ineluctably to that of a central state that in subsequent years came to be regarded as an oppressor. Until the late 18th century Madrid barred Barcelona from the lucrative transatlantic trade with the American colonies.

The presence of the fortress on Montjuïc and, until the mid-19th century, the enormous Ciutadella, symbolized Barcelona's submission

to an essentially foreign power. Resentment was always latent, but many Barcelonians shrugged their shoulders and with stoic pragmatism set about turning their city into the country's economic powerhouse. The political muscle might well reside in Madrid, but by the end of the 19th century it was clear which of the two cities was in better shape.

Even then Barcelona looked north to Europe. As if profoundly depressed at having to drag along the dead weight of bureaucrati-

Watched over by the Temple del Sagrat Cor, the rides of Tibidabo's Parc d'Atraccions whirl through the night.

cally sclerotic Madrid, Barcelona sought inspiration elsewhere. The city's artists went to Paris, and the art nouveau style that would become *modernisme* in Barcelona filtered down across the Pyrenees. In Madrid, virtually nothing of artistic interest was going on, but with the city's Universal Exhibitions of 1888

and 1929 Barcelona seemed bent on getting the rest of the world to sit up and take notice.

The chaos of the 1930s and the civil war of 1936–39 were heady if tragic moments. For the first time in centuries, the city and its region gained real autonomy. The city, whose workers had since the late 19th century imparted a strong leftist tendency to its politics, was for a while converted into an anarchist "paradise." The end of the war and General Francisco Franco's (1892–1975) victo-

ry again brought repression. Nationalist Madrid ruled in the dark years from 1939 to 1975 and, many claimed, even did what it could to make sure Real Madrid, the country's top soccer team, got the better of Barcelona's champs, FC Barcelona, as often as possible.

The return of democracy and the devolution of many powers to the regions in the late 1970s returned Barcelona to a position of control over its own destiny that it had not enjoyed since 1714. Since then, a duel with

Madrid has continued unabated. With Catalan nationalists under Jordi Pujol in power from the first post-Franco elections in 1980 until 2004, Barcelona engaged in a steady campaign of attrition to win a greater share of political and fiscal power from the central state.

Pujol and his successors have made enormous strides, although their sometimes strident nationalism—most eloquently expressed in the language question—does not appeal to all. The Generalitat (regional government) has

Football Club Barcelona is more than just a soccer team; many locals see their support as an expression of Catalan patriotism.

engaged in an unwavering policy of raising the status of Catalan, which was suppressed during the Franco years and earlier periods. Officially Catalan and Castilian (Spanish) have equal standing now, but in practice Catalan is often favored. Public servants are obliged to speak Catalan, and much education is carried

out primarily in Catalan. Although little statistical proof indicates it yet, some fear that in the long term Castilian will be reduced to an imperfectly mastered foreign language in Catalunya. In some parts of the region that was always the case, but in a city like Barcelona, full of Spaniards from other parts of the country, it seems unlikely it will happen any time soon. The Catalans themselves would be the big losers if it did.

In spite of all that has been gained in the past 25 years, the chip on the shoulder remains in place. While the people of Madrid scarcely register the existence of Barcelona or other cities as rivals, barely a day goes by that Barcelona's press doesn't report on some statistic or aspect of urban life in which Barcelona and Madrid are held up for comparative scrutiny. And in local eyes Barcelona doesn't always come up smelling like roses.

The city is watching as its jealously guarded status as economic and industrial powerhouse

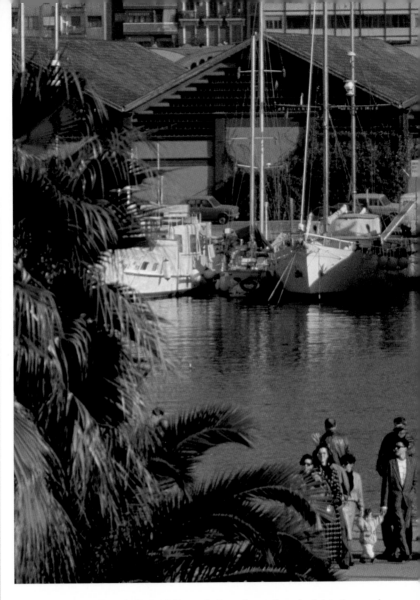

of the country is rapidly eroded by Madrid.

All sorts of economic statistics have Barcelona commentators predicting hard times as Madrid overtakes the port-city in production, exports, attraction of foreign investment, and so on. They point to the impressive expansion of Madrid's metro system, while in Barcelona the creation of one line to the airport is years behind schedule. The collapse of several blocks of flats due to tunneling for the modest extension of another line only served to rub salt into the wound.

Meanwhile conspiracy theorists are convinced that the year-long delay in the projected high-speed AVE rail link between Madrid and Barcelona is because of foot-dragging by a Spanish government that is unsympathetic to Catalunya. The new Socialist government in Madrid did give the residents of Barcelona some cause for cheer when it approved a long–sought city charter that will mean much more funding for the Catalan capital.

Barcelona, on the Mediterranean Sea, has developed its waterfront into a pedestrian-friendly area.

A NEW ERA

But are things really so bad? Visitors from Madrid frequently express admiration for the seemingly endless urban reform projects being carried out in the city, and central Barcelona probably breaks records for the quantity of scaffolding, road works, and building sites.

The 1992 Olympics served as an excuse for a massive program to regenerate the city. Although the waterfront and Montjuïc were the principal beneficiaries, the momentum created has not stopped; controversial plans to re-inject life into the old city areas of El Raval, the Barri Gòtic, and La Ribera with new streets, squares, and renovated housing, continue unabated. In 2004, Barcelona staged the Fòrum, an international cultural fest, in the long neglected northeast corner of the city.

The event was largely staged to speed redevelopment of the area, which has turned half–abandoned industrial wasteland into a chichi residential district with high-rise hotels, a marina, parks, and one of Europe's biggest convention centers.

And it is not only the physical appearance of the city that is changing. Until the 1990s, Barcelona was a fairly homogeneous city, made up in equal measure of Catalans and Spanish internal migrants. The rising tide of immigration into Europe from Africa, Asia, Latin America, and Eastern Europe has hit Barcelona with the same force as many other cities across the Old Continent, and roused similarly conflicting sentiments. The influx of North Africans, Pakistanis, Asians, East Europeans, and South Americans has put a multicultural face on the city that in 1990 would have been quite unimaginable.

Moreover, around 3.5 million tourists a year flock to the city, and their presence fuelled

The opening ceremony of the successful 1992 Olympics that, for many, put the city on the modern map.

a hotel building boom that only now is slowing down and has confirmed Barcelona as one of Europe's favorite holiday destinations.

This convergence of people, permanent and transient, is the changing the face of the city, a fact reflected in the soaring housing prices and the appearance of new restaurants and bars that seem to spring up out of nowhere every day. Where 15 years ago the presence of foreign cuisines was thin, you can now eat Japanese, Middle Eastern, French, Greek, Pakistani, Thai, Tibetan, and others at will. The Passeig del Born area is jammed with watering holes, and the waterfront, an ugly, tangled mess at the end of the 1980s, has been transformed out of sight. The long, gray years of Franco's dictatorship, which ended only three decades ago, already seem long forgotten. ∎

History of Barcelona

EVIDENCE OF SOME TWO THOUSAND YEARS OF HISTORY CAN STILL BE MADE out in the fabric of the city of Barcelona. Roman Barcino was a small but thriving town, but in the Middle Ages the city reached its apogee as head of a vigorous Mediterranean merchant empire. Things began to go downhill after Spanish unification under the Crown of Castilla. By the 19th century Barcelona had again picked up steam as Spain's leading industrial and business city, a position it has managed to occupy, albeit in increasing competition with the capital, Madrid, ever since.

ANTIQUITY

Archaeologists have revealed that Stone Age tribes were wandering about the Pyrenees as long as 70,000 years ago. As the millennia swept by and the tribes became more sophisticated and less fearful, they began to move into the more exposed plains.

These Iberian tribes were joined from about the seventh century B.C. by fresh blood—Celts migrating across Europe from the east. How they rubbed along is difficult to tell. To outsiders such as the Greeks, who landed in Catalunya about a century later, they already seemed well integrated. The mix resulted in what historians refer to as the Celt-Iberians.

It appears at least one of these Celt-Iberian tribes, the *Laietani*, lived in the area around present-day Barcelona for several centuries, but no one knows if they actually settled. Given the Celt-Iberian penchant for creating settlements on defensible hilltops, the most likely location

This 13th-century depiction of St. Ursula and the virgins traveling to Rome shows Catalan confidence in crossing the Mediterranean in the wake of Jaume I's conquest of Mallorca.

for any such village would have been Montjuïc.

The arrival of Phoenician and Greek traders along the Spanish coast had a telling effect on Celt-Iberians. Exchange with the Greeks was especially important and in Catalunya they set up trading depots at Rodes (near modern Roses) and Emporion (Empúries). You can still see vestiges of the latter today (see p. 237). The use of coinage and a great deal of Celt-Iberian art (particularly in ceramics) were clearly inspired by contact with the Greeks.

It is said that the great Carthaginian general and father of the legendary Hannibal (247–181 B.C.), Hamilcar Barca (died 228 B.C.), established the first settlement on the site of Barcelona but no evidence of this

has come down to us. Even less likely is the claim that the mythical Hercules himself founded the city!

What is sure is that the sworn enemy of the Carthaginians, Rome, landed troops in Spain in 218 B.C. in an attack on Hannibal's rear. Hannibal had invaded Italy from the north that same year in the opening stages of the Second Punic War and in the first years of this conflict, he marched from victory to victory. But reinforcements from Carthaginian Spain, cut off by the Roman armies that had marched south from Emporion, could not reach him. The war in Spain was over by 206 B.C., and the peninsula's destiny forever changed as it was then slowly absorbed into the burgeoning Roman Empire.

It is not entirely clear just when Barcino was formed, but there is little doubt it began life as a garrison, as did many other Roman towns. It was planned around the standard north–south axis *(decumanus)* and crossroad *(cardo),* with the forum and temple near the intersection. Peace had long reigned in the area when Caesar Augustus (63 B.C.–A.D. 14) arrived around 15 B.C. He must have liked his reception in the prosperous provincial center because he bestowed it with the rather magnificent sounding title of *Colonia Julia Augusta Faventia Pia.* Four hefty columns of the temple raised to worship the emperor still stand today (see p. 67).

DARK TIMES

The first walls were raised around Barcino as early as the first century A.D.—probably no more than a perfunctory measure, as the *Pax Romana* rendered warfare or invasion unlikely. By the fourth century storm clouds were gathering across the length and breadth of the increasingly troubled empire. Stouter walls were raised, and it was as though the citizens of Barcino, among them a growing Christian minority, could do little more than prepare themselves and await the onslaught.

And come it did. Like locusts, waves of barbarian marauders swarmed into Spain from the north, bringing death and destruction on the country and then moving on. The Christianized Visigoths, who first arrived in 415 and made Barcelona their temporary capital, were intent on staying. They spread their control across Spain but their hold on power was always tenuous. Small in numbers and prone to violent internecine squabbling, the Visigoths brought little stability to the former Roman provinces.

The marked Visigothic tendency toward assassination and treachery was of no help when a Muslim army landed at Gibraltar in

After repeated campaigns, Count Ramon Berenguer I (R. 1035–1076) bought the French lands of Carcassonne and Béziers.

711. Inspired by their faith and the prospect of endless loot, the mixed Berber and Arab army swept across the entire Iberian Peninsula, encountering little effective resistance. The people of Barcelona mounted the ramparts of the city, but their stand was futile. Barcelona succumbed as easily as the rest and the Muslim advance was only finally checked by the Franks at Poitiers in France 21 years later.

COUNTS OF BARCELONA

The Franks threw the Muslims back across the Pyrenees, and in 801 Louis the Pious (778–840) liberated Barcelona. From then on a rough line running from Barcelona to the northwest marked the divide between Muslim-occupied land to the south and a cluster of Christian counties to the north. Together, the northern lands came to be known as the Spanish March, a Frankish buffer zone designed to keep the Muslims at arm's length.

These were momentous times in Europe, for the Frankish king (and father of Louis the Pious), Charlemagne (742–814), had been proclaimed Holy Roman Emperor in 800. The counts who dominated the Spanish March were either direct imperial appointees or at least required the emperor's blessing to rule. Although theoretically agents of the imperial Crown, in reality they had a large degree of autonomy and cheerfully engaged in local spats. By the middle of the ninth century, the struggle for supremacy south of the Pyrenees had been reduced to a two-horse race, represented by Sunifred (died 848), the Count of Urgell, and Bernat, head of the Septimania dynasty. The latter's allies controlled many of the counties of what would one day come to be known as Catalunya.

Bernat's death in 844 created a power vacuum into which Sunifred's son, Guifré el Pelós (Wilfred the Hairy, circa 840–897), stepped some 20 years later. Between 870 and 878 he and his brothers took control of almost all the counties south of the Pyrenees, including Barcelona.

In subsequent centuries, Guifré came to be venerated as the father of the Catalan "nation" as medieval propagandists sought to create a suitably heroic history for the principality. No doubt an able warrior and astute politician, he was no Catalan nationalist. Indeed, the earliest surviving documented references to "Catalunya" date only from the 12th century and Guifré actively sought imperial blessing for his conquests. He knew how to win good publicity, though, and was particularly assiduous in founding religious institutions across Catalunya. Some of these grand churches and monasteries, such as Santa Maria de Ripoll and Sant Joan de les Abadesses, remain standing today. In return, the only class in society with serious education, the clergy, spared no effort of the imagination in eulogizing their hirsute benefactor. To this busy frontier warlord who founded the Casal de Barcelona (House of Barcelona) and conquered much of what would later be called Catalunya Vella (Old Catalunya) was thus attributed the birth of Catalunya, a nation that would never truly be.

Under Guifré's successors, the Comtes de Barcelona (Counts of Barcelona), the city slowly expanded and became their preferred residence. Devastation came in 985 when the Muslims, under the great general Al-Mansur (938–1002), mounted their last successful raid on the city. Calls for aid to the Franks, still theoretically suzerains of the Spanish March, went unheeded and so, understandably, the counts felt themselves released from even nominal bonds of allegiance. By the end of the 11th century, the counts of Barcelona were firmly in control of a solid chunk of territory encompassing Old Catalunya and French land extending as far as Carcassonne and Béziers. To the south, Tarragona was wrested from the Muslims in a campaign that led to the fall of Tortosa and Lleida.

Finally, in 1153, the white flag went up over the last Muslim stronghold, Siurana de Prades, and the re-conquest of Catalunya Nova (New Catalunya) was complete. Early in the 13th century, a diplomatic campaign had seen the Catalans take control of vast areas of Occitania in southern France, and their influence extended well into what is now Provence.

CROWN OF ARAGÓN

A turning point came in 1137 when Count Ramon Berenguer IV (1113–1162) married the heiress to the throne of neighboring Aragón. It is odd that until this time the rulers of the House of Barcelona had not thought to proclaim themselves kings of Catalunya. For almost three centuries Catalan rulers, or *comtes-reis* (count-kings), would continue foremost as kings of Aragón and secondly as counts of Barcelona. Catalunya quite clearly existed, but it was as though someone had forgotten to label it properly.

Under the terms of the union, each party retained a high degree of independence, preserving many of their own laws and customs. The deal was a good one for the more populous and prosperous Catalunya, allowing it to pursue the expansion of its nascent commercial empire while the Aragonese formed a bulwark against the Castilian kingdom that dominated central Spain. Aragonese nobles soon came to resent

Count Ramon Berenguer III rides tall outside the city walls; the first written records of Catalunya date from his reign (1097–1131).

the Catalans and centuries later would burst Barcelona's bubble by engineering a union with Castilla. For now, though, the Catalans were embarking on their Golden Age.

Imperial adventure

It might seem odd that the most spectacular expansion of Catalan territory and trade should come in the wake of a sinister defeat. After a long and complex series of events, and

against his will, Pere I (1174–1213) found himself at the head of a Catalan army facing off the French in the Battle of Muret in 1213. The result was an unmitigated disaster as, against all expectations, the Catalans were trounced, and Pere died in combat. In one fell swoop all the careful work of the previous century was undone. The French took control of much of Occitania, leaving the Catalans with Roussillon, Cerdanya, and part of Provence (including the city of Montpellier).

The day Pere died, his young son Jaume was captured by the French. Pope Innocent III interceded on his behalf and the five-year-old was returned to Catalunya, where he was proclaimed king. Jaume I (1208–1276) finally took the reins of command in 1225, when he reached his majority. Young Jaume was nothing if not energetic. He gave no thought to avenging his father, because he had more ambitious plans. In a sense the path before him was clear, for although Barcelona lacked a

With Ramon Berenguer IV's marriage to the infant Petronilla of Aragón in 1137, the Counts of Barcelona also became the Kings of Aragón and a major force.

decent port, it was already an important trading center with a growing merchant marine and navy. The city's single greatest handicap, however, lay in the Balearic Islands, whose North African masters used them as an extortionate customs post and pirate base. As long as this obstacle remained in place, Catalan merchants could never hope to seriously compete with the Genovese and Venetians for a piece of the lucrative eastern Mediterranean trade.

And so in 1229 Jaume El Conqueridor (The Conqueror) set out with a fleet of 150 vessels and 2,000 men to take Mallorca. The campaign was an unqualified success, and the merchants of Barcelona immediately began to cash in. Ibiza fell six years later, but the easternmost of

his brother Frederic for the possession of Sicily make for confusing reading.

After much bloodshed and with the royal coffers suffering, the Crown of Aragón ended up at the head of a confederation that was to all intents and purposes a major mercantile empire. On the mainland her territories included Catalunya, Aragón, Valencia, Murcia,

Jaume I, El Conqueridor, led Catalunya and Aragón on a campaign of conquest recorded in his *Llibre dels Fets* (Book of Deeds).

the islands, Menorca, held out until 1287. The conquest of that island proved a bloody, ignoble, and largely futile chapter in what may fairly be termed Catalan imperial history.

The Aragonese had remained aloof from Jaume's island campaign but had their eyes on another objective, the Muslim fiefdom of Valencia. Jaume embarked with equal vigor on the conquest of this fertile coastal strip, which he completed by 1245. However, he enraged the Aragonese, who wanted the conquered territory placed under their laws, by creating a new kingdom of Valencia with its own statutes, curiously similar to those of New Catalunya.

From Jaume I's death until the early years of the following century, the Crown of Aragón's overseas possessions grew—in fits and starts and often against the will of the Aragonese. The wars, revolts, and intrigues that at one stage saw a French army invading Aragón and the count-king Jaume II fighting

Roussillon, and Montpellier. Beyond, the largely Catalan offensive effort had netted the Balearic Islands, Sicily, and Sardinia (invaded in 1323). For a brief moment Catalan duchies also controlled Athens, Malta, and Gozo.

Historians remain divided as to the utility of the effort. There is no doubt that Catalan trade profited; Barcelona's merchants by now ranged across the entire Mediterranean. They dominated the western half and established trading posts in North Africa and as far off as the Middle East. However, the purchase price had been high and the maintenance was still more prohibitive. Revolts were the order of the day in Sardinia and, to a lesser extent, from Sicily to Valencia. Attempts to take Corsica and penetrate Muslim Andalucía ended in costly failure.

Home front

Whatever the pros and cons of royal empire-building, Barcelona was a prime beneficiary. From the time of Jaume I's "great deed"—the invasion of Mallorca—the city had become a boom town. The count-king's need for money and men to realize his conquests put

the wealthy merchants of the city in a strong bargaining position. Jaume's decision to gradually shift municipal control of the city into the hands of its citizens must inevitably be seen in that light. In 1249, the first city assembly was authorized, and by 1274 it had taken definite shape. Five *consellers* (ministers), who were elected for a year from a representative assembly, ran the city's affairs. They formed a tightly knit oligarchic group acting in the interests of the premier merchant class. In one form or another, the Consell de Cent (Council of One Hundred), as the assembly came to be known, ran city hall until 1714.

In 1283 another key institution sat for the first time: the Corts Catalanes, a kind of regional parliament. It was matched by similar institutions in the other constituent parts of the Crown of Aragón, including Aragón and Valencia. Members of the Corts came from three social classes: nobles, clerics, and high-ranking citizens. Initially, the Corts were called into session yearly (later every three years), generally by the count-king, to consider his proposals and, more often than not in the early days, to rubber-stamp them. The Corts also passed laws and the budget, and increasingly the count-kings turned to them for funding, in return for which the Corts extracted a greater say in law-making and other privileges. It could hardly be described as democracy at its best.

As the Corts sat so infrequently, an executive council in permanent session emerged. Made up of a dozen *diputats* (deputies), their main roles were to collect taxes (or *generalitats)* and keep the royal finances oiled. Over the centuries this Diputació de la Generalitat, later simply called the Generalitat, took on greater political responsibilities and eventually made its seat the Palau de la Generalitat (see pp. 77–78), where the Catalan regional government still sits today.

By the middle of the 14th century, Barcelona was a major city with a population of 50,000. Jaume I had extended the city walls as far southwest as La Rambla—in those days a sewage-clogged stream. This wall became the city's main defensive bulwark. At the same time, the economic nerve center of the city had shifted beyond the cramped city to the area now known as La Ribera. Pere III (1319–1387) again extended the walls to take in La Ribera and, southwest of La Rambla, the higgledy-piggledy suburban sprawl known as El Raval. Those walls were eventually knocked down in the 19th century, but the layout can still be identified today: Start in the south where Avinguda del Paral.lel heads west from the waterfront and follow Ronda de Sant Pau, Ronda de Sant Antoni, Ronda de l'Universitat, Ronda de Sant Pere, and, finally, the boundary

**Left: Jaume I in Barcelona's Ajuntament.
Right: Palma de Mallorca was already an impressive city when Jaume I's war vessels convened outside its walls to invade.**

formed by the Parc de la Ciutadella.

At either end of this medieval city grew the two great arms of Catalan mercantile wealth. The traders, grown rich on the back of military expansion, congregated around Carrer de Montcada, which to this day is lined with Gothic and Renaissance mansions that once were home to the most powerful families of the city. The street was laid out to connect the main road northeast out of Barcelona with what was then the waterfront. By contrast, the long, broad Passeig del Born was a hive of commercial activity. Catalan mariners used to say: *"Roda el mon i torna al Born"* (Go around the world and come back to the Born.) For centuries this space was the center of much of the city's grand theater. From early medieval jousts to the grim autos-da-fé (burning of heretics by the Inquisition) that began late in the 15th century, the Born was certainly never dull.

On the other side of town, one of the great monuments of Gothic architecture was raised—the Drassanes, or shipyards. They now house the fascinating museum of maritime history (see pp. 102–104). These shipyards were among the greatest in Europe and furnished not only vessels for the merchant fleet but a good number of the Crown of Aragón's warships. They would continue to play a key role long after the Crown of Aragón had thrown in its lot with that of Castilla to create a united Spain.

So, by the time Pere III built the new city walls, Barcelona had become a rich and prosperous city, with its own civil administration and seat of the regional parliament. Not everyone fared equally well, however. The townsfolk were divided roughly into three groups: the so-called *ciutadans honrats* (honorable citizens), a moneyed, aristocratic elite; a middle class made up of traders, professionals, shipbuilders, lawyers, and others; and finally the lower classes, *menestrals,* made up of artisans and laborers. These people formed the bulk of the city's population and did most of the work.

While the artisans and skilled workers had some protection and representation in their guilds—a medieval combination of trade union and mutual support society—unskilled laborers had precious little. Riots broke out frequently, with the biggest disturbances in

1285, 1334, 1348, and 1391. That the people had any energy at all to riot in 1348 (the year the bubonic plague decimated Europe) is a source of considerable surprise. What lay behind the riots is not clear. The 1391 pogrom was as savage as it was inexplicable. There is, however, little doubt that the distribution of wealth was uneven.

The latter half of the 14th century was a strange time in Barcelona. The Black Death of 1348 had decimated the city's population and foreign wars continued to drain the coffers, and yet it was now that much of the Gothic city you see today was built. Somehow, Pere III and his immediate successors found the funds to initiate ambitious new building programs and continue older ones.

The city was getting prettier, but this was not mirrored in its murky politics. The Consell de Cent, whose members decided on their own replacements from one year to the next, remained an old money club to which

DE LA CIUDAD E   BARCELONA·1690

By the Middle Ages, Barcelona had become one of the Mediterranean's leading ports. Its shipyards, the Drassanes, were probably second only to the great Arsenale of Venice.

not even wealthy Johnnies-come-lately had access. Thus two factions emerged, the Biga and the Busca. The latter was made up of the frustrated aspirants to power who wanted not so much to shake the establishment Biga as simply be a part of it. Corruption was rife and several count-kings meddled in the city's affairs, pitting factions against one another and even fomenting riots in the name of reform. No doubt royal backing for the Busca came attached to a price that the latter was happy to pay.

When the Busca finally grabbed control of the Consell de Cent in the mid-15th century, the group enacted important fiscal reforms, but they did not last. In any case, events were fast overtaking them.

THE CALAMITY OF 1714

Catalunya's decline had begun even before the union of the Crowns of Aragón and Castilla in 1479 (signaling the end of Catalunya as a fully independent entity), engineered by the Aragonese against the will of the Catalans. That it retained wide autonomy and commanded respect is reflected in the stately receptions frequently accorded Barcelona's emissaries to the Castilian court now and in later centuries.

However, where it counted Castilla gradually assumed control, especially under the rule of Charles I and Philip II, who presided over the zenith of Spanish glory, that brief moment when continental domination and American gold combined to make Spain the greatest power on Earth. The introduction of the Inquisition in Barcelona and laws that excluded direct trade between Catalunya and the Americas made it perfectly clear who was master.

Exhausted by continuing war and negligent economic policy at home, Spain quickly slipped from its exalted position after the death of Philip II. And struggle as it might against the tendency, Catalunya inexorably slipped with it. Wars and revolution, including the popular peasant rising, or the Guerra dels Segadors (Reapers War) of 1640–1652, only served to devastate the Catalan countryside. On this occasion royal troops reduced Barcelona during a siege in what must have

Besieged Barcelona had no hope of holding out against Madrid's forces at the tail end of the War of the Spanish Succession in 1714.

been seen in hindsight as a dry run for the disaster still to come.

The death in 1700 of Charles II left Spain without an heir. Like vultures, all Europe came to the table to play, and thus ensued the War of the Spanish Succession (1702–1714), in which Catalunya threw in its lot with an anti-

REAWAKENING

The shock had been considerable but the city slowly became accustomed to the new situation. From the late 18th century, when finally the ban on direct trade between the Latin American colonies and Catalunya was lifted, until 1898, when Spain lost the last of those colonies—Cuba, Puerto Rico, and the Philippines—in a humiliating defeat by the U.S. Navy, Barcelona recovered to the point of becoming Spain's leading city. It had been a bumpy ride. Napoleon's occupation and the Peninsular War (1808–1814) had been disastrous for the entire country, and the faltering industrialization (textiles, shipbuilding, iron, the first Spanish railway, cork and wine production) had brought wealth to some and slum misery to most.

Nevertheless, in the final 20 years the city's fathers were in ebullient mood. Having knocked down the city walls, they embarked on an ambitious urban development plan, creating the elegant grid-plan district between Barcelona and the then separate town of Gràcia. L'Eixample (the Extension), as the new area is still known, fueled a building and property boom. In 1888 the city hosted a Universal Exhibition.

The euphoria of those heady days was accompanied by political renewal. The Renaixença (Renaissance) began as a cultural movement in which a minority of intellectuals fomented interest in the Catalan tongue and literature. At the same time, *modernisme* (or modernism, the local version of art nouveau) exploded onto the Barcelona art scene and was regarded by many as further evidence of Catalan renewal. Modernisme's great exponents, especially in architecture, tended to be Catalan nationalists. In 1892 a loose political movement promulgated the Bases de Manresa, the blueprint for a Catalan government and self-rule.

WAR & PEACE

Barcelona was bubbling by the beginning of the 20th century. Indeed, all Spain was in ferment. A century of political uncertainty, coup and counter-coup, and economic mismanagement had left the country increasingly ripe for conflict.

Barcelona could hardly remain aloof and events seemed to be spinning beyond control.

French coalition. The French prevailed and a Bourbon king, Philip V, ascended the throne. The allies left Catalunya to its fate, which took the form of a merciless siege and bombardment of Barcelona in 1714. On September 11, the city surrendered and Philip V abolished every trace of Catalan autonomy. An absolutist in the mold of Louis XIV, Philip set about creating a fully centralized state. Catalunya lost its privileges, overseas possessions, even its language, the use of which was prohibited.

The city's population doubled to one million in between 1900 and 1930, and the restless and growing industrial working class turned increasingly to the radical left, especially the anarchists. In July 1909, a call-up of reservists to boost beleaguered Spanish forces in their ill-organized campaign in northern Morocco sparked a week of violence in Barcelona, the Setmana Tràgica (Tragic Week), in which anti-clericalism was especially vented with the torching of churches across the city. Violence both on the right and the left was becoming the norm, not only in Barcelona but also elsewhere in the country. In Barcelona, calls for self-rule in Catalunya grew louder by the day.

Fears of a general workers' revolt led General Miguel Primo de Rivera to stage a coup in 1923. His dictatorship lasted until 1930 but achieved little more than to stall the inevitable. Catalan nationalists saw their opportunity with the 1931 election victory in Madrid of a leftist coalition. Under Francisco

U.S. intervention in Cuba's struggle for independence from Spain in 1898 inflamed Barcelonians, who took to La Rambla to demand war.

Macià and Lluís Companys, the Esquerra Republicana de Catalunya party (ERC, Republican Left of Catalunya) proclaimed a republic within the newly declared Spanish republic. Madrid quashed this but within a year had granted limited self-rule. The struggle between right and left intensified. In February 1936, when the leftist Popular Front coalition won the national elections, Companys again proclaimed the Catalan republic. It was all in vain. In July of the same year General Franco launched an army rebellion in Spain's North African enclaves. His aim was to topple the left-wing republican government in Madrid and install a Nationalist government in its stead. The Spanish Civil War had begun.

By May 1937, it was clear that the war was not going particularly well for the Republicans. In Barcelona, a burgeoning communist party and its militia gained the upper hand and, with Companys' blessing, openly began an assault on the anarchists and the POUM. After three days and the loss of 1,500 lives, the latter two groups surrendered

"Anarchist Books are Arms in the Fight against Fascism" proclaims the propaganda.

Years of agony

For the next three years Spain went through the agony of civil war. In Barcelona the army attempted to rise up in support of Franco but it was quickly defeated by the police, who were loyal to the government, and bands of armed anarchists.

Thus began a surreal period. Lluís Companys, nominal head of the recently resurrected Generalitat, was powerless to prevent a coalition of anarchists and Trotskyist militia (Partido Obrero de Unificación Marxista, Workers Party of Marxist Unification) from taking control of the city. The former in particular, with their red-and-black flags, were dominant. Factories, public transportation, and social services all ended up in anarchist hands. Revolution hung in the air as the anarchists and POUM were as much interested in creating a new social order right away as defeating a common enemy.

and were disarmed. Several months onward the central republican government set up shop in Barcelona.

The writing was on the wall, however. The last great clash of the war, the Battle of the Ebro, which was fought out along that river in southwestern Catalunya in the summer of 1938, brought yet another defeat for the Republicans, who were now virtually incapable of defending Barcelona. Nationalist troops, watched in silence by those people in Barcelona who had opted not to flee into exile in France, marched into the city in January 1939. Two months later the civil war came to an end.

For the next 36 years Spain was to live in the vice-like grip of General Franco. A great believer in central government, Franco abolished all the usual things: the Generalitat, the use of Catalan, the right to hold demonstrations, and so on. The repression was at its bloodiest during the 1940s—Companys was executed in 1940 in Montjuïc castle. Opposition was never completely silenced, however. Strikes and protests began to occur as early as the 1950s and continued through the 1960s. At the same time Franco was

During his brief dictatorship (1923–1930), General Miguel Primo de Rivera cracked down on the radical left and Catalan nationalists, but to little avail.

encouraging the massive migration of people from the poorer regions of Spain, such as Andalucía and Extremadura, to Barcelona. About three-quarters of a million swelled the population of Barcelona and its satellites during the 1960s alone.

Rebirth

The death of Franco in 1975 sparked a remarkable process that brought Spain in from the cold and returned to Catalunya a degree of self-rule not seen since before 1714. In 1978 a system of devolution of power to the regions was agreed upon. The following year, a specific Autonomy Statute for Catalunya was given royal ascent by King Juan Carlos I, the constitutional monarch at the head of the Spanish state since Franco's death.

President of the Catalan Generalitat from 1980 to 2004, the wily Jordi Pujol addresses the regional parliament.

In 1980 the first regional elections were held and Jordi Pujol, at the head of a right-of-center Catalan nationalist coalition, became president of Catalunya. He astutely ruled until 2004, when the former mayor, Catalan Socialist leader Pasqual Maragall, won elections at the head of a three-party coalition.

Maragall continues Pujol's fight for increasing financial self-sufficiency from Madrid and the reassertion of Catalan identity, particularly in the use of the Catalan language. While he was mayor, the 1992 Olympic Games put Barcelona in the international spotlight; the event was judged a big success. As regional president, Maragall faces economic and political challenges, not least from his extremist Catalan coalition partners who ultimately seek independence from Spain. ∎

The arts

AN OVERWEENING SENSE OF CONFIDENCE ABOUT THE CITY'S PROSPECTS has on two occasions spurred a building and design frenzy in Barcelona. The activity unleashed has left us with two remarkably rich and distinct artistic legacies: the Gothic of the old center and the sometimes delirious *modernista* whims of the late 19th and early 20th centuries. The city is also home to a rich collection of paintings from the early medieval Romanesque period. In the 20th century the city was awash with genius—Pablo Picasso and Joan Miró laid the foundations of their careers here, and Salvador Dalí remained true to his Catalan roots throughout his life.

ARCHITECTURE

As if caught in a time warp, central Barcelona remained faithful to Gothic styles of building long after they had been abandoned elsewhere. This legacy and the wonderful outpouring of imagination that came with *modernisme* (modernism) are the main sources of visual feasting in the streets of the Catalan capital.

Roman Barcelona

Barcino, the town known to us today as Barcelona, was a standard example of Roman garrison town planning. Rectangular and crisscrossed by a north–south axis (the *decumanus*) and an east–west thoroughfare (the *cardo*), the city center was made up of a forum (roughly where Plaça de Sant Jaume is today) and a temple, of which several columns remain standing. Aside from lower levels of sections of the city wall and towers, and a small cemetery, the best view of excavated ancient Barcino is in the basement of the Museu d'Història de la Ciutat (see pp. 68–71).

Visigoths and, for a short time, Muslim invaders, followed the Romans in charge of Barcelona, but virtually nothing remains to testify to their presence.

Romanesque

It was in the early Middle Ages that a new and vigorous building style known as Romanesque swept across Christian Europe. Lombard artisans from northern Italy began transmitting it across Catalunya and to Barcelona from about the 11th century.

Romanesque is appealingly simple and forceful, and survives today almost exclusively in churches—generally consisting of a simple rectangular plan with no transept—and some elements of monasteries. Characterized by the use of stone to create angular and largely unadorned buildings, the softening touch comes with the semicircle—arches, vaults, doorways, and windows all take this shape. A tall, square-based bell tower flanks many a Catalan Romanesque church and, again, the semicircle tops all its openings. At the back of the church was added a semicylindrical apse. With time, builders became more ambitious and raised grander buildings; some churches were blessed with triple and even quintuple apses. Doorways might be adorned with a series of arches within arches, and the occasional item of stone and wooden statuary was added to enliven things.

Monastery cloisters were often of great elegance. Double sets of columns seem to parade around the perimeter of the courtyards, topped by capitals with increasingly rich adornment representative of biblical stories or other religious imagery.

The comparative lack of sculptural ornament on the walls and ceiling also needs to be understood in light of the fact that church interiors were frequently covered in brightly colored frescoes, while the altars might be surrounded by wood panels, also richly painted with images of Christ, the Apostles, and religious episodes. Most of that has disappeared, but a visit to Barcelona's Museu Nacional d'Art de Catalunya (see pp. 186–88) is a polychromatic eye-opener.

In Barcelona examples of the Romanesque style are few (seek out in particular Església de Sant Pau del Camp, see p. 98.) Those with a hunger for it can sate themselves in northern

The towering columns of the temple dedicated to Caesar Augustus are among the few reminders of Roman presence.

Catalunya—largely beyond the scope of this book, although you'll find mention of one worthy exception, Cardona (see p. 238).

Gothic heights

The building of a Mediterranean trading empire brought enormous wealth to Barcelona in the 13th and 14th centuries, although the latter was marked also by several serious reverses, not the least of them being repeated waves of the bubonic plague. It was,

Close to the hearts of Barcelonians, Santa Maria del Mar in La Ribera is also one of the finest examples of austere Catalan Gothic.

however, a boom time, reflected in an explosion of new and ambitious building. Increasingly sophisticated techniques gave rise to what is now termed Gothic construction.

These methods were first developed in France and then spread to the rest of Europe. Engineers perfected load-bearing and weight-

filled the immense spaces with filtered daylight. There was a marked tendency to overwhelm with ornament. Inside and out, churches were covered with sculptural whimsy. In the great cathedrals the volume of adornment matched their dizzying height.

In Barcelona, Catalans applied their own spin to Gothic. Although there are exceptions, Catalan Gothic is characterized by breadth and sobriety. The extraordinary Església de Santa Maria del Mar is virtually as wide as it is high, creating a generous sense of volume that is often lacking in the classic Gothic churches farther north. And, like most other Gothic buildings in Barcelona, it is only sparingly decorated; bare surfaces predominate inside and out. Studying its western entrance is one way of comprehending what sets apart the Catalan version of Gothic. Aside from the entrance, the facade is virtually bereft of decoration and instead of a forest of densely decorated pinnacles, all that rises above it are two austere, octagonal bell towers. In Barcelona, only the main facade of the Catedral breaks with this local norm and reflects more elaborate tastes. The great Cistercian monasteries outside Barcelona (see pp. 212–15) were also more inspired by French models and contrast greatly with their Catalan Gothic counterparts.

One key characteristic to emerge from the importance attached by Catalan builders to breadth is the development of the wide, flat arch, a common feature of many Gothic structures in Barcelona. Where designers opted for rounder arches, they still seem to have been determined to stretch them to the limit—the 48-foot-high (15 m) arches in the Saló del Tinell, for instance, are among the largest ever built without reinforcement. Equally impressive are those that mark off the shipbuilding halls of the Drassanes, the city's medieval shipyards, a remarkable legacy of that era in Barcelona. Gothic private mansions, albeit often with baroque modifications, still grace the old city too, particularly along Carrer de Montcada in La Ribera (see pp. 124–29).

The city's energetic spurt of monumental building was largely over by the end of the 14th century, although the Palau de la Generalitat was a later addition, built under the guidance of Marc Safont (active in the 15th century).

distribution techniques, and the greater use of pillars and arches, buttresses, and ribbed vaulting in the ceiling resulted in far loftier buildings than ever before.

In religious construction engineers aimed high and churches seemed to soar heavenward. They were designed to leave their visitors awestruck; even today one's eyes are inevitably drawn upward. Huge rose windows of stained glass, assisted by ranks of narrow windows with pointed arches along the aisles,

Baroque

The Renaissance made little impact on Barcelona's architecture, which remained rooted in Gothic tradition long after it had been consigned to the past in other parts of Europe. The arrival of the more boisterous baroque period in the latter stages of the 17th century had more of an effect. A handful of churches (such as Església de la Mercè and Església de Sant Felip Neri) were built in a comparatively sober version of the style, which had sprung out of the Renaissance in Italy. Several other buildings, including some of the Gothic mansions on Carrer de Montcada, were the subject of baroque modifications. Apart from its clear roots in classicism, the style is dominated by use of curves; round, porthole-style windows are one easily noticeable element.

Modernisme (art nouveau)

Barcelona's next moment of architectural greatness came toward the end of the 19th century. The city's population was exploding, the property market was booming, and the wealthy business class was flush.

In this optimistic climate, the local version of art nouveau flourished from the 1880s until about 1910, then tapered off into the 1920s. In part influenced by Japanese painting, art nouveau sought to emulate nature in architecture, painting, and the decorative arts, insomuch as it represented a rejection of straight-laced and straight-lined building—especially the imitation of classical models. In Barcelona, the movement came to be called modernisme, and its protagonists were a broad mix of designers with a still wider spectrum of interpretations of what this new "freedom" meant.

While the inspiration in nature and its harmonious forms remained a constant, modernisme's leading exponents also sought their muses in the past—not in the classical lines of Greece or Rome, but in the rich heritage of Spain and its Gothic and Islamic building cultures. Drinking at the fount of this knowledge, modernista architects felt no compunction about adapting what they learned.

The scaly, fish-like appearance of Gaudí's Casa Batlló (finished 1906) is perhaps the weirdest product of this modernista genius.

They never slavishly aped any one style or period but rather sought to create new expression through a dynamic mix of old and new, using raw materials until then largely disdained, such as unclad brick and wrought iron. Barcelona's modernista architects helped revive the nearly extinct figure of the artisan. This is especially apparent in the "handmade" decoration and, sometimes, construction of their buildings. The relatively new building materials of steel and iron were exploited to the full: as frames on which to hang walls and in decoration. Glass and ceramic tiles also played a key role, both used in ways that reflected past glories but in abruptly novel style. Architects fostered the old skills of the craftsmen, whose knowledge had been handed down from generation to generation, starting with the medieval guilds. Of all these tradesmen, the sculptor Eusebi Arnau (1864–1934) was one of the most outstanding. He left his mark in the Hospital de la Santa Creu i Sant Pau (see p. 163), the Palau de la Música Catalana (see pp. 120–21), and many others.

The modernistas got an enthusiastic response from Barcelona's moneyed families and many splendid results, although not to everyone's taste then or now, can still be seen dotted about the city, especially in l'Eixample (the Extension), the new grid-plan part of town developed outside the former city walls at the turn of the 19th century.

The top names in modernista architecture were all to some extent Catalan nationalists. Riding on a wave of renewed popular interest and sentiment in all things Catalan, the modernista architects frequently saw their projects as a means of giving vital expression to a renewed Catalan identity.

Towering above them all was the (some would claim divinely) inspired Antoni Gaudí (1852–1926), the figure who has come to symbolize modernisme. More than any of his peers, this eccentric figure went out on a limb in the pursuit of the style's ideals. If you had to summarize his credo, it would be "there are no straight lines in nature." None of Gaudí's rivals displayed his technical daring. He alone created pillars that lean with the sinewy power of ancient tree trunks, undulating floors, ceramic ceilings, serpentine benches, and chimney pots that look like *Star Wars* characters on acid.

Although he had projects beyond Barcelona and even a handful outside Catalunya, the bulk of Gaudí's handiwork is on display in this city. Important examples include the Palau Güell (see pp. 92–93), La Pedrera (see pp. 145–47), Casa Batlló (see pp. 142–43), Park Güell (see pp. 166–67), and Barcelona's call sign, the incomplete Sagrada Família church (see pp. 158–62). Palau Güell was one of his earliest commissions and is a fine introduction. Although in many respects a solemn edifice, it is nevertheless loaded with innovation. The gentle parabolic arch is a key Gaudí item, and he is faithful to modernisme in his expansive use of bare brick and wrought iron. The former has its roots in Islamic Spain. The Muslims built mostly in brick, and as the Christians reconquered the peninsula, Mudéjar (Muslims living in Christian territo-

The sleek white lines of the MACBA modern art gallery helped breathe new life into the traditionally neglected district of El Raval.

ry) tradesmen passed on this tradition.

La Pedrera, Casa Batlló, and Park Güell are all marvelously playful gems, executed for three different masters. The fantastical rooftop of La Pedrera has to be seen to be believed, and each of the apartments below is a singular dream home. Living in Casa Batlló wouldn't be too bad either, but the exterior, which has the appearance of a scaly dragon, is so bizarre that even after years of living in Barcelona one cannot help but regard it with admiring bemusement. Park Güell, one of Gaudí's last commissions, was supposed to be a select little suburb for the well-to-do, but funding and interest ran out. Its ceramic-lined stairways,

decorated with strange beasts, lead you into a fairy-tale world of design fantasy.

That tale ends with the Temple Expiatori de la Sagrada Família (Expiatory Temple of the Holy Family). Conceived originally as a pseudo-Gothic offering from Barcelona's pious citizens a God thought to be increasingly displeased with the not-so-faithful, it soon turned into the century's most ambitious art-architecture project. Gaudí took over the job two years after it was launched in 1882.

He stuck with the Gothic theme insofar as he sought inspiration for the church in the grandeur of the past. Not content merely to create a neo-Gothic church, he applied his belief that architecture should follow nature's lines and designed a structure of extraordinary harmony and lightness. Increasingly convinced he was embarked on a supreme mystical mission, Gaudí devoted the last years of his life to the Sagrada Família. When he was run over by a tram in 1926, he was barely a quarter of the way through. Amid much controversy, work continued slowly, but the end is now in sight.

But Gaudí was not alone. What is perhaps most striking is that modernisme, however brief may have been the movement's life, was so densely rich with genius. At least two of Gaudí's contemporaries require mention: Lluís Domènech i Montaner (1850–1923) and Josep Puig i Cadafalch (1867–1957).

The most cursory examination of a few key creations by these two and Gaudí reveals just how broadly were interpreted the "rules" of modernisme. A visit to Domènech i Montaner's Hospital de la Santa Creu i Sant Pau (see p. 163) and Puig i Cadafalch's Casa Amatller (see p. 143) is instructive. The former combines a microcosm of urban planning and joyous decoration (in ceramic tiles) with Gothic nostalgia. The latter is a rectilinear curve ball—straight off an Amsterdam canal with its squared-off gables, and just as full of colorful fantasy as its more outlandish neighbor. Domènech i Montaner's Palau de la Música Catalana (see pp. 120–21) is a must-see landmark, a lavish celebration of the decorative arts in a way Gaudí buildings never could be.

To the present

After the exuberance of modernisme, which was sputtering to a close long before Gaudí drew his last breath, anything else was bound to seem a little staid. The uncertain years between the World Wars, civil war, and the long night of the Franco years put the brakes on inventive building. In spite of the unceasing town renovation programs under way since the 1992 Olympics, serious inspiration has been in fairly short supply. The Museu d'Art Contemporani de Barcelona (called MACBA) (see p. 96) and the Teatre Nacional de Catalunya (see p. 170), by leading local architect Ricard Bofill (born 1939) are two striking exceptions. A battalion of international heavyweights are leaving their mark also. After Norman Foster (Torre de Collserola, see p. 182) and Arata Isozaki (Palau Sant Jordi, see p. 193) in the 1990s, another wave is crashing over Barcelona; Jean Nouvel's cucumber-shaped Torre Agbar (see p. 170) and Herzog &

de Meuron's triangular Edifici Forum (see p. 116) will be joined by a Frank Gehry complex for the future high-speed train station in La Sagrera District. Gehry had already contributed his waterfront Peix (see p. 116).

PAINTING & SCULPTURE

It is probably fair to say that, while much art of high quality was produced in Barcelona and Catalunya down through the centuries, greatness has only ever been associated with the city in modern times. Three intensely different figures with some connection to Barcelona (although only one born and bred) are the 20th-century stars that shine over an otherwise unexceptional panorama.

Middle Ages

The Romanesque churches littering the northern Catalan countryside once boasted brightly colored frescoes that have now largely disappeared. Some of the most remarkable survivors are on display in Barcelona's Museu Nacional d'Art de Catalunya (see pp. 186–190).

Romanesque painting nearly always dealt with religious subjects and always in a seemingly childlike fashion. To understand the predilection for such an apparently naïve style one has to travel into the early medieval European mind. Mostly illiterate, brutish, and short-lived, the God-fearing Europeans got their religious education in this way; the medium was less important than the message.

Imagery of Christianity's key figures (Christ, the Virgin, the Evangelists, the Apostles, and the saints) were repeated over and over, accompanied by biblical episodes (mostly from the New Testament). Their unreal two-dimensionality served to underline that such divine beings were on a level far removed from that of common mortals.

The counterpoints to the murals were wooden sculptures, most often of the Crucifixion of Christ or the Virgin Mary with the Christ Child on her lap. Although you can rarely see it now, they were brightly painted. In stone, the most exquisite work was done on the sarcophagi of eminent corpses. Some remarkable works, especially later in the Gothic period, were produced in other materials such as alabaster.

Initially artists (regarded as skilled trades-

men) remained anonymous, although certain works are now associated with particular workshops. As Romanesque gave way to Gothic in the 13th and 14th centuries, these artisans began to sign their works.

The passage from Romanesque is sometimes barely perceptible to the untrained eye: The key is the growing humanity and thematic suppleness of Gothic works. More lifelike figures with human expression and movement appear, and an increasing variety of themes, many secular (like the conquests of Jaume I), are illustrated. Also, frescoes gave way to wooden panels and other longer-lasting bases.

Among the most important Catalan artists of the Gothic period were Ferrer Bassà (circa 1290–1348), Bernat Martorell (died 1452), and Jaume Huguet (1415–1492). A few of their works can be seen in city collections.

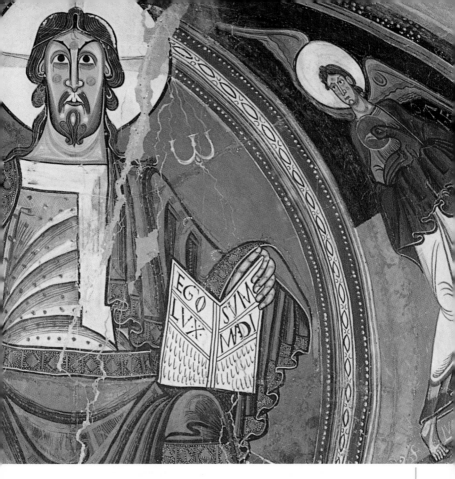

"I am the Light of the World" proclaims Christ in this fine Romanesque fresco in the Museu Nacional d'Art de Catalunya.

Lackluster centuries

Largely due to Barcelona's marginalization, little of greatness was achieved between the 15th and early 20th centuries. By the middle of the 19th, realism was all the rage but produced pedestrian work. Modernisme closed the century with a dreamy, whimsical movement from which little more than talented dilettantes emerged, among them Ramón Casas (1866–1932) and Santiago Rusiñol (1861–1931). At the forefront of the bohemian scene in early 1900s Barcelona, neither was destined for immortality. Noucentisme (literally Twentieth-Centuryism!) came as a conservative reaction to the perceived excesses of modernisme and preached a return to classic forms and subjects.

The movement soon fragmented and some of its senior protagonists—Joaquim Sunyer (1874-1956) and Isidre Nonell (1876-1911)—set off in other directions and were influenced by France's Cézanne.

Pablo Picasso

Lapping up the tavern lifestyle of the modernistas was young Pablo Ruiz Picasso (1881–1973). Born in Málaga, he spent his formative years in Barcelona before moving to Paris in his early 20s. He later settled there and last visited Barcelona in 1934 (see pp. 122–23).

By the time Picasso moved to France, he had begun a seemingly inexorable advance from one artistic phase to the next that would continue through to his final days. He started with his Blue and then Pink (or Rose) Periods, in which those colors shaded and informed all his output. The former tended to the melancholy, while the Pink Period had a lighter air.

With "Les Demoiselles d'Avignon" (1907), Picasso broke with tradition, introducing a deformed, even shattered perspective that would spill over into cubism. In the 1920s he flirted with surrealism. One of his best known works, "Guernica," portrays the 1937 German

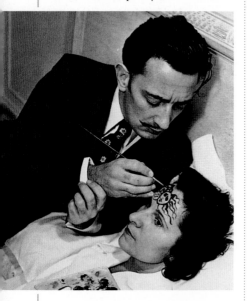

As obsessed with his lifelong companion, Gala, as he was with his art, Salvador Dalí sometimes managed to combine the two.

bombing of the Basque town, Gernika. It hangs in Madrid's Centro de Arte Reina Sofía.

In 1957 Picasso concentrated on a pair of projects. The most intriguing is his series of studies of "Las Meninas," (which hangs in Madrid's Prado museum) by Diego Rodríguez de Silva Velázquez (1599–1660). The other is a more lighthearted series called "Pichones" (Pigeons). Both can be seen in the Museu Picasso (see pp. 125–28). Also a gifted sculptor, ceramicist, and graphic designer, Picasso kept pumping out work until his death.

Joan Miró

Born and raised in central Barcelona, Joan Miró (1893–1983) was an altogether different character. Unsure about his talent, Miró got

off to a slow start. Although he too spent time in Paris, he summered on the Catalan coast, turning out paintings that ranged from the seemingly realist to the naïve. Then, in the early 1930s, he proclaimed that "painting must be murdered" and turned to collage, lithography, and other media.

During World War II Miró turned to the themes for which he is best known: women, birds (the link between earth and the heavens), and stars (imagination). His arrangement of distinct lines and shape in primary colors depict these and other figures in their essence. Miró was also a sculptor and ceramicist and left several public works scattered about Barcelona. For more, see pp. 194–96.

Salvador Dalí

Completing the grand trio is Salvador Dalí i Domènech (1904–1989), who was born and died in Figueres (see pp. 230–33) in northern Catalunya and barely deigned to visit Barcelona. This larger-than-life figure and self-promoting showman with the extravagant moustache was a rapid-fire genius, whipping off his works with disconcerting speed. His nightmare landscapes and hallucinatory scenes reveal, if nothing else, a tormented mind, although they form only a part of a greatly varied opus.

Contemporary art

Rapidly becoming the grand old man of Barcelona's contemporary art scene is Antoni Tàpies (1923–). The one constant feature in this artist's work is the use of unlikely materials in three-dimension collage effect. His grand works may be loaded with anything from wood and sand to rice, and he achieves a texture so heavy that the observer is tempted to touch his "canvases." He is still working today.

The best place to get your finger on the pulse of what else is going on in the art scene is to visit the MACBA art gallery (see pp. 96–97). A short list of the more established local figures includes Susana Solano (1946–), Jaume Plensa (1955–), Joan Hernández Pijuan (1931–), and Jordi Colomer (1962–). ∎

Catalan native Joan Miró poses at one of his numerous one-man shows (1966).

Festivals in Barcelona

CROWDS JOSTLE IN FRONT OF THE PROUD ROMAN GATES NEAR THE cathedral waiting, as it were, for all hell to break loose. Around 10 p.m., a pyromaniac's dream evening begins as towering, fire-spitting dragons, squat and equally scintillating monsters, and band after band of demons armed to the teeth with high-caliber fireworks launch themselves onto the onlookers in an unnerving spectacle of hellfire and noise. The braver (or more foolhardy) tempt fate, challenging the bursts of flame in what is known as the *correfoc*, fire-running. The parade makes for Via Laietana and then heads on to the waterfront where it reaches its culmination at the Gates of Hell.

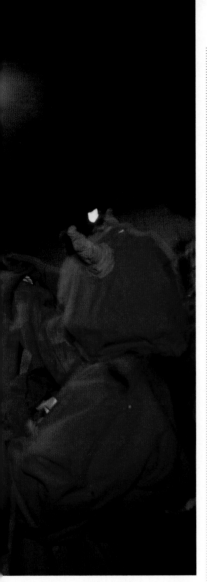

During Barcelona's biggest festival, the Festes de la Mercè, wild characters throw themselves into the pyrotechnical madness of the *correfoc*, or fire-running.

Among the more colorful sets of characters are the *gegants* (giants) and *capgrossos* (big heads). On one afternoon of the festivities a grand parade of gegants, striding by in stately pairs, such as Moorish prince and Christian princess, takes place along La Rambla. They are accompanied by a merry band of impish capgrossos, marching bands, traditional dance groups, horsemen, and many others. The Festes de la Mercè also provides a fine opportunity to see *castellers,* human castle-builders, in action (see pp. 82–83). All over the city you can see musical performances, from folk to rock, classical to electronic. The floodlit cathedral makes for a dramatic stage back-drop. And most of it is free.

The Festes de la Mercè is the biggest of Barcelona's bashes, but the calendar is full of festive opportunities. What Christmas Day is to children in northern European countries and elsewhere, **El Dia dels Reis** (Three Kings' Day, or the Epiphany) is to Catalan children, when they receive gifts and have inordinate amounts of attention lavished on them. On January 5, the eve of the holiday, Barcelona's kids are treated to the **Cavalcada dels Reis** (Kings Parade). The Three Kings (aka the Three Wise Men) land at Moll de la Fusta in Port Vell (see pp. 105–109) and parade around the center of town, much to the delight of young onlookers, especially if they manage to catch some of the candy hurled into the crowd.

A couple of weeks later, the feast day of St. Anthony, patron saint of domestic animals, is marked by the **Festes dels Tres Tombs** (Festival of the Three Circuits). Horseback riders and mule-driven carriages meander around a circuit in the Raval area, including Ronda de Sant Antoni, named after the saint.

Barcelona's other patron saint, Eulàlia, gets her turn amid the **Carnestoltes** (Carnival) celebrations in February. It is a fun-filled week of parades, music, and parties, marking the end of winter but also the onset of Lent, tradi-tionally a period of fasting and sobriety in the run-up to Easter. If the innocent fun of Barcelona's Carnival is too slow for your

The correfoc, a distinctly Catalan festive activity, is one of the climactic points in Barcelona's biggest yearly festival, the September **Festes de la Mercè,** a four-day feast of fun to see off the summer.

Held in honor of one of the city's co-patron saints, Nostra Senyora de la Mercè (Our Lady of Mercy), this is a perfect opportunity to see some of the classic elements of a Catalan *festa major,* which just about every town celebrates once a year.

Among the outlandish figures of the Festes de la Mercè are the *capgrossos* (big heads).

liking, head down to Sitges (see pp. 216–18) for what is basically a wild street party.

Easter itself is not celebrated with the same passion as in some other parts of Spain. If you do want to see a traditional Spanish Easter procession, with heavy floats bearing images of the Virgin Mary, solemn members of religious confraternities dressed in flowing *sotanas*, *capirotes* (those long pointy hats), and bearing staffs, and penitent barefoot women dressed in black and dragging crosses and chains wrapped around their ankles, head for Església de Sant Agustí in El Raval on Good Friday afternoon.

Sant Jordi (St. George) the dragon-slayer is Catalunya's patron saint, and his feast day is celebrated on April 23 in very gentle style. Men traditionally give women flowers while women present men with books. Book and flower stalls pop up all over town, and Catalan publishers profit from the occasion to launch new titles.

Another big festival with fire in its blood belongs to yet another saint, **Sant Joan** (St. John the Baptist). His feast day, June 24, is a public holiday that most locals use to sleep off the night before, marked by bonfires and fireworks displays all over town (beware of children throwing firecrackers about the place!). Locals munch on *coca de Sant Joan*, a sweetish pastry, drink, and generally make merry on a night that is also commonly known as La Nit de Foc (Fire Night).

As the full heat of summer breaks over the city, some of its *barris* (quarters) put on their party clothes. By far the busiest shindig is the **Festa Major de Gràcia.** Around August 15 the locals literally dress up a dozen or so of its narrow streets to different themes—the best-dressed street gets a big municipal pat on the back. Meantime, people set up trestle tables in the streets and load them up to groaning point with food and drink. Every night the area heaves to the joyous din of competing bands of various descriptions.

No sooner has Gràcia packed everything away and cleaned up the streets than another district takes up the baton. The **Festa Major de Sants,** which kicks off around August 24, depending when the weekend falls, is not as big an event as its Gràcia counterpart but gets busy enough. Then follows the **Festa Major de la Barceloneta** in early October and the **Festa Major de les Corts** shortly after. ■

Gegants, the giant figures of the Festes de la Mercè, line up outside Gaudí's La Pedrera building, itself dressed in festive mood.

Food & wine

SUDDENLY THE GOURMETS OF THE WORLD HAVE DISCOVERED BARCELONA. Led by that indefatigable kitchen wizard and doyen of *nueva cocina española*, Ferran Adrià, a new wave of young, uninhibited chefs is taking the world by storm. Even the haughty French are taking their chefs' hats off. Adrià is taking cooking to undreamed-of shores. But Catalan cuisine has always been one of Spain's most delicious. And the newly multicultural Barcelona is peppered with establishments offering exotic cuisines.

As long ago as the 13th century Catalans were writing recipe books, wine guides, and manuals on good table manners. The most venerated tome on the subject of fine eating was Robert de Nola's *Libre del Coc* (15th century, not in print), much of which still holds good.

Barcelona's markets have long been awash with variety. The Greeks and Romans brought the fundamentals: wheat, olives (and hence the oil), wine, and salted fish. The Muslims from North Africa introduced the eggplant, artichoke, red pepper, and various spices. It's conceivable that they introduced rice and pasta to the Iberian Peninsula, too. Extension of the Catalan merchant empire from the mid-13th century to the 15th century opened markets and palates to new taste sensations from around the Mediterranean, while discovery of the Americas added still more previously unknown basics such as potatoes, tomatoes, and corn. All of these elements have been absorbed into Catalan traditions.

Apart from the staples (wheat, olives, and wine), the basis of much Catalan cooking is defined by geography—seafood along the coast, and meat dishes, stews, and broths in the Pyrenees—and Catalans have no trouble mixing and matching. One of the cornerstones of even the simplest Catalan cooking is *mar i muntanya* (surf and turf), in which meat and seafood are cheerfully thrown together—a common dish is the surprisingly good

The *crema catalana* is without doubt the most emblematic of Catalan desserts.

mandonguilles amb sípia (meatballs with cuttlefish). Catalans like to mix fruit and nuts with their fish and meat dishes, too. Fish is frequently prepared with almonds and you may be offered chicken with pears or apricots, or duck with figs.

Sauces are an important part of many Catalan dishes. Standards include *allioli* (a pounded garlic and olive oil mix resembling mayonnaise), which frequently accompanies rice and noodle or meat dishes; *romesco* (almond, tomato, garlic, vinegar, and olive oil, also used as salad dressing); *sofregit* (a fried onion, tomato, and garlic mix), and *samfaina*, which is basically sofregit with eggplant and red pepper thrown in.

Other traditions run deep. Catalans love their sausages *(botifarra)* and mushrooms *(bolets)*. In the autumn the tasty *rovellons* are particularly sought after. The night before All Saints' Day (November 1) is Halloween to some but in Barcelona it is the *castanyada*, or roast-chestnut evening. In spring, if you head out into the country around Barcelona, you can take part in a *calçotada*, the Catalan version of the barbecue. Calçots are a kind of long spring onion, very tasty when grilled and dipped in romesco sauce.

Although tapas were not originally an intrinsic part of Catalan culinary tradition, they have become a joyous mainstay of many a Barcelona lunch hour.

Barcelona offers a broad variety of dining options for Catalans, who love to eat out.

Among standard Catalan starters are the three *e*'s: *escalivada, esqueixada,* and *escudella.* To make escalivada, red peppers (a favorite ingredient in Barcelona) and eggplant are mixed in with tomatoes—grilled, peeled, and cooled—and served in an olive oil and garlic dressing. Esqueixada is salted cod *(bacallà)* cut into strips, garnished with tomato, red pepper, onion, olives, beans, olive oil, and vinegar. Escudella is made up of stock from various cooked meats and sausages, rice or noodles, beans, and other vegetables. Usually a few bits of the meat and sausage are thrown in. Some restaurants may then serve a second course of the meat used to create the stock, or *carn d'olla* (meat from the pot).

Main meals offer huge variety. Few people haven't heard of paella, a Valencian specialty, but you can try many rice- *(arròs)* based dishes in Catalunya, frequently with seafood or a mix of seafood and meat. Vermicelli noodles *(fideus)* are an alternative base for such dishes, which are known as *fideuà.* One version comes black with the ink of cuttlefish. Beef and lamb dishes abound, along with game and poultry. And although the Mediterranean is rapidly being fished out, a busy import campaign keeps Barcelona's central markets well stocked.

Desserts are not the Catalans' strong point, but try *crema catalana,* custard with a caramelized crust. *Mel i mató* (honey and fresh cream cheese) and *music* (dried fruits and nuts served with muscatel wine) are good, but the eye-catcher is *pijama,* tinned peach with *flan* (creme caramel), vanilla and strawberry ice cream, whipped cream and perhaps some chocolate topping.

You will want to wash all this down with something tasty. Across Catalunya there are ten DO *(denominación de origen)* wine zones. The DO label assures a level of quality and adherence to a complex set of rules on allowable mixes of grape variety and procedure.

In Barcelona's hinterland lies the Penedès region, a major wine-producing section of the country. About 90 percent of Spain's sparkling whites, or *cava,* are produced here. Much comes from big names such as Codorníu and Freixenet, but many smaller firms worth looking out for include Nadal, Canals Canals, and Mas Tinell. One of Spain's leading still wine producers, Miguel Torres, is present in the Penedès. Keep an eye out for Raïmat whites and reds from around Lleida in western Catalunya. Only one wine-making region has the DOC *(denominación de origen calificada)* label aside from northern Spain's Rioja region, and that is Catalunya's Priorat. This area inland from Tarragona produces hefty reds. ■

The Catedral is the centerpiece of medieval Barcelona. Taking its name from the Gothic style that still predominates in its buildings today, this compact area is the chalice that contains 2,000 years of the city's history.

Barri Gòtic

Fans, like these in a Barri Gòtic store, are popular in the summer heat.

Barri Gòtic

BARCELONA'S GOTHIC QUARTER IS NO MERE MUSEUM-LIKE REPOSITORY OF old buildings, but its civic and religious heart. A magnet for the thousands of visitors in town on any given day, the *barri* pulsates equally with the life of its inhabitants and workers. Everyone from Catalunya's most senior decision-makers to a colorful array of urban strays populate the warren of largely medieval streets. Great numbers of bars, restaurants, stores, and businesses keep the area chaotically busy through the day and well into the night. It sounds a cliché, but the Barri Gòtic has something for everyone.

Upon the foundations of Roman Barcino rose medieval Barcelona. To the chagrin of many, little remains of the Romanesque period. The prosperous rulers of the city deemed it appropriate to replace the old with the new, raising the grand Gothic palaces and churches that still dominate today. As prosperity had condemned most Romanesque buildings to

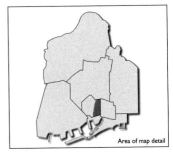

Area of map detail

demolition, so decline from the 15th century onward helped preempt any later impulse to pull down their Gothic replacements. By some estimates, Barcelona's old center is the single greatest treasure of Gothic buildings in the whole of Europe.

Roughly speaking, the core of medieval Barcelona expanded slowly to what is now La Rambla (to the southwest) and Via Laietana (to the northeast). To the southeast it meandered down toward the sea, while to the north it didn't advance much beyond the original Roman walls and Carrer de la Porta-ferrissa. Only in recent times has it come to be known as the Barri Gòtic, and, for neatness' sake, it is considered to extend north as far as Plaça de Catalunya. It is the keystone of a broader municipal division called Ciutat Vella (Old City).

The Barri Gòtic not only contains all that remains of Roman Barcino but many of Barcelona's greater medieval sights. They range from the Catedral and Església de Santa Maria del Pi to the seat of regal power in the complex of buildings around Plaça del Rei,

Countless narrow lanes crisscross the centuries-old Gothic heart of Barcelona.

now transformed into a fascinating museum of the city's history. Smack in the middle of this long-lived quarter stand the buildings that for centuries have housed the regional and city councils—the Generalitat and the Ajuntament. Just to the west, you can explore the cramped streets of what was the *Call*, the city's once busy Jewish quarter. The inquisitive explorer with time to sneak a look into unheralded nooks and crannies will turn up all sorts of little gems; never pass up a chance to glance into the many fine courtyards of medieval mansions scattered about the heart of the Barri Gòtic. ■

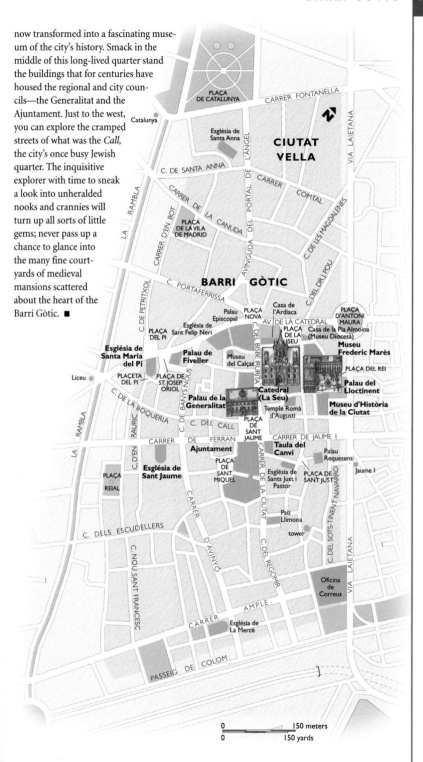

Catedral (La Seu)

Catedral de la Santa Creu i Santa Eulàlia

www.website.es/catedralbcn/

🗺 Map p. 59

✉ Plaça de la Seu

🕐 Closed 1:15–5 p.m.

🚇 Metro: Línia 4 (Jaume I)

Coro, roof & sacristy

🕐 Open 1:30–5 p.m.

💲 $$ (includes access to church)

A CHURCH HAS STOOD ON THIS SITE SINCE THE EARLIEST days of Christianity. The city's first known bishop, Pretextat (circa 343 A.D.) said Mass in a small paleo-Christian church built in the fourth century. Count Ramon Berenguer I and his wife, Almodis, presided over the consecration of its Romanesque successor in 1058, an act that confirmed the supremacy of the counts of Barcelona over Christian Catalan territory. The soaring Gothic facade of the present Catedral de la Santa Creu i Santa Eulàlia comes as something of a surprise; it was only completed along with the pointed central tower late in the 19th century. It's a little disappointing perhaps, although one saving grace is that it was based on an early 15th-century design.

In 1298 work on the Gothic church began and its Romanesque predecessor was slowly dismantled. It took until 1460 to finish the job—apart from the facade and towers. Much of the delay must have been due to the enormity of events that took place in those years. The single most devastating setback was the Black Death (1348), which reappeared several times over the course of the 14th century and decimated the population of Barcelona. Civil war and costly conquests and rebellions in the Mediterranean didn't help. Still, the work was finally done, and the resulting church is 310 feet (93 m) long, 133 feet (40 m) wide, and 93 feet (28 m) high; the bell tower is 177 feet (53 m) high and the main tower 233 feet (70 m).

The main entrance is dominated by a statue of Christ, surrounded by representations of the Apostles. The facade, reminiscent of the great cathedrals of France, is something of a curiosity. Its stone lace work, pinnacles, gargoyles, and other decoration sit at odds with the austerity not only of the rest of this church, but with that of other Gothic churches and nonreligious buildings around Barcelona.

Inside you find yourself in the nave, to either side of which stretch out aisles lined with chapels. These are neatly fitted in between the buttressing that keeps the whole edifice standing.

To the left of the entrance is the **baptistery.** It is said (although believed by few) that Native Americans brought from the newly discovered Americas by Christopher Columbus were baptized in the Gothic baptismal font here.

To the right of the entrance is one of the most significant of the

Right: Illuminated Gothic splendor
Below: Geese make fine watchdogs for the Catedral cloister.

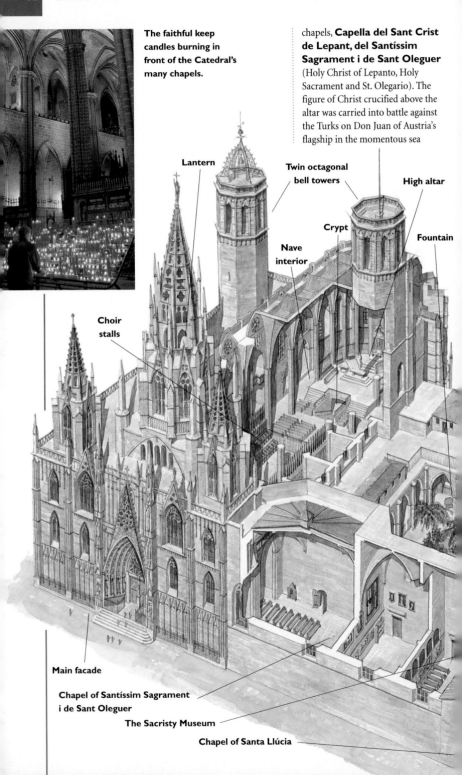

The faithful keep candles burning in front of the Catedral's many chapels.

chapels, **Capella del Sant Crist de Lepant, del Santíssim Sagrament i de Sant Oleguer** (Holy Christ of Lepanto, Holy Sacrament and St. Olegario). The figure of Christ crucified above the altar was carried into battle against the Turks on Don Juan of Austria's flagship in the momentous sea

Lantern

Twin octagonal bell towers

High altar

Crypt

Fountain

Nave interior

Choir stalls

Main facade

Chapel of Santíssim Sagrament i de Sant Oleguer

The Sacristy Museum

Chapel of Santa Llúcia

Sala Capitular

Ⓢ $

Casa de l'Ardiaca

🕐 Closed from 2 p.m.
Sat. & all day Sun

Museu Diocesà

🕐 Closed 3–4 p.m. &
Mon.

Ⓢ $

**CATEDRAL DE
LA SANTA
CREU I SANTA
EULÀLIA**

Cloister

clash of Lepanto in 1571. Apparently, during the battle the figure moved to dodge an incoming Turkish cannon ball, thus creating the slightly odd pose it has today.

Occupying much of the central nave is the **coro,** or choir, which has intricate woodcarving worthy of prolonged examination for its fine craftsmanship. Some of the carvings represent scenes from the Passion and death of Christ. The coats of arms are those of members of the Barcelona chapter of the Order of the Golden Fleece, whose meeting here in 1519 was presided over by Emperor Charles V. Particularly beautiful are the carvings—especially those of the Virgin Mary and Christ Child—on the wooden pulpit on the altar side of the choir stalls. On the other side, the Renaissance reliefs depicting the life of Santa Eulàlia date from the mid-16th century.

In front of the choir stalls a staircase leads down to the **crypt,** which houses the exquisite alabaster sarcophagus of Santa Eulàlia, co-patron saint of Barcelona. The grim story of her gruesome martyrdom, which supposedly took place in pre-Christian Barcelona in the early fourth century, is told in the panels of the sarcophagus. According to one study, a Pisan sculptor, Lupo di Francesco, did the work around 1327.

Above the crypt, the **altar** at the center of the presbytery rests on two sturdy Visigothic capitals preserved from the original church. Behind it is the 14th-century alabaster *catedra,* the seat that symbolizes the spiritual sovereignty of the bishop and the loyalty of the faithful to the successors of St. Peter. It is from this that the word cathedral derives.

Along with the presbytery, the **apse** is the oldest part of the church. Of its ten chapels, the most interesting is the one dedicated to San Benito (third around from the exit to the cloister). It contains the restored series of panels known as the **Transfiguració** (Transfiguration) by Bernat Metge (died 1452), one of the most outstanding Catalan artists of his time. The panels depict various episodes in the life of Christ.

In the **Capella de les Animes del Purgatori** (Souls of Purgatory Chapel), in the northeast transept, an elevator takes you to the **roof** of the cathedral (purchase tickets by the northeast transept.) Walkways allow you to wander across the top of the church and enjoy splendid views over central Barcelona. Watch out for sea gulls and take an umbrella if it's raining. From here a claustrophobic stairwell climbs up inside the main tower.

Back down inside the church, go out to have a look at the **Porta de Sant Iu,** an early example of the ogive (pointed) arch in Catalan Gothic. Plaques in the wall confirm that construction of the Gothic cathedral began in 1298. Returning inside the church, cross the transept toward the cloister. Before heading out, look for the sarcophagi of Count Ramon Berenguer I and his wife suspended from the wall to the left. Virtually next door is the entrance to the modest **sacristy.** Behind it is the church's Treasury, which is unfortunately not open to the public.

The leafy **cloister** is a peaceful haven, entered via a doorway that came from the Romanesque cathedral (evident when viewed from the cloister). During the procession of Corpus Cristi (on the ninth Sunday after Easter Sunday), one of the cloister fountains is adorned with

flowers, and an empty eggshell (supposedly representative of the holy host) is set to dance about on the jet of water. This *ou com balla* (dancing egg) has been a part of Barcelona's tradition since at least the 18th century. The 13 geese in residence represent (according to local lore) the age of the martyr Santa Eulàlia and act as cackling versions of watchdogs when all is shuttered at night.

Several chapels of interest line the cloister. The second on your left after you exit the cathedral is dedicated to the Verge de la Llum (Our Lady of Light), the patron of electricity and plumbing. Mass is held in the chapel on the first Saturday of the month. Directly ahead of you in the western flank of the cloister is a chapel dedicated to the memory of 930 priests and other members of religious orders killed during the Spanish Civil War (1936–39). On the northern side is the **sala capitular** (chapter house), which houses a shop and, in a hall next door, a modest art collection of mostly religious paintings and altarpieces. The 11th-century baptismal font by the shop counter is a rare four-leaf-clover pre-Romanesque piece.

The Romanesque **Capella de Santa Llúcia** takes up the northwestern corner of the cloister. If you step onto the street and look back, you will see clearly that this was a separate structure absorbed into the Gothic project. The giveaway signs are the simple, low facade and semicircular arches above the doorway and window.

Directly opposite the chapel is **Casa de l'Ardiaca,** or archdeacon's house, which is now used to store archives *(not open)*. Enter and go up the stairs to savor the tranquility of its 15th-century courtyard. Inside the glass doors you can look at what remains of the

fourth-century B.C. Roman wall against which the medieval building was constructed.

Palau Episcopal, on Carrer del Bisbe Irurita, also has a fine courtyard. You may be able to take a look inside if its great gates happen to be open.

Across Plaça de la Seu stands **Casa de la Pia Almoina,** once an almshouse that distributed hundreds of meals a day to the needy and now home of the **Museu Diocesà** (Diocesan Museum). Inside is a comparatively thin but well-presented permanent collection of mainly Romanesque and Gothic religious artwork, including altar panels, wooden busts (mostly of the Virgin and Child), and processional crosses. Of most interest are the restored murals dating from 1122 on the first floor and an altar panel by Bernat Martorell depicting John the Baptist (from around 1420) on the second floor. The Pia Almoina was built within what remained of the Roman walls and a tower, which you can appreciate today. ■

The lanes around the Catedral frequently serve as a makeshift stage for Barcelona's street musicians.

Left: Massive pillars soar into the vaulted ceiling of the Catedral, naturally leading visitors to gaze upward toward the heavens.

Roman Barcelona walk

A millennium after the demise of the Romans, the people of Barcelona were still living protected within the walls that testify to their robust imperial legacy. What the Romans called Barcino was a minor city, but enough has survived for us to take a measure of the place.

Start beyond what was the Roman perimeter at Plaça de la Vila de Madrid, site of a modest **Roman Cemetery.** Carrer de la Canuda, which leads east onto Avinguda del Portal de l'Àngel and onto Plaça Nova, may follow the branch road that connected Barcino to the Via Augusta—the imperial road from Rome to Cadiz. Regardless, travelers from the north would have arrived before the city gate on **Plaça Nova ❶.** Not until the third century though would the walls have confronted them; previously the *Pax Romana* had rendered such defenses superfluous.

Two hefty **towers** flank the entrance to Barcino, their lower parts Roman, the upper levels added and modified over the centuries. Jutting out from the left tower is an incipient

A temporary show at the Exhibition Centre Civic Pati Llimona

> 🗺 See area map p. 59
> ► Plaça de la Vila de Madrid
> ⬌ I mile (1.6 km)
> 🕐 1.5 hours
> ► Museu d'Història de la Ciutat
>
> **NOT TO BE MISSED**
> • Gate and walls on Plaça Nova
> • Pati Llimona
> • Temple Romà d'Augusti
> • Museu d'Història de la Ciutat

arch—all that remains of the pair of **aqueducts** that once helped slake Barcino's thirst. The most visible stretch of **Roman wall** fronts Plaça Nova; you can also get a close look at the inside when you visit **Casa de l'Ardiaca** (see p. 65).

To get some idea of the dimensions of the

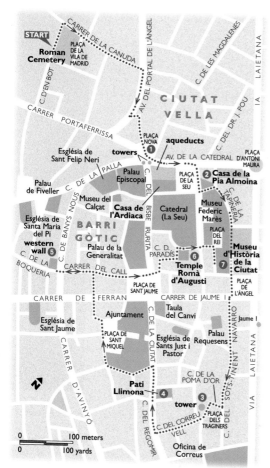

**Part of the Roman wall
remains on Plaça Nova.**

most city gate and wall. If you
wander up to Carrer del Call
(the heart of the former
medieval Jewish ghetto) and
enter the jewelry shop at
No. 5, you can see remnants
of the **Western Wall** ⑤.

From here turn east again,
cross Plaça de Sant Jaume
(the northern edge of which
may overlap with the site of
the ancient forum), and then dogleg your way
around Carrer del Paradís. Inside No. 10 stand
four proud fluted Corinthian columns of what
was the **Temple Romà d'Augusti** ⑥,
which was erected to worship Caesar
Augustus. The best time to call is from 10 a.m.
to 2 p.m., Monday to Saturday. Otherwise,
wander in if the door is open.

To complete your Roman tour, visit the
Museu d'Història de la Ciutat ⑦ (see
pp. 68–71). Continue north along Carrer del
Paradís until you reach the cathedral. Turn
right and go straight ahead to Plaça del Rei.
Just off the square to the south is the museum
entrance. Here you can see an excavated section of the Roman city, including the ruins of
houses, shops, wineries, and public baths. ■

Roman town, follow the line of the wall
around to the east. You will see the outside of
Casa de la Pia Almoina ② (see p. 65),
built into the wall. Follow Carrer de la
Tapineria southeast then continue along
Carrer del Sots-tinent Navarro. To your right
are remains of the original Roman walls fused
with medieval and later construction.

Duck into Carrer de la Poma d'Or and
you emerge onto leafy little Plaça dels
Traginers, dominated by the base of another
defensive Roman **tower** ③. Follow Carrer
del Correu Vell to Carrer de Regomir and turn
right to reach the square of the same name.
Just before it is the civic center known as **Pati
Llimona** ④ *(Closed 2–4:30 p.m.)*, in which
you can see preserved parts of the southern

Plaça del Rei

THE KING'S SQUARE WAS, FROM THE EARLY MIDDLE AGES, home to one of the main residences of the counts of Barcelona and rulers of the Crown of Aragón—the Palau Reial (Royal Palace). Built into the Roman walls, the early structure resembled a fortress, but as the centuries wore on, buildings were raised on all sides of the square. The bulk of what we see today dates from the 14th and 15th centuries; along with the archaeological remains below the square, it constitutes the fascinating Museu d'Història de la Ciutat—a voyage into the first 1,500 years of the city's life in one compact package.

MUSEU D'HISTÒRIA DE LA CIUTAT

Just off Plaça del Rei is the entrance to Casa Padellàs, a 15th-century noble mansion through which you access the Museu d'Història de la Ciutat. The elegant courtyard and staircase are typical of high-class Gothic houses. When you explore the Barri Gòtic, peek through doors opening onto similar courtyards.

From the ticket office you pass into a small museum dedicated to the ancient history of Barcelona and the surrounding area. Here, a handful of Roman sculptures and household items are accompanied by explanatory plans and maps.

The real fun begins after this. Take the elevator down to the excavations: You don't get out at the basement but at "-12" (that's 12 B.C.). From here, an elevated walkway leads right through this underground archaeological treasure chest.

Initially you follow the **intervallum,** the Roman path that separated the wall from the first line of houses (parts of the wall still stand) and allows access to remnants of a fourth-century **tower.** You then enter a small museum space; the model of a patrician Roman house is based on archaeologists' finds showing that there were houses of this magnitude and luxury in the ancient city of Barcino.

Next, wind your way past the remains of laundries and dye shops and a cold-water pool of what was certainly a bigger public bath complex. You soon arrive at part of **Cardo Minor,** one of the city's main cross streets. It is fronted by *tabernae,* or stores, and alongside runs a sewage drain. Then comes a part of town that was dedicated to the production of salted fish and *garum,* a gastronomic delicacy made by pounding fish innards to create a tangy sauce. Prawns, oysters, and other seafood were sometimes added to enhance the flavor. It sounds ghastly, but for centuries this was the Latin world's favorite sauce. It was stored in vats known as *dolia,* whose eggshell-shaped bases can be seen here.

The walk then takes you past remnants of the early church and contiguous religious buildings dating from the fourth to the eighth centuries. Some may find the area that is dedicated to wine production, with its fermentation vats and grape-crushing rooms, of greater interest.

The final part of the walk takes you along the walls of the eighth-century Visigothic bishop's palace and then on up ramps into a pair of vaulted halls containing Roman artifacts and a final room in which 13th-century frescoes discovered in 1998 are on display.

Museu d'Història de la Ciutat
www.museuhistoria.bcn.es

🅰 Map p. 59

✉ Carrer del Veguer 2

☎ 93 315 11 11

🕐 Closed 2–4 p.m. Oct.–May

💲 $

🚇 Metro: Linia 4 (Jaume I)

For centuries the Plaça del Rei (King's Square) and its buildings formed the city residence of the Counts of Barcelona.

You emerge in a ticket hall between the Saló del Tinell and the Capella Reial de Santa Àgata. Head right for the **Saló del Tinell.** It is now occasionally used for temporary exhibitions, so you may be required to pay for a separate ticket. Inaugurated in 1370, the hall is a splendid example of Catalan Gothic. Bereft of the decorative frills so evident in the Catedral, it is a magnificently sober feat of engineering. Seven 48-foot (15 m) arches support the weight of the ceiling and gallery above, backed by buttresses on either side. Those on Plaça del Rei are clearly visible.

The hall was used as a throne room and reception hall for the great and the good when Palau Reial was still a royal palace. After the Crown of Aragón was sub-

sumed into a unified Spain under Ferdinand and Isabella, the hall and indeed the entire palace complex began to lose importance. It is said that the Catholic Monarchs received Columbus in the Saló del Tinell to hear tales of his New World discoveries. By the 16th century, it had been converted for use as a branch of the royal courts. In 1718 the hall and much of the rest of the palace complex was handed over to nuns of the order of Santa Clara. They turned the hall into a chapel and veiled its Gothic splendor in a layer of baroque ornamentation.

During the civil war the nuns were relocated for safety reasons and restorers subsequently removed the baroque overlay. They discovered a set of murals depicting King Jaume I's conquest of Mallorca (see

The Catholic
Monarchs
supposedly heard
Columbus report
on his first voyage
of discovery
beneath the
Gothic arches of
the Saló del Tinell.

pp. 26–27). Executed around the
end of the 13th century, the murals
represent a curious cross between
Romanesque and Gothic art.

From the Saló return to the
ticket hall, from where you enter
the **Capella Reial de Santa
Àgata.** This palace chapel was
begun in 1302, replacing an earlier
Romanesque version and using the

Roman wall as its foundation. It is a
single-nave, Gothic construction,
simple but impressive with ribbed
vaulting and high windows (the
stained glass is modern.) The
impressive *retaule* (altarpiece) is the
work of Jaume Huguet and dates to
1465. The central panel depicts the
adoration of the child Jesus by the
Three Kings while the one above

Roman tipples

The wine of Laietania (the
ancient name for the area
around Barcelona) was known
throughout the empire to be a
simple, inexpensive drop. Standards
fluctuated and various ingredients
were added to enhance quality; sea-
water(!), honey, vinegar, and herbs
were all used. Romans drank an
average of up to a pint (0.75 liter)
of wine a day and served it hot or
cold, to be mixed with fresh water
as desired. In Laietania wine production reached a peak between
the first century B.C. and the second century A.D. ■

shows the Crucifixion. To the sides, six panels illustrate various episodes in the life of Christ and his mother, Mary. Equally magnificent is the *techumbre* (timber ceiling).

From the chapel, return to the ticket hall and exit onto Plaça del Rei by the fan-shaped steps. Cross to the square's northwestern corner to enter the final part of the museum, the multi-story **Mirador del Rei Martí** (King Martin's Lookout), built in 1555—a century and a half after the king's death.

Climb to the top of the tower, which dominates Plaça del Rei, for splendid views over the city. Martí was the last of the Catalan kings, and it is thought the present tower was built partly to replace an older version and partly to commemorate the end of a dynasty.

PALAU DEL LLOCTINENT

The mirador connects Palau Reial to Palau del Lloctinent, built in 1549 as a residence for the *lloctinents reials* (viceroys) installed in Barcelona by Madrid. In fact the viceroys never lived here, but for years various police forces used the building as their headquarters. King Philip V later ceded part of the building to Benedictine monks, who were thrown out by the government in 1838. In 1853 the building became the seat of the Arxiu de la Corona de Aragò (Archives of the Crown of Aragón, transferred to Carrer Almogávares 77 in 1994).

Although it was tacked on to Palau Reial halfway through the 16th century, the style of the Renaissance building reflects its Gothic surroundings. ■

The bell tower of Capella Reial de Santa Àgata soars above the mix of Gothic and Roman defenses. The sacristy was actually built in the remains of a Roman tower.

Palau del Lloctinent

⬆ Map p. 59
✉ Carrer dels Comtes de Barcelona
🕐 Closed to the public
🚇 Metro: Línia 4 (Jaume I)

Museu Frederic Marès

Museu Frederic Marès

www.museumare.bcn.es

⬛ Map p. 59

✉ Plaça Sant Iu 5–6

☎ 93 310 58 00

🕐 Closed from 3 p.m. Sun., & Mon.

💲 $

🚇 Metro: Línia 4 (Jaume I)

Left: Among the works found in the museum's upper floors is this lithograph of the Virgin of Montserrat, a symbol of Catalunya.

HOUSED IN PART OF THE FORMER PALAU REIAL, THIS museum contains the extraordinary collection of Frederic Marès i Deulovol (1893–1991), sculptor, traveler, and eccentric. The building itself became home to the Inquisition when the Catholic Monarchs (Ferdinand and Isabella) ordered the Holy Office to set up a Barcelona branch in 1484. That move was made against the will of the locals, who rightly predicted a flight of Barcelona's Jews (converts to Christianity or otherwise) and their wealth, and saw in the Inquisition's arrival a move to tighten central control over Catalunya. The Inquisitors were finally ousted in 1834.

Access the museum from Plaça de Sant Iu via a shady courtyard that flourished during the 15th century as a luxuriant garden of fruit trees and rare birds. The café here makes a pleasant spot to take a break from sightseeing.

Marès concentrated primarily on his collection of medieval wooden polychrome sculptures and busts, of which there are both Romanesque and Gothic examples. These occupy much of the **first and second floors** of the building—the two predominant figures are Christ on the Cross and the Virgin

Mother and the Christ Child. Most of the items that are exhibited here are from Catalunya or other regions of Spain. In an underground hall of the museum stands a proud Romanesque portal taken from a 13th-century church in Aragon and reconstructed here.

The collection takes a leap into the 19th and 20th centuries on the **top two floors.** Here you will find enormous diversity, from toy soldiers and old playing cards through to a room, once Marès' study, that is dedicated to the collector's own sculpture. ∎

Barcelona's Jewish Quarter

In the 600 years since Joan I abolished the city's Jewish quarter in 1401, virtually every sign of its once busy existence has disappeared. But with a little imagination, you can still capture some of the atmosphere of the area as you wander its claustrophobic lanes.

Documents referring to a street that led to the *callem judaicum* (street where Jews live) demonstrate the presence of a strong Jewish community here from at least the 11th century. For Catalans, the Latin word *Calle,* shortened to *Call,* came to mean Jewish quarter. The Lateran Council of 1179 promulgated severe restrictions on Jewish people in Europe, and the Barcelona Call, delimited by Carrers del Call, de Sant Honorat, de Sant Sever, the Baixada de Santa Eulàlia, and the Roman wall, was closed off. A second Call, Call Menor (lesser Call), was later founded around Carrers dels Tres Llits and de la Lleona.

The Jewish people were under the direct protection of the king and within the Call. Beyond the Call, they had to submit to a series of regulations, including the display of a distinguishing sign. Not all of Barcelona's Jews lived in the Call, however: Many had houses elsewhere in the city, and some had small farms. Most of the men were either artisans (cobblers, jewelers, tailors, and so on) or professionals (doctors, lawyers, and translators). Within the two Calls four public synagogues (including one for women only and another for migrant French Jewish people) and two small private ones served religious needs.

The main synagogue (Carrer de Marlet 5, www.calldebarcelona.org, closed 2:30–4 p.m.) was unearthed in the 1990s. All that remains are two vaulted medieval halls.

In 1160 a certain Abraham Bonastruch struck a deal with Count Ramon Berenguer I

Hebrew inscription on Carrer de Marlet, one of the few reminders of the medieval Jewish ghetto, or *Call*

to build a bathhouse much along the lines of the public baths common in the Arab world. Of these Banys Nous (New Baths)—the Banys Vells (Old Baths) were near the Santa Maria del Mar church—nothing remains. The 18th-century house with sgraffito decoration marks their exact location on the corner of Carrer dels Banys Nous and Carrer de la Boqueria.

A rare reminder of the Jewish presence is a stone inscription in Hebrew on Carrer de Marlet. It reads, "The Pious Foundation of Samuel Ha-Sardí. His light burns permanently." Medieval foundations of this sort were generally hospices for the poor and ill.

In 1391 a pogrom broke out in Seville and spread across the Iberian Peninsula. The Barcelona Call was sacked on August 5 and 7. Ten years later, Joan I ordered the abolition of the Call and allowed Jewish people (including *conversos,* those converted to Christianity) to live where they chose. The town fathers moved in to repair the damage, and soon Christians bought up many of the houses. Many Jews maintained positions of importance in Barcelona society, but this was to change.

Toward the end of the 15th century Ferdinand and Isabella installed the Inquisition in Barcelona and the Holy Office was diligent in its search for enemies of the faith in the early decades of its presence. As Jewish people had been ordered to convert or leave in 1492, most of those remaining in Barcelona were conversos and many of them wealthy contributors to Catalan public finances. The Inquisition doubted the sincerity of their conversion, however, and made life intolerable for them. As the Catalans had feared, the Jews fled, taking their wealth and skills with them. ∎

Hebrew literature (left) in a Call shop; St. George's image at Carrer del Call (right)

Curious little shops, such as the Sombrería Obach, fill the streets of the Call.

Plaça de Sant Jaume

NAMED AFTER A CHURCH DEDICATED TO ST. JAMES THAT stood here until its demolition in 1824, this square has been at the center of the city's political life since at least the 14th century. In Roman times the forum lay just to the north, but by the early Middle Ages the square was little more than a discreet widening in the streets. That all began to change when construction started on what is now the Ajuntament (city hall) on the south side of the square, and the Generalitat opposite it in the following century. The square only took on its present form in 1823. Until then, much of what is now open space had been occupied by a church and cemetery.

Ajuntament

www.bcn.es

 Map p. 59

✉ Plaça de Sant Jaume

☎ 010 80 711 77 00

🕐 Closed Mon.-Fri. & p.m. Sat.–Sun.

🚇 Metro: Línia 4 (Jaume I)

In 1274 the Consell de Cent (Council of One Hundred) had been formed from leading citizens to run city affairs, all with the consent of the count-kings. Construction of the Gothic Casa de la Ciutat, as the **Ajuntament** is also known, began in the 14th century, but to look at it from the outside, you'd never know. Apart from the elegant windows and portal facing Carrer de la Ciutat, once the main entrance, virtually nothing of the Gothic facade remains.

The 19th-century edifice is a rather uninspiring, neoclassic effort, while the flank facing Plaça de Sant Miquel and the offices attached to the back are almost inconceivably ugly. Some of the architectural meddling was the result of damage caused by a bombardment during a popular uprising of 1842 that was, needless to say, put down with little ceremony.

Fortunately, inside the building a great deal of the original Gothic splendor remains intact, even if it has been tinkered with repeatedly over the centuries. As you enter the courtyard you will probably be directed to the right, where you proceed up the **Escala d'Honor.** This regal staircase leads up to the

Gothic gallery, from which you enter the onetime meeting hall of the Council of One Hundred, **Saló de Cent.** For centuries thereafter the town council held its plenary session here. (A plaque on the left wall commemorates the first session held here in 1373.) The broad vaulting is pure Catalan Gothic and the timber ceiling demonstrates fine work. Not all that you see is the real McCoy, however. The wooden seating was added at the beginning of the 20th century, as was the grand alabaster retable at the back.

The modern city council now sits in the rather more modest **Saló de la Reina Regente,** built in 1860 to the right of the Saló de Cent in honor of the then regent of Spain, Maria Cristina.

To the left of the Saló de Cent is the **Saló de les Croniques.** Here the series of 20th-century murals brings to life episodes of Catalunya's colorful efforts to extend its mercantile empire into Greece and the Near East. Temporarily unemployed knight errant Roger de Flor and 8,000 of his merry men had set off on a quixotic mercenary mission to fight the Ottoman Turks in the service of the tottering Byzantine Empire. In spite of Roger's successes, the Byzantines didn't feel obliged to pay up and the ensuing disagreements led to the assassination of Roger in 1305.

Shortly thereafter the Companyia Catalana a l'Orient (Catalan Company in the East) was formed; one of its aims was to avenge Roger. In what became known as the *Venjança Catalana* (Catalan Revenge), troops torched and pillaged the area around Constantinople (although they failed to enter the city). They then established themselves in the new duchies of Athens, Thebes, and Neopatras. The first two lasted under the patronage of the Catalan rulers of Sicily until the 1380s, but Byzantium retook Neopatras in 1335. The adventure was immortalized in purplish prose by the chronicler and propagandist Ramon Muntaner (1265–1336), who took part in some of the episodes. Scenes depicted include the taking of the Acropolis in Athens.

From the Saló de les Croniques a staircase leads back down to the courtyard, where there is a series of statues of women. One of them, although you may have trouble making out the connection between art and reality, is by Joan Miró.

Facing the Ajuntament is the **Palau de la Generalitat,** medieval home to the Diputació de la Generalitat (or permanent council of the Corts Catalanes—Parliament—which first met in 1283) and today seat of the regional Catalan government.

The building has evolved strangely over the centuries. After the pogrom of 1391 and the decree scrapping the neighboring Jewish

Carrer del Bisbe Irurita, which follows the ancient Roman street into the city, connects Barcelona's political and religious centers, Plaça de Sant Jaume and the Catedral.

Palau de la Generalitat

www.gencat.es

🗺 Map p. 59

✉ Plaça de Sant Jaume

🕐 Open 10 a.m.–1 p.m. 2nd & 4th Sun. (except Aug. & Dec.) and all day (no tours) April 23, Sept. 11 & 24

🚇 Metro: Línia 4 (Jaume I)

Anyone who knows the steps can join the sardana circle; dancers just spread out to allow newcomers in.

quarter in 1401, some members of the Diputació acquired houses in the area, particularly along Carrer de Sant Honorat, which before had marked the limit of the Jewish quarter. The bulging wall of the Generalitat on that street is a reminder of the building's origins. Several of these houses were then connected by a garden to Carrer del Bisbe Irurita. In the following years a more organized plan to house the Diputació evolved.

The facade on Carrer del Bisbe Irurita by Marc Safont, sporting sculpted episodes in the story of St. George and the dragon, is the finest. It was once the main entrance and was completed in 1425. Sant Jordi, as he is called in Catalan, is the region's patron saint. The covered walkway across Carrer del Bisbe Irurita looks genuinely Gothic but was actually built in 1926. Today the palace's ceremonial entrance is directly on the square, but the facade is a rather disappointing Renaissance-era makeover.

If you are in town when the Palau is open to the public, take advantage. You enter from the rear (Carrer de Sant Sever) and pass through several rooms with low vaulted ceilings before emerging upstairs in the raised courtyard

known as the **Pati dels Tarongers,** a late Gothic orangery. The 16th-century **Sala Daurada i de Sessions,** leading off the courtyard, is a splendid meeting hall lit up by huge chandeliers. The most spectacular of the Palau's seemingly endless halls, though, is the Renaissance **Saló de Sant Jordi,** whose murals were added this century. It is used to receive visiting dignitaries. Finally, you descend the staircase from the magnificent Gothic gallery that frames the **Pati Central,** the final courtyard from which you exit onto Carrer del Bisbe Irurita.

Back on Plaça de Sant Jaume notice the distinguished financial institution, La Caixa, facing the Ajuntament across the square on the corner of Carrer de la Ciutat. Monetary transactions have been carried out on this site for at least 600 years, for on this spot was the **Taula del Canvi** (literally "change table"), the money-moneychangers' center. Established in 1401, it was one of Europe's earliest public banking institutions, where the city administration kept its funds and citizens deposited savings, paid taxes, and took out loans. It remained active until the 18th century. ■

Dancing the sardana

If it can be said that the passion of flamenco rules the heart of southern Spain, then it is true to say that Catalans dance to the beat of a different drum. The unkind would remark that the *sardana* reflects a chilly sobriety for which Catalans are known elsewhere in Spain. Dancers hold hands in a circle and, accompanied by about ten musicians playing various kinds of flutes, bob about in rather controlled fashion—a series of steps

to the right, one back, and then the same to the left. When they get carried away, the dancers raise their arms in the air for a moment. Up to ten musicians playing various kinds of flutes accompany them.

Many Catalans find it boring, but others turn up for a twirl at noon on Sundays in front of the Catedral, one of the best chances you will have to see the dance, whose origins lie in old folk dances of northeastern Catalunya. ■

Església de Santa Maria del Pi to Plaça Reial

BY THE 11TH CENTURY, BARCELONA BEGAN TO BURST ITS Roman walls. It would be another two centuries before new walls were raised, so in the meantime *ravals,* or satellite hamlets, sprang up beyond the walls. One grew around the Romanesque predecessor of the grand Gothic Església de Santa Maria del Pi. A brief stroll away you cross into another world. Plaça Reial, laid out on the site of a former Capuchin convent, is now a focal point of nocturnal entertainment, an elegant space that received an early touch of Gaudí magic.

Founded in 1322 to replace a Romanesque church, the austere Gothic structure that dominates busy Plaça del Pi and Plaça de Sant Josep Oriol was dedicated to the Virgin Mary. Plaça del Pi got its name from a pine tree (*pi* in Catalan), a descendant of which still graces the square, and the church soon came to be known as **Santa Maria del Pi** (Holy Mary of the Pine Tree).

The facade is a forbidding wall of stone, broken only by the immense rose window and the grand entrance portal. It is typical

The huge rose window is about the only decorative concession in the otherwise austere Església de Santa Maria del Pi.

Església de Santa Maria del Pi

🗺 Map p. 59

✉ Plaça de Sant Josep Oriol

🕐 Closed 1–5 p.m. Mon.–Fri.; 1–4:30 p.m. Sat.; 2–5 p.m. Sun. & holidays

🚇 Metro: Línia 3 (Liceu)

Gaudí first set to work in Barcelona with a commission to create the Plaça Reial's lampposts.

Barri Gòtic's balconies afford views for often sleepless locals.

of the most sober of Catalan Gothic, eschewing virtually all exterior ornament. Think back to the ornate Catedral; the difference is notable. Inside, a vast, broad nave opens up before you, almost 56 feet (17 m) wide. Flanking it to either side is a series of chapels ensconced in between the buttresses that help keep the huge structure standing. High above soars the ribbed vaulting that holds together the ceiling. Look back to the entrance

to admire the long flat arch supporting the choir—a feature of Catalan Gothic and no mean feat of engineering. The church was filled with artworks of enormous value, many of them dating from the 14th century, but most were lost in the early volatile days of the civil war in 1936, when leftists torched this and other churches across the city.

Several religious brotherhoods *(confraries)* have their headquarters in this church. Members of one of

We want to sleep!

The squares of the central Barri Gòtic burst with history, stores, and tempting cafés. Some are also full of an endless din, and Plaça Reial and the surrounding streets were a nocturnal no-go zone until well into the 1980s. Although things have improved here and elsewhere in what was a decidedly unsavory part of town, the racket from revelers until the small hours drives local citizens to despair. Combined with all-night street musi-

cians (especially the bongo brigade), the decibel count in a city already known as one of the noisiest in the world must be impressive. Local police seem unwilling or unable to impose much order on either the noise or the petty crime that also afflicts the area, and the long-suffering tenants frequently vent their frustration by hanging out plaintive placards of protest on their balconies. Spare them a thought and watch your pockets. ■

these brotherhoods, the Arxiconfraria de la Puríssima Sang (Archfraternity of the Most Pure Blood), dedicated themselves to the task of accompanying the condemned to their place of execution and lending them spiritual solace in their final moments.

Directly opposite the church on Plaça del Pi is an attractive 17th-century building with 18th-century sgraffiti. It once housed one of the city *gremis* (guilds). The **square** gets busy on many evenings with a market offering all sorts of enticing food products. Running north of the square is narrow **Carrer de Petritxol,** which has been home to chocolate and pastry shops since the 18th century.

Around the corner from Plaça del Pi is another pleasing square, **Plaça de Sant Josep Oriol;** the entire western flank is occupied by the side of the church. Several cafés set up tables outside in what is doubtless one of the prettiest little corners of the old city. Facing the right flank of the church across the square at No. 4 is a smart 16th-century mansion, **Palau de Fiveller,** built in 1571 for the influential aristocratic Fiveller family. The facade was reworked in the 18th century so horses and carriages could drive right inside.

Following the line of the church south through Plaça de Sant Josep Oriol you turn onto the less inviting Placeta del Pi, behind the church's apse, and then proceed down Carrer d'En Rauric to reach the unusually rectilinear **Carrer de Ferran.** This is no medieval thoroughfare, but was sliced through here in 1823 and named after Spain's anachronistically absolutist king, Fernando VII (Ferran to the Catalans). Along it is the facade of the **Església de Sant Jaume,** which started life as a synagogue and was later turned into a church

and convent by Jewish converts. Joan Miró, one of Spain's great 20th-century artists, was born in 1893 in an apartment in Passatge del Credit, a covered arcade that runs south of Carrer de Ferran close to Plaça de Sant Jaume.

For those not expecting it, stumbling onto **Plaça Reial** (Royal Square), with its solid porticoes and slender palm trees, comes as quite a surprise. Nineteenth-century neoclassic facades mask grand rambling apartments. French and Castilian models inspired the design of the square, and it is hard to picture the convent that stood here previously. Look for the lampposts nearest the central fountain; they are the earliest known commission undertaken by Antoni Gaudí. The square and some of its southern back-streets contain some of Barcelona's classic restaurants and bars, while a muddle of lanes runs down to the busy Passeig de Colom and the waterfront from here (see pp. 99–116). ∎

Modernisme penetrated medieval Barcelona too, as this shop on Carrer de Santa Anna testifies.

Towers of strength

Catalans have cornered the market in one highly bizarre sector of the construction industry—human castles, or *castells*. *Castellers* have been raising these "edifices" to extraordinary heights for 200 years in the southwest of Catalunya, particularly around Tarragona and the Penedès region. This unique folkloric activity supposedly has its roots in medieval siege tactics, but is now just an amateur sport, although it's taken very seriously.

The first golden age came in the 1880s, when *colles* (teams) of several hundred people would form complex castells of varying dimensions as high as ten stories. The second golden age came in the 1990s, when the activity seemed suddenly to grab the attention of Catalans across the region. At the last count there were 78 colles.

Several teams are active in and around Barcelona. They and other teams across the region (the best are from Valls and Vilafranca del Penedès) compete in town fairs and on holidays from about February through October. Every two years (even years) a championship competition is held at the Tarragona bullring. During the Festes de la Mercè in September you can see local and outside teams competing in Barcelona's Plaça de Sant Jaume.

Castellers attempt to build human layers as high as possible and then to dismantle the lot without collapsing in an undignified heap. The "basement" of the *tronc* (trunk) is a broad concentric scrum known as a *pinya* and upon this the castellers build their castle, which can be of many different types. About the best ever

Recipe for a *castell* (human castle):
Strong arms, steady legs—and bare feet

achieved is a *tres de deu*, or three by ten—that means ten levels of people standing on each other's shoulders. Other difficult formations include the *quatre de nou* (four by nine) and *cinc de vuit* (five by eight). Often the pinya does not provide sufficient support, and so the second level will be buttressed by castellers forming the *folre* (lining). *Manilles* (literally "handcuffs," but here it means another layer of people) are occasionally added at the third level. Where neither manilles nor folre are employed (which is harder), the castell is *net* (clean).

The successful *quatre de nou amb folre* will require a good 500 participants and look like this: at the base a populous pinya pushing into the center and on their shoulders the smaller folre. Above are four stories each of four people with their arms locked around each other's shoulders. The seventh level consists of two people, above whom one person crouches to form the penultimate story. The *agulla* (pinnacle) is a lightweight child, the *anxaneta*, who scrambles up the structure to the top and waves his/her hand to indicate the castell has been completed. The anxaneta then scuttles back down and each level lowers itself by sliding down the lower stories. A castell that is successfully disassembled wins greater admiration than one that collapses.

Some teams aim to make broad, squat castells (like *nou de set*, or seven stories of nine people each), while others try for slender *torres* (levels of two people), or *pilars* (levels of one); the latter two rarely rise beyond six levels. ■

More places to visit in Barri Gòtic

ESGLÉSIA DE LA MERCÈ

One of Barcelona's few baroque houses of worship, this church is also home to the image of Nostra Senyora de la Mercè (Our Lady of Mercy), the city's co-patron saint. She was elevated to this exalted role when, it is said, she single-handedly warded off a bout of the plague in 1637. More curious still, Our Lady was made commander-in-chief of the city's defenses toward the end of the siege that ended the War of the Spanish Succession, and Catalunyan autonomy, in 1714. She was forgiven this failing and is the religious focal point of the city's biggest annual party, the Festes de la Mercè, held in late September to mark the end of the summer. The church is actually a curious mix: A Renaissance flank on Carrer Ample (which was transferred from another church in 1870) accompanies the main baroque facade. The whole edifice was built over an earlier Gothic structure.

Map p. 59 Plaça de la Mercè 1 Closed 1–6 p.m. Mon.–Sat., 1:30–7 p.m. Sun. & holidays Metro: Línia 4 (Jaume I)

ESGLÉSIA DE SANTA ANNA

Back in 1141, members of the military order of the Holy Sepulchre began construction of a monastery dedicated to St. Anne. It lay beyond the Roman walls, which still served as the city's northern defense perimeter, and a small "suburb" soon grew around the church and its cloister and gardens. The church you see today is largely Gothic, although some Romanesque elements are visible, and the shady if somewhat unkempt Gothic cloister comes as a lovely surprise. The complex is hidden away on a little square off Carrer Comtal and much ignored by the passing tourist trade.

Map p. 59 Plaça de Ramon Amadeu Closed 1–6:30 p.m., from 2 p.m. Sun. & holidays Metro: Línies 3 (Drassanes) & 4 (Jaume I)

ESGLÉSIA DE SANT FELIP NERI

Again hidden away from the main stream of visitors to the city, but barely a hop, skip, and jump from the Catedral, this modest baroque church was built in the mid-18th century. Look for the bullet holes in the wall: In one of the city's sadder chapters, the Nationalists used this square for the summary execution of Republicans rounded up in the city following its fall in January 1939. The shady square was once a medieval cemetery; looking onto it is the Gremi de Sabaters, the medieval cobblers' guild—look for the stone standard depicting the lion of St. Mark, the shoemaker's patron saint. Inside today is the fusty, little-visited **Museu del Calçat,** or Shoe Museum *(Closed Mon.),* where you can see everything from Roman sandals to elegant silk slip-ons of the 18th century.

Map p. 59 Plaça de Sant Felip Neri Closed p.m. Metro: Línies 3 (Liceu) & 4 (Jaume I)

ESGLÉSIA DE SANTS JUST I PASTOR

Traditionally claimed to be the oldest church in Barcelona (apart from the Catedral), it is thought to have been founded in 801. The present structure was raised about six centuries later in typical Catalan Gothic style, with one broad nave and a lack of fussy decorative effects. To this church was accorded an unusual privilege: From the 11th to the 15th centuries, court cases that could not be resolved by standard judicial process could be dealt with in a Trial of God. The two parties would come to the church and vow to fight it out according to the rules stipulated by this privilege, which also covered what arms could be employed. God ensured that the guilty party lost.

At the junction of narrow streets that forms Plaça de Sant Just in front of the church is a medieval fountain. If you follow the dead-end Carrer del Bisbe Caçador to the end and find the gates open, you can enter the magnificent Gothic courtyard of **Palau Requesens,** also known as Palau de la Comtessa de Palamós. Look up at the narrow windows; some of them are Romanesque and others are Gothic.

Map p. 59 Plaça de Sant Just Closed noon–6:30 p.m. Metro: Línia 4 (Jaume I) ■

Barcelona's main boulevard, La Rambla is undeniably the city's center stage. Off to its west is El Raval, an enclave of Gaudí fantasy, modern art, and late-night watering holes where just a frisson of the dark old days lingers on.

La Rambla & El Raval

A permanent resident peers out from the front of a house in La Rambla.

La Rambla & El Raval

LA RAMBLA UNDERGOES FIVE NAME CHANGES ALONG ITS LENGTH, suggesting that more than a little history lies behind the impassive hotel facades and colorful street theater of Barcelona's best-known avenue. The broad pedestrian-only promenade, which runs southeast toward the old port from central Plaça de Catalunya and is flanked by two narrow (and often choked) traffic lanes, bubbles with activity.

During their short stay in eighth-century Barcelona, the Muslims applied the Arabic name *al-raml* (stream) to the unimpressive rivulet that dribbled into the Mediterranean beyond the city's western wall. By the time Jaume I raised new walls alongside it in the mid-13th century, that stream was reduced to a stinking sewage ditch. Beyond it sprawled the fetid mess of El Raval, a shantytown that would later be incorporated into the city.

Jaume's wall was thus deprived of its defensive intent, and in its shadow La Rambla gradually took shape. First, starting in the 1530s, came convents and churches. Later, nobles built mansions here. When the wall was finally pulled down in the mid-19th century, the gaps were filled with new housing.

What stretches before us now is a year-round carnival. Daytime strollers, tourists, and the occasional three-card trickster are replaced at night by hedonists, hookers, and one or two petty thieves (watch your valuables). In the predawn hours the pleasure-seekers wend their animated way past newsstands, already open, to Plaça de Catalunya for a cab home.

To the west of La Rambla lies El Raval. Poorest of the old city's quarters and home to the shadowy, down-at-heel red-light district of Barri Xinès, the area is changing fast. New streets have been laid out and buildings are being restored. A wave of migrants has altered the face of El Raval. With the creation of the MACBA modern art museum and other galleries, an infusion of young blood has brought refreshing life to what was long a neglected slum. A tribe of new bars, cafés, restaurants, and clubs attests to the trend. Most tourists fail to move beyond Gaudí's extraordinary

Area of map detail

Palau Güell, just off La Rambla, but other lesser-known gems, some admittedly still in need of a polish, await discovery. For all its roughness, a wander around El Raval adds a rewarding dimension to knowledge of the city. ■

Universitat

CARRER DE PELAI

CARRER DE VALLDONZELLA

RONDA DE SANT ANTONI

Sant Sever i Carles Boromeo

PLAÇA DE CASTELLA

CARRER DELS TALLERS

Centre de Cultura Contemporània de Barcelona (CCCB)

C. DE MONTALEGRE

Museu d'Art Contemporani de Barcelona (MACBA)

Catalunya

Font de les Canaletes

PLAÇA DELS ÀNGELS

pharmacy

LA RAMBLA

Convent dels Àngels

C. DELS ÀNGELS

Reial Acadèmia de Ciències i Arts (Poliorama)

CARRER DE LA RIERA ALTA

C. DE J. COSTA

Tabacos de Filipines

Església de Betlem

C. DE SANT ANTONI ABAT

Sant Antoni

CARRER DEL CARME

Palau Comillas (Palau Moja)

CARRER DE LA CERA

Antic Hospital de la Santa Creu (Biblioteca Nacional de Catalunya)

C. DEL CARME

Palau de la Virreina

EL RAVAL

CARRER DE LES CARRETES

CARRER DE LA RIERA ALTA

Capella de l'Hospital

CARRER DE L'HOSPITAL

PLAÇA DE LA GARDUNYA

Museu de l'Eròtica

Mercat de la Boqueria

RONDA DE SANT PAU

RAMBLA DEL RAVAL

RAMBLA DEL RAVAL

Antiga Casa del Dr. Genové

Antiga Casa Figueres

Casa Bruno Quadros

Església de Sant Agustí

Liceu

CARRER DE SANT PAU

Gran Teatre del Liceu

LA RAMBLA

CARRER DE SANT PAU

Església de Sant Pau del Camp

Hotel Orient

PLAÇA REIAL

CARRER NOU DE LA RAMBLA

Palau Güell

Paral·lel

AVINGUDA DEL PARAL·LEL

CARRER DE

BARRI XINÈS

L'ARC DEL TEATRE

Teatre Principal

AVINGUDA DE LES DRASSANES

Centre d'Art Santa Mònica

Drassanes

LA RAMBLA

Museu de Cera

Many distractions await pedestrians along La Rambla's central section.

0   200 meters
0   200 yards

Rambling along La Rambla

La Rambla is Barcelona's drawing room. For more than a century townspeople have gathered along the lively pedestrian boulevard to chat, stroll, or duck into a café to pass the time. Unofficially divided into five segments (which is why some call it Las Ramblas), its colorful parade of buskers, impersonators, puppeteers, and posing human statues also makes it a popular first stop for visitors.

They say that if you slake your thirst from the late 19th-century drinking fountain, **Font de les Canaletes,** at the top end of La Rambla, you will surely return to Barcelona. This initial stretch, known as **La Rambla de Canaletes,** was the last to be cleared in the second half of the 19th century, when the final vestiges of Jaume I's wall were demolished and new housing was raised. Some of those buildings remain, such as Nos. 134–136, which stand next to where the Santa Anna gate once stood, and Nos. 125–129 across the road. The **pharmacy ❶** at No. 121 retains its distinctive *modernista* decor.

The second stage of the street is known as **La Rambla dels Estudis,** after the early 16th-century academic institute, the Estudis

La Rambla, Barcelona's famous pedestrian street, is lined with cafés and vendors.

> 🗺 See area map p. 87
> ▶ Plaça de Catalunya
> ↔ 0.75 mile (1.25 km)
> 🕐 1 hour
> ▶ Museu de Cera
>
> **NOT TO BE MISSED**
> - Palau de la Virreina
> - Mercat de la Boqueria
> - Museu de l'Eròtica
> - Gran Teatre del Liceu
> - Hotel Oriente

Generals, that occupied the area until 1844. Several striking buildings line this part of La Rambla. Number 115, the **Reial Acadèmia de Ciències i Arts (Poliorama),** was established as a seat of learning during the Enlightenment in the 18th century and

La Rambla appears a leafy, meandering river from atop the Monument a Colom.

received its present look in an 1883 makeover. A little farther down at No. 109 is the large, imposing 19th-century **Tabacos de Filipinas** building, the headquarters of the company in control of Philippine tobacco imports and destined for conversion into a hotel. Next door is the baroque **Església de Betlem ➋**, part of a 16th-century Jesuit compound that included a religious college. The present church dates from the end of the 17th century and is one of a few outstanding examples of baroque architecture in the city. The interior decoration was lost when anarchists torched the church in the Spanish Civil War in 1936.

Across La Rambla is one of three grand private residences built along the boulevard in the late 18th century, **Palau Comillas (Palau Moja).** You can see temporary exhibitions

here and peer into the courtyard from the main entrance on Carrer Portaferrissa.

This street takes its name from the Iron Gate, a city gate that once stood here. It was lso called after the iron bar used to close it at night. The same bar had a double function as one of the official yardsticks of medieval Barcelona. This section of La Rambla is also known as La Rambla dels Ocells (Birds), since here you can buy a feathered companion at one of various stands.

Next, the street comes to be known as **La Rambla de Sant Josep,** after a Carmelite convent that stood here until the mid-19th century. Flower stands abound, explaining the second sobriquet of La Rambla de les Flors. **Palau de la Virreina** ❸, another fine mansion begun in 1772 and named after the widow of the Viceroy of Peru, fronts it. One of the most outstanding baroque residences in Barcelona, it is now used in part to stage temporary art exhibitions. On the first

On Sunday the market comes to Plaça Reial, where people can trade stamps, coins, and an assortment of knickknacks.

floor you'll find an information and ticketing shop for events around the city.

Next door spreads the grand expanse of the **Mercat de la Boqueria** ❹, a modernista palace of metal and light, and a colorful place to do grocery shopping. It stands on the site of a Carmelite convent founded in 1586. Across the road at No. 83 is yet another modernista delight, **Antiga Casa Figueres,** adorned with marvelous mosaic and stucco ornamentation. A couple of other extraordinary buildings from the same period are the narrow, blue-tiled **Antiga Casa del Doctor Genové** at No. 77 and the former umbrella-makers' house, **Casa Bruno Quadros,** clad with model umbrellas, at No. 82.

Back up a little at No. 96 is a more recent curio on this street of curios—the **Museu de**

The elegant Gran Teatre del Liceu on La Rambla, rebuilt after a fire in the 1990s, is the city's main opera house.

l'Eròtica ⑤. Here you can see ancient phalluses, paintings, and figurines depicting unending variants on copulatory poses contained in the "Kama Sutra," some rather remarkable porn movies of the 1920s, and a chamber dedicated to sadomasochism.

A Joan Miró mosaic in the pavement marks Plaça de la Boqueria, the convergence point of a couple of streets with La Rambla. This also indicates the next stage of the avenue, **La Rambla dels Caputxins,** named after Capuchin monks who had a monastery here. Most interesting now is the **Gran Teatre del Liceu** ⑥ (see pp. 98 and 263), the city's premier lyric theater that was reopened in late 1999 after being burned several years earlier. Various elements of *modernista* decoration have been retained and the best way to see them is to enjoy a high-quality opera performance during a stay in town.

A little farther down at Nos. 45–47 is the **Hotel Oriente** ⑦ (see p. 251). Once a

Franciscan religious college, the building was converted into a hotel in the middle of the 19th century. The former cloister and refectory have been preserved and lend much to the faded elegance of the place.

Virtually opposite the hotel is the entrance to the 19th-century **Plaça Reial** (see p. 81). Off to the west down Carrer Nou de la Rambla is **Palau Güell** (see pp. 92–93). From here onward the avenue gets decidedly seedier. Late into the night, groups of unhappy-looking hookers huddle among a couple of sad strip clubs, strangely out of place amid the bustle of the street stands on the pedestrian strip that runs down the middle of La Rambla.

You pass another theater, the **Teatre Principal** and a nondescript square of the same name as the street enters its final incarnation as **La Rambla de Santa Mònica,** named after the convent that has now been converted into an arts center, the **Centre d'Art Santa Mònica.**

Across La Rambla and down an alley is the last attraction before you reach the end, the **Museu de Cera** ⑧ *(Closed 1:30–4 p.m.),* a wax museum with figures ranging from Salvador Dali to Don Quixote.■

Gaudí's almost obsessive use of the parabolic arch reaches a pinnacle in the high ceiling of the Palau Güell.

Palau Güell

ONE OF ANTONI GAUDÍ'S EARLIEST MASTERPIECES STANDS just off La Rambla. Even before entering, it is clear that this is no ordinary work of architecture—the two parabolic arches that serve as the entrance are unmistakable Gaudian signatures. His main patron, the wealthy industrialist Eusebi Güell i Bacigalupi (1846–1918), commissioned the building in the early 1880s as an annex to his prime residence on La Rambla. The result is a typically bizarre stylistic mix, as Gaudí looked to past conventions (especially Gothic and Islamic art) to inspire his fresh *modernista* take. You must join a guided tour to explore the entrails of this singular animal.

Palau Güell

- Map p. 87
- Carrer Nou de la Rambla 3–5
- 93 317 51 98
- Closed for restoration until Dec. 2006
- $
- Metro: Línia 3 (Liceu)

While waiting for the next tour to start, it is worth inspecting the **vestibule.** The pavement appears to be brick but in fact the "bricks" are made of red pinewood, which deadened the clatter of horses' hoofs. The walls are largely unclad brick, unusual as conventional wisdom of the time held that this was an ignoble, not to say, ugly material. Gaudí had earthy but innovative taste, hence the extensive use of black wrought iron throughout the building. Another odd feature here is the use of ceramic tiles to clothe the ceiling.

The tour begins at the rear of the vestibule down ramps to the **stables** below ground level. Here again, unclad brick lends warmth to the slightly bizarre landscape of columns with mushroom-like capitals. A spiral ramp winds back up into the vestibule, from which the tour continues up a rather gloomy gray marble stairway. After passing through a small chamber, the **Escala d'Honor,** or principal stairway, leads up to the main floor of the house.

Here a series of three **antechambers** looks onto the street and screens off the central salon where the Güell family would receive visitors before ushering them farther into the house. Again the wrought iron is of note, particularly the lamps. Remember to look up, especially in the tiny third room, as the ceilings are magnificent constructions of timber and iron.

The **central salon,** entered through splendid doors, is a curious space indeed. On a square base, four parabolic arches soar three stories and end in a dome, giving the sensation of being in a tiny cathedral. Here the Güell family held chic parties and occasional political meetings. Sometimes the room became the family chapel; its altar was destroyed during the civil war.

From the salon a passage leads to the **dining room,** a sumptuous affair of walnut paneling and furniture. The space next door to the dining room is dominated by a **tribune** fronted by four parabolic arches atop columns. It pushes outward from the rear of the building in the form of a semicircular balcony whose ceramic decoration can be admired from the little **terrace** that opens out from the dining area.

A couple of flights of service stairs climb from the dining area up

onto the **roof** of the building. On the way you can peer down into the central salon from several different angles. The roof itself presents the kind of weirdness one expects from Gaudí. Ranks of bizarrely shaped chimney pots, some coated with a dazzling and fragmented array of brightly colored tiles, can only leave you guessing as to whether Gaudí was simply giving in to an almost childlike playfulness or had other more complex intentions. No two chimney pots are alike—each is a separate work of art.

From the roof you can gaze across the old city's rooftops west toward Palau Nacional (see pp. 186–88) on Montjuïc and east toward the Catedral (see pp. 60–65) and Església de Santa Maria del Mar (see pp. 131–32). ∎

The bizarre battalion of chimney pots is the icing on the Palau Güell cake.

El Barri Xinès

Nowadays, Barcelona's biggest concentration of streetwalking ladies of the night hangs out around the Camp Nou soccer stadium, and yet the Barri Xinès (Chinese Quarter—a strange term having nothing to do with Asia but meaning red-light district) still sputters along, living off a long and colorful reputation as the naughtiest part of town. It is a bedraggled and at times dispiriting area today, roughly occupying El Raval from Carrer de Sant Pau south.

Ladies of the night still frequent the Barri Xinès.

Poor Barcelonians share cramped housing with floods of migrants from North Africa and Pakistan. Petty drug-traffickers hawk their wares in wangling whispers; the unwary or unlucky are relieved of their wallets and purses. And although the sex trade is largely carried on elsewhere in the city, a small group of diehards still plies the lower half of La Rambla into the small hours. The girls, and boys who want to be girls, mostly look like they have seen better days but nevertheless can occasionally be seen stealing off into the back streets with clients who tend to be unsteady on their feet.

In a sense, it was always thus. Back in the years before World War I and again in the 1920s and '30s, the Barri Xinès was the place to go for smoky, low-lit entertainment. Everyone from cigar-puffing magnates to local gangsters, artists such as Picasso to pickpocketing lowlifes, tumbled in to the area's questionable taverns and lipstick whorehouses. A well-known bordello was Madame Petit at Carrer de l'Arc del Teatre 6, while the drinking houses and louche cabarets of Carrer Nou de la Rambla were especially well patronized.

Then came the civil war and Franco. Much of the activity ceased from 1936 as the austerity of war replaced the chaotic hedonism that had marked the 1920s. With Franco in charge from 1939, a new Puritanism was inevitable and by 1950 many of the brothels and taverns had been shut down.

In spite of this, a sparkling handful of classics survived. Some keep comfortingly late hours and even retain just a whiff of the old spirit. For all the tired tawdriness of the Barri Xinès, a nocturnal tour of some of these establishments—increasingly under assault by tourists and in the growing company of trendier new watering holes—is something of a highlight for night owls.

Back in 1820, **Bar Marsella** (*Carrer de Sant Pau 65*) opened its doors, and it seems barely anything has changed since. It still serves *absenta* (absinthe), a beverage hard to find because of its supposed narcotic qualities. The drink is a complicated aniseed affair into which you melt sugar cubes with water to produce the full pleasing effect.

One of Picasso's personal favorites was the **London Bar** (*Carrer Nou de la Rambla 36*), with its *modernista* decor and floorshow. It still attracts the occasional good jazz act and you can sip your preferred tipple at the bar until 5 a.m. People have been cramming in here to do so since 1909.

A more conspiratorial air predominates in the claustrophobic **Bar Pastís** (*Carrer de Santa Mònica 4*). French singer Edith Piaf is the mascot. In business off and on since the end of World War II, if they aren't playing Piaf records, chances are the live music will be just as Gallic. ∎

Apartment blocks of Barri Xinès

Colorful food stand on El Raval

Museu d'Art Contemporani de Barcelona (MACBA)

NEVER LET IT BE SAID THAT ART AND THE REAL WORLD
have nothing to do with one another. In 1995 this inspired little
treasure trove of contemporary art was opened as part of a plan to
breathe new life into the top half of El Raval. The result has been
spectacular. Tourists and art lovers flock to the museum, and the
area has shaken off its seediness without losing the charm.

MACBA

www.macba.es

🏛 Map p. 87

✉ Plaça dels Àngels 1

☎ 93 412 08 10

🕐 Closed Tues. & from
3 p.m. Sun.

💲 $$

🚇 Metro: Linies 1 & 2
(Universitat)

The bright white architectural
knight was designed by American
Richard Meier. Neither as ambi-
tious or outlandish as Paris's
Pompidou Center, Meier's creation
still shows considerable functional
panache. The main entrance is a
pleasing interplay of vertical planes,
while a curvaceous bulge caps the
opposite end and juts into the
square. Skateboarding kids animate
the area in front; serious art lovers
prowl around inside.

The structure and idea are
simple. On the first floor an ever
changing arrangement of the
gallery's permanent collection
forms the core and expresses the
museum's aims: to present an inter-
national sketch of modern art
trends with a strong Barcelona spin.
A spiral staircase and graceful
ramps for the disabled lead up to
two floors above, reserved for
temporary exhibitions.

Although works from the per-
manent collection are in constant
rotation, a few general observations
can be made. It is divided into four
periods. The first extends from the
late 1940s to 1968, and among the
artists represented are Alexander
Calder, Paul Klee, Hans Hofmann,
and Àngel Ferrant. Two particular
trends are represented: the infor-
malism of Barcelona's Antoni
Tàpies (and others) and construc-
tivism. Informalism is rooted in

surrealism and its protagonists abandoned themselves to spontaneous, unstructured creation. Many of Tàpies' works use materials such as sand, marble dust, wood, and acrylic paint to produce heavy, three-dimensional whimsy you can almost taste. Among the more order-seeking constructivists was Madrid's Pablo Palazuelo.

The second period, from 1968 to the mid-1970s, is a blossoming of revolt and questioning in art (mirroring a similar feeling toward Franco's regime). Catalan conceptual artists Francesc Abad and Francesc Torres feature alongside figures like Italy's Mario Merz and Germany's Dieter Roth, whose striking 1970 "Schokoladenmeer" (Ocean of Chocolate) is an embodiment of the ferment.

The next period extends to the end of the 1980s, and here the line between media and material blurs. Metalwork, photography, painting, and just about anything else blend in a creative mix. Yet the likes of Miguel Barceló and Jean-Michel Basquiat rediscovered painting as a primary art form.

The final period takes us from 1990 to the present. One of the characteristics of present-day art, as represented in the MACBA, is the growing use of video and digital forms in artistic creation.

The **Centre de Cultura Contemporània de Barcelona** (*Carrer de Montalegre 5, tel 93 306 41 00*) behind the museum is a complex of auditoriums and exhibition areas in a former 18th-century hospice. It hosts a changing program of exhibitions and organizes many other activities and performances.

Across Plaça dels Àngels stands the former 16th-century **Convent dels Àngels** (*Carrer dels Àngels 3–7*), restored in 2000 and used for a variety of exhibitions. Opening times are irregular. ■

Temporary exhibitions and rotating elements of the permanent collection mean that the MACBA is always full of surprises.

Cool art & café circuit

The arrival of the MACBA and CCCB has attracted an arty crowd to this part of El Raval. Some have opened small private galleries in the area, particularly on Carrer d'Elisabets, Carrer dels Àngels, and Carrer del Doctor Dou. Others just come to drink and chat, and they have a growing choice of places in which to do so.

For coffee or cocktails a popular spot is **Mamacafé** (Carrer del Doctor Dou 10). Just west of the MACBA on Carrer de Joaquim Costa is a trio of late-night bars for post-gallery repose: **Casa Almirall** at No. 33 is a fine *modernista* relic; **Granja de Gavà** (No. 37) is a quieter little place; while **Benidorm,** at No. 39, is a groovy lounge-room-like bar that fills with local journalism students. ■

More places to visit in La Rambla & El Raval

ANTIC HOSPITAL DE LA SANTA CREU

As early as the 12th century, ailing locals were treated here in a house converted into a hospice. By 1401 it had been decided to bring together all of Barcelona's medical centers under one roof. The new buildings were slowly raised around a central cloister (1417), and although the dominating style is Catalan Gothic, some of the dependencies still extant today were added as late as the 16th and 17th centuries. In its late medieval heyday, the hospital complex was said to be one of Europe's finest. Apart from caring for the sick, the hospital also took in orphans and the insane. That hospitals should have such varied social functions was standard practice in medieval Europe.

The fine Gothic chambers now house the **Biblioteca Nacional de Catalunya** (Catalunya's National Library). The library is the single most complete collection of docu-

The Way of the Cross is celebrated in the Antic Hospital de la Santa Creu.

ments (around three million) tracing the region's long history. On April 23 and one day in September, guided tours of the entire library take place all day.

Next door to the main hospital buildings is the **Capella de l'Hospital,** the former hospital chapel now used for temporary art exhibitions. There is an organ above the

entrance to this now bare, single-nave affair, although off to the right are a couple of still richly decorated niches.

🅰 Map p. 87 ✉ Carrer de l'Hospital
🕐 Library: Closed from 2 p.m. Sat. & Sun. Chapel: Closed 2–4 p.m., Sat. & from 2 p.m. Sun. 🚇 Metro: Línia 3 (Liceu)

ESGLÉSIA DE SANT PAU DEL CAMP

Now surrounded by the inner-city slums of El Raval, the Romanesque Church of St. Paul in the Fields seems incongruously named. When it was built, though, in 1117, it was well out of town. What makes this somewhat rundown relic interesting today is the exquisite little cloister, whose twin sets of slender columns are topped by unusual lobed arches vaguely resembling clover leaves. The Visigothic ornamentation around the main entrance was probably a leftover from an earlier church.

🅰 Map p. 87 ✉ Carrer de Sant Pau 99
🕐 Closed 1–4:30 p.m.; p.m. Sat., & Sun.
🚇 Metro: Línies 2 & 3 (Paral.lel)

ESGLÉSIA DE SANT AGUSTÍ

When the Augustinian friars' monastery was demolished to make way for the Ciutadella after the War of the Spanish Succession, they set to building a replacement in El Raval in 1728. The style is a restrained baroque, along classical lines, but the facade was never completed. Indeed much of the exposed side of the church is more akin to a demolition site than a monumental house of worship.

🅰 Map p. 87 ✉ Plaça de Sant Agustí 2
🕐 Closed 2–4 p.m. 🚇 Metro: Línia 3 (Liceu)

GRAN TEATRE DEL LICEU

Built in 1847, Barcelona's magnificent opera house was destroyed by fire in 1994 and resurrected five years later. If you can't catch a night at the opera, make a day visit to admire the Salo dels Miralls (Hall of Mirrors) and its marble staircase. www.liceubarcelona.com

🅰 Map p. 87 ✉ La Rambla dels Caputxins 51-59 ☎ 93 485 99 00 🕐 Guided tours 10:00 a.m.; unguided 11:30 a.m., noon & 1 p.m.
💲 $$ 🚇 Metro: Línia 3 (Liceu)■

Port Vell (Old Port) looks brand new. Where once was neglect now stands a busy entertainment complex. The waterfront is also alive with memories of the past—in maritime and history museums and seaside warehouses.

The waterfront

A fisherman bent over his nets is a rare sight on the revamped Barcelona waterfront.

The waterfront

THEY USED TO SAY THAT BARCELONA HAD TURNED ITS BACK ON THE SEA. Strangely for a seafaring city, a defensive *muralla de mar* (seawall) was raised in the 16th century, shutting the citizens off from the Mediterranean. With no natural harbor at its disposal, Barcelona had always had to satisfy itself with an imperfect artificial port. Nevertheless, it grew to be one of the great maritime trading cities in medieval Mediterranean Europe. Decline set in from the 16th century, but new wind filled Barcelona's sails from the late 18th century on, when transatlantic trade boomed. As this ebbed in the early 20th century a morose air of slow decay descended upon the waterfront. However, a visitor to the city in the 1970s would not recognize its coastline today, such has been the waterfront's phoenix-like rise from the half-abandoned industrial gloom that long preceded the city's frenetic bout of urban renewal.

While the area's commercial operations have been relocated away from the center down along the coast to the southwest, extending as far as the mouth of the Llobregat River, Port Vell (Old Port) has been transformed into a showcase for contemporary Barcelona. Wandering along its lanes can be rewarding.

Passeig de Colom, the busy boulevard along whose length once stood the seawall, has been cleared of all the industrial clutter that once blighted the waterfront. A forest of pleasure boat masts sways in front of Moll de la Fusta (Wood Dock), which was formerly lined with designer bars but is now scheduled for

The sun sets behind the Torre de Jaume I and World Trade Center in Port Vell.

CARRER DE DOCTOR TRUETA

ersitat
mpeu
abra

PARC
DE
CARLES I

AVINGUDA D'ICÀRIA

VILA OLÍMPIC

adella
plca

CARRER DE SALVADOR ESPRIU

ARC DE
CASCADES

PARC DEL
PORT OLÍMPIC

AVINGUDA DEL LITORAL

Platja de la Nova Icària
Platja del Bogatell
Platja de la Mar Bella
Platja de la Nova Mar Bella

Peix

LONETA
eloneta

PORT OLÍMPIC

Moll de Xaloc

Escullera del Poblenou

Area of map detail

further change. On the other side of the Rambla de Mar pedestrian bridge looms the Maremàgnum complex, with bars, restaurants, stores, movie theaters, and a shark-infested aquarium.

The water no longer laps at the slipways of the Gothic Drassanes (shipyards), now home to a modern and engaging maritime museum, but none of the building's splendor has been lost. Nearby, the Monument a Colom (Christopher Columbus's statue) seems to keep watch over it all from his high perch at the end of La Rambla.

Farther north, just before the tight grid-pattern lanes of 18th-century La Barceloneta, stand former warehouses that today harbor seafood restaurants by the shore and an intriguing museum dedicated to the history of Catalunya. Following the shore, you stroll toward the city beaches, which stretch north past the Olympic port (built for the 1992 Games) and on along the coast from La Barceloneta. Once filthy and unkempt, these beaches nowadays fill to the brim with sun-worshipping locals. The great news for sunseekers is that there are plenty more fine sandy strands, easily reached by regular train services, spreading along the coast to the north and south of the city.

An extraordinary display of maritime memorabilia lies beneath the Gothic arches of Barcelona's medieval shipyards.

Museu Marítim (Drassanes)

IN 1570 A GRAND NEW GALLEY SLID DOWN THE SLIPWAY OF the Drassanes Reials, Barcelona's Royal Shipyards. This jewel of naval production, 197 feet (60 m) long and carrying a crew of 400, was unusually large by the standards of the day and would serve as the flagship of Don Juan of Austria in the classic sea battle of Lepanto in 1571. The reconstruction of the vessel at the heart of this outstanding maritime museum alone makes a visit worthwhile.

Museu Marítim
www.museumaritimbarce
lona.com
- Map pp. 100–101
- Avinguda de les
  Drassanes s/n
- 93 342 99 20
- $$
- Metro: Linia 3
  (Drassanes)

The **Drassanes** are a singular work of civic Gothic architecture. Construction of the shipyards began on this site in the reign of Jaume I in the 13th century, not long after the Venetians began building their famed Arsenale. All the great maritime cities developed shipyards from about this time but few have survived as well as these.

Expansion came in the late 14th century under Pere IV. At the time the sea washed up at the entrance to the parallel halls of the yards, lightly inclined so that completed vessels could be easily let down slipways into the water. Additions were made in the 15th century and the whole area was fortified around the end of the 17th century. In the

18th and 19th centuries the shipyards passed into the hands of the army, who used them for artillery production and training. In 1941 the army handed the structure over to civilian authorities, and the idea of a naval museum was born.

Since 1987 it has been restored and the modern museum created, so that today the majestic Gothic arches extend their protective mantle over an engaging and varied collection. Headphones with commentary in the language of your choice are provided, along with a brochure.

To enter the building, you pass through a shady courtyard that hosts what looks like a timber sunfish. It is in fact a life-size model of the Ictineo I, an early submarine created by the Barcelona inventor Narcis Monturiol i Estarriol (1819-85) in 1859. Into this piece and a second, bigger version of the model (a model stands in the open air near the IMAX cinema in Maremàgnum), he invested his life savings and gradually went broke in the effort.

Inside you enter what was the central part of the shipyards. Here begins an imaginative voyage into the history of this city and the sea. First up is a series of fishing vessels, from typical Catalan coastal boats to the oddly podgy *polveiro*, used in Galicia (northwest Spain) for centuries for fishing octopuses.

The next section deals with the evolution in timber vessel construction. A sturdy Brazilian fishing raft (*jangada*) takes center stage. Around it, models and panels describe how the Egyptians, Greeks, and Romans built this kind of vessel, and how their medieval successors developed the techniques. They are followed by more models, tools, and displays on the manufacturing of vessels that were used in 19th-century Catalunya.

La Imatge del Món (The Image of the World) section is the most intriguing for its navigational charts. The parchment copy of Abraham i Jafuda Cresques's 1375 chart covers the known world; it's strong on Europe but less on the rest. Maps were partly the result of dogma and contained all sorts of references, not just geographical. On Cresques's chart, we see the Queen of Sheba and other Biblical characters. The Red Sea on this and other maps is colored red, while Ireland is often green. You can see this on the 1439 Vallseca chart used by the Florentine explorer Amerigo Vespucci (1454-1512). Here too are models of the three ships Christopher Columbus took in 1492. The *Pinta, Santa Maria,* and *Niña* were a new kind of vessel, built for speed and to withstand the rigors of ocean voyages. There follows a section devoted to Magellan's discovery of the strait that opened the way from the Atlantic to the Pacific in the 16th century. A handful of navigational instruments completes the panorama.

From Atlantic exploration, we return to the Mediterranean and the world of the galley. Scale models are dwarfed by the full-scale replica of Don Juan of Austria's flagship galley, which led the Christian allies to victory over the Turks in 1571, the last great sea battle dominated by galleys. Follow the audiovisual commentary as you climb aboard (after walking around the underside of the raised vessel) and you will probably feel queasy at the appalling conditions in which the galley crews, made up of slaves, prisoners—even the occasional desperate volunteer—suffered. More than 200 oarsmen

The decorative pomp of Don Juan's flagship belies the horrible conditions in which galley crews slaved to power the vessel.

A modern fresco depicts Jaume I's fleet on its way to conquer Mallorca.

of vessels. They grew out of the custom of painting eyes on ships' prows, still common on small fishing boats. It was believed that these figures, like the eyes, would help guide and protect the ship and her crew from the cruel caprices of the sea and war. The lion became common on the armadas of England, Spain, and the Netherlands in the 16th century. This mascot was supposed to symbolized both the ship's and crew's courage and power. While the English tended to paint their lions gold, the Dutch preferred a fiery red.

The route then takes you to displays on waterfront Barcelona from the mid-18th century on. Apart from the models of great ocean-going sailing vessels, life-sized dioramas reproduce something of the period's atmosphere. Officers' quarters, chambers below the decks on a merchant vessel, a sailing school, workshops, and the like await.

remained chained to benches, three or four across, for the duration of their time at sea. They rowed during battle, when the ship had to make complex maneuvers, or when there was no wind. The men ate, drank, and slept where they sat; they say you could *smell* a galley from miles away.

Climb back down for the next stage of the permanent exhibit, called La Navegació a Vela (Age of Sail). Apart from model vessels and a 10-minute audiovisual display, the most curious items are the seven *mascarons*, wooden figures that for centuries adorned the bows

Finally you move into the age of steam. This section has numerous models, from the earliest belchers to transatlantic liners. Interspersed with them lie charts, captains' logs, and other paraphernalia. Models range from the grand *Royal Edward*, built in Glasgow shipyards in 1908 for a Canadian company, to one of the modern Transmediterránea fast ferries that today zip between Barcelona and the Balearic Islands. ∎

Don Juan of Austria

Half-brother of King Philip II of Spain, Don Juan (John) of Austria (1547–1578) was a military man with a mission. When he drew up his forces (Spanish, Papal, and Venetian) to face the Turkish armada off Lepanto in Greece in 1571, it was largely his will to win that kept the allies together and helped carry off a splendid victory. Had Philip not been so distrustful of the allies, they and Don Juan might well have gone on to break the back of Ottoman Turkish power in the eastern Mediterranean. Instead, Don Juan would end up in the unenviable position of governor of Spain's rebellious Dutch provinces until his death. ∎

Port Vell

The modern
waterfront
of Port Vell at
night

NOWADAYS IF YOU STAND IN THE SHADOW OF THE Monument a Colom and look toward the Mediterranean, the view is very different to that of pre-Olympics Barcelona. Back in the 1980s, Port Vell (Old Port) was a disastrous tangle of half-abandoned warehouses, dumps for empty containers and rusty scrap metal, and creaking rail yards. The 1992 Games provided the city fathers with the excuse they needed to give the waterfront a facelift. They succeeded.

Across the partly subterranean Ronda del Litoral freeway, the Moll de la Fusta quay looks on to a revamped parking lot for yachts, the Port de Barcelona. Perhaps here the authorities have gone too far—the desolate shells of what were until the mid-1990s a series of little designer bars, sorely missed by many of Barcelona's night owls, now play unofficial host to homeless people. Eventually they will be replaced by tourist information stands and a possible extension of the Museu Marítim.

Behind the port looms a modern pleasure center built on Moll d'Espanya (Spain Dock). To get to it, cross the stylish **Rambla de Mar** bridge (it opens up occasionally to let yachts pass), its wavy design nicely in keeping with the water it spans. Thousands stroll across here every day to crowd into **Maremàgnum,** a cornucopia of stores, eateries, and bars. Across the water to the south, Barcelona's snazzy World Trade Center is a hive of activity.

Behind Maremàgnum (to the north) is a movie theater complex and then the star of the show, L'Aquàrium. Beyond that stands the city's wide-screen IMAX theater.

L'AQUÀRIUM

The Aquarium is an extraordinary sea show and makes a pleasing diversion from the city's grand monuments, museums, and galleries. Those of you who don't have

L'Aquàrium
www.aquariumbcn.com
🗺 Map pp. 100–101
✉ Moll d'Espanya
☎ 93 221 74 74
💲 $$$
🚇 Metro: Línia 3
(Drassanes)

the chance to dive in the Mediterranean, Red Sea, Caribbean, or Great Barrier Reef are compensated here with the 21 tanks that make up this underwater world for landlubbers. Open since 1995, it claims to be Europe's biggest aquarium (as does the one in Genoa, Italy), containing more than 8,000 fish, including 11 sharks.

The tanks contain about 1.3 million gallons of seawater, regularly filtered, treated, and topped off. Artificial lighting, controlled by a central computer, is adjusted constantly to reflect as closely as possible what happens in nature. New fish, when introduced to the aquarium, are not simply thrown in the deep end; they go through a quarantine period in which they are checked for disease and given time to grow accustomed to a new diet. More than two tons of feed (fish, shellfish, plankton, vitamins, and seaweed) is on the marine menu every week.

Ticket in hand, you head down a series of ramps to the tanks. Before doing so you may wish to buy the detailed and colorful "Guide—L'Aquàrium," a useful illustrative handbook to what you are about to see. Less detailed labeling in Spanish, Catalan, and English appears throughout the display.

The first ten tanks re-create various Mediterranean environments. Indeed, it is claimed that the collection of Mediterranean species here is the most extensive in Europe.

Tank 1 simulates a shallow-water rocky area just off the coast, characterized by transparent water and lots of light, which fuels the growth of algae and other vegetation. Fish here seek out protection among the rocks, although some, such as the black scorpion fish, have different defense methods (the scorpion fish has nasty spikes.) Other common inhabitants include sea bass and two-banded bream. A nastier customer is the moray eel, which delivers a mean bite to anything that disturbs it. The Romans used to use the toxins in moray blood to make poison.

Tank 2 is dedicated to sandy coastal areas. Various kinds of rays dominate, along with several species of fish that bury themselves in the sand, such as the wide-eyed flounder. You can also see an assortment of crustaceans and snails, including the *Spinus murex,* from which the Romans extracted the purple dye for their togas.

Tank 3 re-creates the specific environment of the Ebro Delta, in southern Catalunya, where freshwater from the river mixes with seawater in extensive lagoons. The fish that live in these waters have evolved in such a way that they can cope with varying levels of salinity. Among them are gilthead bream, corb, sole, and meagre. Eels, which breed in the Sargasso Sea, also migrate in and out of the area.

Eleven sharks and thousands of other fish patrol the tanks of Europe's biggest aquarium.

Next is a rocky environment made up of tunnels and caves. Several breeds of fish favor this dark ambience, and crustaceans, such as hermit crabs, lobster, and prawns, simply love it.

Tank 5 is dominated by algae and various fish breeds, such as the ornate wrasse, that prefer a weedy environment. A couple of smaller tanks next to it contain shark eggs, crabs, and sea horses.

The following five tanks are dedicated to a variety of Mediterranean environments ranging from shallow plains reaching out from the shoreline to the mid-sea depths. Everything from striped red mullet to the big, spiny St. Peter's fish inhabits these waters. Some, like the pilot fish, happily swim around the depths without ever having to explore the seafloor.

Things get a good deal more colorful in the next two tanks. Beautiful red coral, found in many parts of the Mediterranean, dominates **Tank 11**. Swimming around in here are cardinal fish and a few other species. **Tank 12** contains a Red Sea environment, and its inhabitants are a riot of color, from the bright yellow butterfly fish to the Arabic angelfish and various types of surgeonfish. Small white-tip reef sharks are in perpetual motion, because otherwise they would drown from lack of oxygen. You can also make out at least one giant clam.

All sorts of beautiful coral and shoals of brightly colored little fish dominate **Tank 13**. Yet another carnival of color is presented in **Tank 14,** dedicated to the Caribbean, containing yellow surgeonfish, French angelfish, royal gramma, and sergeant majors.

Then comes a taste of the tropical waters of Australia's Great Barrier Reef. Residents are a mixed bunch, with such eye-catching

members as imperial angelfish and harlequin tuskfish. The tropical theme continues in **Tank 16,** which takes you to Hawaii and further polychrome characters, including Picasso fish and surgeonfish.

Tank 17 is altogether another story, taking you to murkier depths where more dangerous fellows lurk. They include the incredibly ugly rockfish, several species of scorpion fish, and other poisonous critters.

Next comes the star attraction —the 263-foot-long (80 m) **tunnel** that leads you through a huge tank full to brimming with all sorts of Mediterranean deep-sea species. These range from the menacing sandbar sharks through majestic rays to the enormous and oddly oval-shaped sunfish. This tank and tunnel afford the opportunity to

The ultramodern Maremàgnum complex, full of fast-food joints, restaurants, shops, and bars, provides striking views across the harbor to the city.

Revelers cross the Rambla de Mar for the nightlife of the Maremàgnum.

observe these grand creatures up close and from just about every conceivable angle. What better view of a shark's sharp dental set than from below?

The next couple of tanks can be viewed about halfway through the tunnel. The first concentrates on a coralline environment similar to that of the Illes Medes or the Medes Islands, off the Costa Brava north of Barcelona. The area is a popular dive spot, and here you can see a few of the fish species encountered in the protected marine reserve—among them

Grande Dame of the Sea

Docked by the Ramba de Mar bridge that links the Port Vell shoreline to the Maremàgnum, a tall three-master rides at anchor. Restored by the Museu Marìitim in the late 1990s, the *Pailebot Santa Eulàlia* was launched in 1918 under the name. For decades, it operated from Catalunya and in the Balearic Islands. Today it is again in full working order and used for a variety of official events in and beyond Barcelona. When the ship is docked at home, climb aboard (*closed Mon.*) and inspect the rigging at close quarters. Drop below deck aft into the sleeping quarters, feel the water lapping against the sides of the hull, and admire photographs of an era long past. ■

You should be able to witness the antics of several octopuses.

When you finally emerge from the tunnel one tank awaits inspection, this time the re-creation of an atoll in the South Seas. In its warm waters gathers a predictably colorful assortment of little fish. After the blue-water magnificence of the shark tunnel, this seems to serve as a sweetener to bring you back down to Earth before heading upstairs.

The fun is not quite over, for an interactive zone called **Planeta Agua** (Planet Water) upstairs is worth some time. Here you can see families of penguins in a peaceful Antarctic setting; one can only wonder what they make of their human observers. A series of tanks re-creates mangrove swamps and other freshwater environments in which a variety of water creatures circulate, including a couple of versions of the piranha. Children in particular should enjoy the open tank full of rays. An aquarium guide will give you rubber gloves and supervise as you caress the rays on their way around the tank. Several interactive displays reveal the weird and wonderful, such as the weedy sea dragon (a bizarre relative of the sea horse) and lumpy rockfish. Inside a whale diorama are models of truly odd deep-ocean creatures and some huge crabs. ■

conger eels, scorpion fish, grouper, and trigger fish.

Tank 20 plumbs the depths to visit the few species of fish that live on the Mediterranean seafloor-- you can't always see a great deal in this tank as the lighting is kept low to simulate the deep-sea conditions.

Ship docked at the Maremàgnum complex

Locals and visitors enjoy a Sunday morning boat trip around the harbor.

All at sea

While wandering around the waterfront, it is tempting to get a seaward perspective on Barcelona. **Golondrina** excursion boats (Tel 93 442 31 06) leave from Moll de les Drassanes in front of the Monument a Colom. A trip to the breakwater (rompeolas) and lighthouse (faro) on the seaward side of the harbor takes about 40 minutes. Or you could opt for the longer sailing on a glass-bottom catamaran around to Port Olímpic, which takes about an hour and a half. Departures are more frequent in summer, but in slower periods there may be as many as three a day to Port Olímpic. The lighthouse run is more regular and can leave hourly when there is demand. ■

When Columbus sailed the ocean blue

Christopher Columbus (1451–1506) must have been exultant on the day in January 1492 when he received the order to attend an audience with the Catholic Monarchs of Spain, Ferdinand and Isabella. Having just taken Granada, the last Moorish stronghold in the country, they were in high spirits. Columbus, who had been present at the siege, now finally heard the words he had prayed so long to hear: The monarchs announced they would back his plan to search for a western ocean route to India and Cathay (China).

Columbus was born in Genoa, northern Italy. An avid fan of the adventures of Marco Polo, he moved to Portugal as a young man and became a senior navigator. From 1486 onward he was based in Spain, and he set out from Palos in August 1492 with his little fleet of three ships, the *Santa Maria*, *Pinta*, and *Niña*.

Ever since that first voyage, controversy has surrounded Columbus. A brilliant naviga-

Columbus (left) set out from Spain (above) convinced he would find a new sea route to India.

Day and night, Columbus's stoic figure gazes out to sea from its perch at the foot of La Rambla.

tor, he was also an autocratic and ruthless commander, and his almost mystical religiosity and inflexibility won him few friends. Columbus discovered Cuba and other Caribbean islands but was convinced he had crossed the seas to Cathay: He refused to countenance the possibility that he had discovered hitherto unknown lands.

In mid-1493 he arrived in Barcelona to report to the Catholic Monarchs, who happened to be in residence at the time (at this stage they had no fixed court). It was a lively exercise in show-and-tell—his display of gold, spices, exotic birds, and some captive natives left Ferdinand and Isabella suitably impressed. They immediately authorized a second voyage, which, with 17 ships and 1,500 sailors and passengers (including friars and investors), set sail in September of the same year.

This and a third voyage kept Columbus busy until 1500, by which time he had explored more of the Caribbean and landed on the South American mainland (Venezuela). Although he may by now have realized that he had discovered a new world, he insisted otherwise. Meanwhile, the Spaniards had colonized Hispaniola (modern Haiti and the Dominican Republic) and, under Columbus's brothers who were in charge on land, were making themselves unpopular as they extracted gold and reduced the local populace to slavery. Their methods were so harsh that a commission of inquiry arrested Columbus (who was ultimately responsible for his brothers' excesses) and sent him back to Spain. Exonerated, he was sent on one last mission of exploration, but this proved largely a failure. His last years in Spain were ones of sad decline. He died in Valladolid but was buried in Seville: Later his remains were moved to Santo Domingo in Hispaniola.

In 1888 the tall **Monument a Colom,** which you can climb for splendid views, was opened on Plaça de la Porta de la Pau (Gate of Peace Square) in the presence of town officials from Barcelona and Genoa. At the time, a popular line of thinking claimed Columbus was actually a Catalan, and even today some historians maintain this is the case. ■

La Barceloneta

THE NARROW STREETS AND APARTMENT BLOCKS OF "Little Barcelona" were first designed by the French military engineer Prosper Verboom in 1715, but the Spanish engineer Juan Martín Cermeño did not carry out his plans until 1753. Aimed at relocating dispossessed citizens from La Ribera after construction of the Ciutadella fortress, the area wound up becoming a poor if ebullient quarter housing mostly sailors, fishermen, and their families. Even today, it is said the city's best fish is served here.

Museu d'Història de Catalunya

www.mhcat.net

- Map pp. 100–101
- Palau de Mar, Plaça de Pau Vila 3
- 93 225 47 00
- Closed Mon. & from 2:30 p.m. Sun. & holidays
- $
- Metro: Línia 4 (Barceloneta)

Originally, streets of consistently uniform, two-story houses (so as not to obstruct the firing line of cannon in the Ciutadella, see pp. 133–35) were quickly built. With time and a growing population, they were subdivided into as many as four tiny apartments, and a few of these still remain today. Higher apartment blocks (up to five stories) gradually replaced the smaller houses and gave the quarter the claustrophobic feel it has today.

A wander around La Barceloneta, whose centerpieces are the baroque **Església de Sant Miquel** (built in 1755 on Plaça de Sant Miquel) and the century-old market, **Mercat de la Barceloneta** (on Plaça de la Font), is to step a little out of time, for the place retains the lively community feeling of the old fishermen's quarter.

Barcelona's still important fishing fleet ties up at nearby **Moll dels Pescadors** (Fishermen's Dock), opposite the promenade known as Passeig de Joan de Borbó, which is, appropriately, lined with seafood restaurants.

Along the top end of the street is what remains of the Magatzems Generals de Comerç, the old port's warehouses. They are now home to the Museu d'Història de Catalunya, an introduction to the history of Catalunya.

MUSEU D'HISTÒRIA DE CATALUNYA

The museum's permanent exhibition is spread out over the third and fourth floors; temporary exhibitions are occasionally held too. It is worth picking up a returnable guide in your language at the ticket desk as most of the explanations throughout the museum are in Catalan only.

On the **third floor** you start with simple implements from prehistoric times. There are Bronze Age bracelets, ceramic items, coins, and household objects from Iberian tribes as well as from Greek and Roman settlements. Maps and illustrations accompany the recounting of ancient history in Catalunya, and displays include life-size cutaway remakes of a Roman boat and the atrium of a Roman house.

Next are displays dedicated to the rise of Christianity and the Visigothic period, followed by the arrival of the Muslims in Catalunya. The story continues with the Middle Ages: Models of churches and castles are accompanied by explanations of monastery life, a mock-up of Jaume I's field campaign tent, and accounts of Catalunya's expansion in Spain and the Mediterranean. You can even try on some armor.

Other sections are devoted to Romanesque and Gothic art, Jewish and Muslim communities in Catalunya, and the region's gradual absorption into the Spanish Crown. You finish up at the War of the Spanish Succession with scenes of the siege of Barcelona. The city's surrender to the Bourbon king Philip V marks the end of autonomy for Catalunya.

Up on the **fourth floor** the story continues with industrialization in the 18th and 19th centuries and the Napoleonic wars. Photos from late in the 19th century onward shed light on what Barcelona must have been like more than a hundred years ago and help trace the most recent stages in the city's history. They touch on themes such as *modernisme*, child factory labor, internal migration from the rest of Spain, and the growth of Catalan nationalism in the run up to the civil war.

Old typewriters, cameras, and phones are on display, as well as newspapers from prewar years. Next is the civil war and afterward, so you can take cover in a Barcelona air raid shelter. Or you can see newsreels in a postwar, Franco-era movie theater. Or sidle up to a bar and watch 1950s TV.

The display culminates in the end of Franco and the declaration of Catalunya as an autonomous region within Spain (the country is divided up into 17 such "autonomous communities.") After all this history, you might be tempted to try the terrace restaurant-bar on the same floor. ∎

Burnished hues at sunset along Passeig de Joan de Borbó (above)

Roy Lichtenstein's head

Just off Plaça d'Antoni López at the end of Via Laietana stands Roy Lichtenstein's contribution to Barcelona's skyline, his Barcelona Head sculpture. An abstract painter and frontrunner in America's pop art movement, Lichtenstein (1923–1997) made a hit with his vastly enlarged comic-strip characters, characterized by black-rimmed primary colors and the Ben Day screen dots simulated with a stencil. This abstract sculpture bears many of the traits of this comic-strip painting, which became something of a trademark for Lichtenstein. ∎

Life's a beach

Until the late 1980s, Barcelona's beaches were a dispiriting affair. Cluttered with rubbish and lapped by heavily polluted water, they were hardly inviting, although hardier locals refused to be deterred. Amid the neglect and industrial waste was some cheer, however. The two beaches lining La Barceloneta's seaward side, **Platja de Sant Sebastià** and **Platja de la Barceloneta,** were long famed for their *chiringuitos,* little makeshift seafood eateries that set up on the sand. Some were so close to the water that you got your feet wet while you ate!

All good things come to an end, though, and the chiringuitos disappeared along with all the garbage that the town authorities removed in a drive to remake the face of the waterfront. Today, the beaches are kept immaculate and the water, although not transparent, is much cleaner than it once was. And while the old chiringuitos are gone, little snack bars have again set up along the beaches.

Palms have been planted and a pleasant pedestrian-only promenade takes you to Port Olímpic and beyond to further city beaches. Strollers mix with seemingly suicidal inline skaters, street performers, and a cheerful assortment of locals and visitors. On midsummer weekends the beaches are packed.

Stretching beyond the bar-lined mooring for expensive yachts that is Port Olímpic (see p. 116) is a string of four more beaches, each separated from the other by *moles* (breakwaters). **Platja Nova Icària** and **Platja del Bogatell** are family beaches. Where the latter joins **Platja de la Mar Bella** there is a small nudist strip, although sunbathers who prefer to keep one or two items of clothing about them mingle in freely enough with the in-the-altogether crowd. The northern end of the beach and its neighbor, **Platja de la Nova Mar Bella,** tend to be less crowded than the others, if only because a lack of public transportation makes them a little inaccessible. Since 2002, a string of hip summer chill-out bars (offering a limited menu of food) have appeared along these beaches. They keep a hedonistic, suntanned crowd drinking cocktails, chatting, and dancing from the afternoon well into the Barcelona night.

This is only a taster of the local beach scene. Beyond Barcelona to the southwest and northeast lie strings of wonderful beaches. Indeed, the entire Catalan coast is festooned with them. The most accessible lie on *rodalies,*

A much-needed cleanup that began in the 1980s has given La Barceloneta a fine beach.

local suburban train lines. Trains run with surprising frequency from, among other stops, Plaça de Catalunya downtown. Among those to the south are beaches at **Sitges** (see pp. 216–18) and beyond at **Vilanova i la Geltrú** and **Calafell.**

Heading north there is a long succession of beaches along the rail line to **Blanes.** These tend to be narrower, but in general are clean and all have showers. Most are within about an hour's rail travel of central Barcelona. ■

In a good year, you can catch some rays as late as the end of October.

More places to visit on the waterfront

PORT OLÍMPIC

Perhaps the most astounding thing about Port Olímpic and the residential area surrounding it, Vila Olímpica (the athletes' village during the 1992 Games), is what you can no longer see.

The creation of the new pleasure port for the sailing events in the Olympic Games and the village next door were only part of a much broader urban renewal program. Nowadays, expensive yachts from all over the world call in at Port Olímpic either for brief stays or complete refits. Awaiting their crews along the landward side of the port is a line of restaurants, eateries, and bars, the latter of which keep thumping until early in the morning, especially in summer.

Behind the port rise two landmark skyscrapers, the Torre Mapfre office block and the chic, high-rise Hotel Arts Barcelona (see p. 251). Below them a couple of discos, a casino,

Frank Gehry's "Peix" is an eye-catching feature on the Port Olímpic waterfront.

and restaurants are fronted by the striking bronze-colored sculpture known as **"Peix"** ("Fish"). This scaly contribution to Barcelona's seaside is the handiwork of Frank Gehry.

After the athletes left, the housing in Vila Olímpica was sold off as private apartments. The quality of the apartments, it turns out, was not always of the highest, but the surrounding redevelopment revolutionized this part of the city. Before, the working-class Poble Nou district straggled down to the seaside in what had been known to Spaniards since the mid-19th century as the Catalan Manchester. Beneath the not entirely successful housing of Vila Olímpica lies buried the memory of another world: Chemical, textile, and alcohol factories, docks and warehouses stocked with wine, flour, and other goods made this area one of the least appealing of the city.

To sip a beer at the port today or stretch out on one of the beaches, you would be hard pressed to imagine the smoky industrial landscape that once occupied the whole area. Little more than one old factory chimney, now dwarfed by modern skyscrapers, is left as a reminder of the way things were.

▲ Map pp. 100–101

TELEFÉRIC AERI

Looking like some creaking old remnant of a bygone industrial age, an imposing metal tower rises high above Barcelona's old port inland from Platja de Sant Sebastià. This is **Torre de Sant Sebastià**, the start/end point for an aerial excursion linking the sea with Montjuïc (see pp. 183–202). The **cable car** that goes over the water from the tower passes via a second tower, **Torre de Jaume I**, by the **World Trade Center**, and continues to the Miramar observation point on Montjuïc. The views are spectacular. Round-trip tickets cost only marginally more than one-way trips.

▲ Map pp. 100–101

DIAGONAL MAR & FÒRUM

A brand-new high-rise residential and congress district has been created in the northeast corner of the city. The area is known as Diagonal Mar, and its core is known as the Fòrum, after the world cultural event that was staged here in 2004. One of Europe's biggest congress centers, sculpted parks, a protected beach, and the landmark triangular Edifici Fòrum are the highlights in this once neglected part of town.

▲ Map inside front cover

Watched over by the Gothic Santa Maria del Mar, this eastern wing of the old city is the custodian of rare jewels, from Picasso and pre-Columbian art collections to the *modernista* fantasy of the Palau de la Música Catalana.

La Ribera

The *modernista* skylight of the Palau de la Música Catalana

La Ribera

CENTURIES AGO, THE MEDITERRANEAN ate much deeper into Barcelona's land than today. Nowhere was this more the case than in La Ribera (The Shore), the logical center of international medieval trade as vessels from around Europe called in to do business.

Area of map detail

PLAÇA D'URQUINAONA

Urquinaona

C. DE TRAFALGAR

RONDA DE SANT PERE

CARRER DE TRAFALGAR

Palau de la Música Catalana

Església de Sant Francesc de Paula

CARRER DE SANT PERE MÉS ALT

Església de Sant Pere

VIA LAIETANA

CARRER SANT PERE MITJÀ

PLAÇA DE SANT PERE

CARRER SANT PERE MÉS BAIX

LA RIBERA

AVINGUDA DE F. CAMBÓ

PLAÇA D'ANTONO MAURA

Mercat de Santa Caterina

C. DELS CARDERS

C. DE COLOMINES

C. DE CORDERS

Capella d'En Marcús

Museu de la Xocolata

CARRER DEL COMERÇ

Jutjats

PLAÇA DEL ÀNGEL

Jaume I

CARRER DE LA PRINCESA

Museu Tèxtil i d'Indumentària

Museu Picasso

Museu Barbier-Mueller d'Art Precolombí

Palau Dalmases

CARRER DE MONTCADA

C. DE MONTCADA

Galeria Maeght

CARRER DE L'ARGENTERIA

PASSEIG DEL BORN

PLAÇA DE SANTA MARIA DEL MAR

Església de Santa Maria del Mar

FOSSAR DE LES MORERES

PLAÇA DE MONTCADA

La Llotja

VIA LAIETANA

PLAÇA D'ANTONI LÓPEZ

PLAÇA DEL PALAU

PASSEIG D'ISABEL II

AV. MARQUES DE L'ARGENTERA

Barceloneta

Estació de França

CARRER DE LA FUSINA

Mercat del Born

PASSEIG DE PICASSO

Arc de Triomf

AV. VILANOVA

Arc de Triomf

C. DELS ALMONGÀVERS

PASSEIG DE LLUÍS COMPANYS

PASSEIG DE LLUÍS COMPANYS

Palau de Justícia

C. DE BUENAVENTURA MUÑOZ

PASSEIG DE PUJADES

Museu de Zoologia (Castell dels Tres Dragons)

Cascada

L'Hivernacle

Museu de Geologia

Estany

L'Umbracle

PARC DE LA CIUTADELLA

"El Desconsol"

PLAÇA D'ARMES

Parlament de Catalunya

Zoo de Barcelona

PASSEIG DE LA CIRCUMVAL.LACIÓ

CARRER DE WELLINGTON

Ciutadella V Olimpi

CARRER DEL DOCTOR AIGUADER

RONDA DEL LITORAL

0   200 meters
0   200 yards

The first settlement, beyond the then city walls, clustered around the original Església de Santa Maria del Mar as early as the tenth century. It came to be known as Vilanova de Mar—Newtown on Sea. Farther inland, another satellite of the city, Vilanova de Sant Pere, grew around the monastery of Sant Pere de les Puelles, and the two nuclei grew in tandem. While tradesmen, artisans, and storekeepers concentrated around what is today Carrer de la Princesa, seafarers and businessmen with trade interests abroad moved into Vilanova de Mar. By the 13th century much of the wealth pouring into the city as a result of Jaume I's conquests and the rapid growth in sea trade was ending up in what by now had come to be called La Ribera.

As early as the 13th century, the denizens of La Ribera had acquired a measure of independence from the city's mayoral control. Toward the end of that century, Carrer de Montcada—soon to be the wealthiest address in town—was carved out to link Vilanova de Mar with the burgeoning commercial district

Trendy bars, cafés, and restaurants now line Passeig del Born, once the scene of jousts and executions.

inland. A century later the increasing opulence of La Ribera made the soaring Gothic remake of Santa Maria del Mar almost inevitable.

The good times continued into the 16th century, but things began to turn sour as the Atlantic gained in preponderance over the Mediterranean and Barcelona was completely excluded from American trade. Worse was to come. When Philip V of Spain besieged Barcelona into submission at the end of the War of the Spanish Succession in 1714, he pulled down more than a thousand houses in La Ribera to make way for a huge fortress, the Ciutadella, whose guns were to be trained on the rebellious city. This odious symbol of central control was destroyed and replaced in the late 19th century by what is now the Parc de la Ciutadella. What remained of La Ribera had become the crowded, working-class quarter it remains today, to some extent.

Modernista Palau de la Música Catalana is a central pillar in the city's cultural life, while once moneyed Carrer de Montcada has become an alley of museums, with Museu Picasso leading the way. Few give any thought to the grim fortress that preceded Parc de la Ciutadella, with its museums, zoo, and, ironically, the Catalan regional parliament at its heart. ■

Palau de la Música Catalana

Palau de la Música Catalana

www.palaumusica.org

🅰 Map p. 118

✉ Carrer Sant Pere
mès Alt 11–13

☎ 902 442882

🕐 Closed from 3:30
p.m Oct.–May;
guided tours every
half–hour

💲 $$

🚇 Metro: Línies 1 & 4
(Urquinaona)

DECLARED A WORLD HERITAGE SITE BY UNESCO IN 1997, this remarkable theater is not only one of the best places in Barcelona to attend performances of classical and choral music, it is also a sumptuous high point of *modernista* architecture and art.

Even as you approach this extraordinary building, you cannot help being taken aback: Indeed, it is barely contained by the narrow medieval streets it dominates. Here among the many stores dedicated to the wholesale rag trade, it beckons the great and the good from across the city to its concerts.

The "palace" figures prominently in the memory of the city and is by no means merely a music hall. Built between 1905 and 1908 by Lluís Domènech i Montaner, it amply demonstrates that Gaudí had no monopoly on the fanciful during this exciting period of artistic fervor in Barcelona. A battalion of the best artisans joined with Domènech i Montaner to create a decorative homage to Catalunya. Commissioned by the Orfeó Català choral

Right: Playful ceramics and sculptures adorn the facade of Domènech i Montaner's original *modernista* concert hall.

Below: Notoriously poor acoustics don't deter music lovers from concerts at the Palau de la Música Catalana.

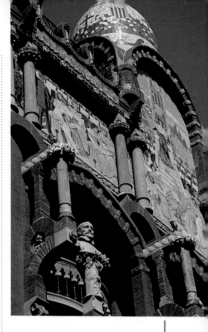

society, the building symbolized a reawakening in Catalan nationalism, at the time embodied in the Renaixença (see p. 33). The Orfeó had emerged late in the 19th century out of a desire to marry popular Catalan song with classical music and to awaken broad interest in home-grown production, while elevating it to international levels. Its founders also wanted to bring the greatest classical music from all over Europe to audiences in Barcelona.

From the outside, the building is almost too rich in detail and is difficult to appreciate in its cramped location. In the decades after it was built, many critical voices opined it was so gaudy that only the wrecking ball could remedy the situation. Thankfully, no one paid any heed.

Exposed brick and mosaics are decorative constants. The voluptuous climax is in the sculpture that bulges from the corner of the building, as if leaning over a balcony. It is a modernista allegory for popular song: a nymph surrounded by representatives of the people. Complementing this outburst in stone are busts of composers, mosaic-clad columns, and a ceramic frieze of singers of the Orfeó.

Inside, the theater is all light and color. The low-slung arches, reminiscent of Catalan Gothic, lend a slightly more sober air to the building, but don't be deceived. Ascending the stairs, the almost serpentine qualities of Domènech i Montaner's inventive decoration are in evidence everywhere.

However, nothing can really prepare you for the **auditorium,** consisting of stalls and two circles that seat about 2,000 people. The walls are made up substantially of sheets of vividly tinged stained glass; unfortunately this has made the hall poor in terms of acoustics, as has been universally recognized since the Palau opened in 1908. (A

smaller second stage with better acoustics, the Palau Petit, was added to the building in 2004.) An enormous shimmering skylight drips down from the ceiling, resembling a work in progress on a potter's wheel. Where there is no room for glass, the walls have a layer of glazed ceramics, whose dominating feature is a series of floral motifs.

Among all the decoration, the proscenium, framing the stage, is a metaphor for the universal genius of music and Catalan resurgence. Above a bust of Beethoven on the right explodes a vast sculpture of Richard Wagner's Valkyries. Facing that sculptural ensemble is another of Anselm Clavé (1824–1874), founder of the Orfeó, and an allegory of one of his Catalan songs.

The back of the stage, above which is mounted an organ, is a symphony of *trencadís* (mosaic of pottery fragments, a common device in modernista decoration) in shades of red and orange. Growing out of them are 18 sculptures of young maidens playing instruments, sculpted by Eusebi Arnau. It is as though the music never stops. ∎

Young Picasso

With his piercing dark eyes and voracious appetite for work, women, and life, the young Picasso was a live wire and lost no time in becoming acquainted with all sides of city life—and painting them.

Portrait of Picasso as a young man

Born in Málaga, southern Spain, the precocious Pablo Ruiz Picasso (1881–1973) began demonstrating his talent early on. His father, José Ruiz Blasco (1838–1913), had a respectable job as a drawing teacher in the town's school of fine arts until he transferred to a similar post in the northwestern city of La Coruña in 1891. A handful of young Pablo's earliest efforts from Málaga survive, but the extent of his potential really became apparent during the family's four years in La Coruña. José Ruiz could smell genius and enrolled his son in art school.

When his father moved to Barcelona to teach drawing at the city's fine arts school in La Llotja (see p. 138), the teenage Picasso followed with the rest of the family and was signed up at the same school. They moved into a flat on what is now Carrer de la Reina Cristina, near the old port, before shifting to Carrer de la Mercè 3. Pablo displayed prodigious capabilities, portraying family members (including his mother, from whom he took his preferred surname, Picasso) and churning out the academic work of model portraiture. In 1896 his father rented studio space for him in Carrer de la Plata (a restaurant now occupies the spot).

Packed off to Madrid in 1897 to study at the Acadèmia de Bellas Artes de San Fernando, the teenager quickly tired of school and, conveniently out of reach of the family, gave free rein to his own instincts. Picasso's school became the Prado art gallery, where he studied and aped grand masters such as Velázquez and El Greco. He took to the streets, putting onto canvas the faces and scenes that came to him, and acquired a taste for taverns and brothels, which provided entertainment *and* material.

In Picasso's mind, however, the following six months spent staying with a friend in the village of Horta de Sant Joan, in southern Catalunya, was the most fruitful period in his apprenticeship. There he submerged himself in the light and color of the countryside and broke with the constraints of academic painting.

Back in Barcelona in early 1899, Pablo rented studio space on Carrer dels Escudellers Blancs, just behind Plaça Reial, but he moved around in the ensuing years. He immersed himself in the bohemian, avant-garde world of the Els Quatre Gats tavern (see p. 249), the favored haunt of leading *modernistas* and other artistic types, and scene of Picasso's first exhibitions. With these like-minded souls he whiled away moments of diversion in the bars and brothels of the Barri Xinès, especially along Carrer Nou de la Rambla, where for a while in 1902 he had a studio at No. 10. He also was very fond of the sailors' brothels of Carrer d'Avinyò, said to have inspired his very famous 1907 painting, "Les Demoiselles d'Avignon."

As Barcelona's artists looked to Paris, it was only a matter of time before Picasso would try his luck there. The first trip came in 1900, followed by a brief stint in Madrid and repeat trips to Paris until, in April 1904, he moved to the French capital for good.

In the following years he returned several times to Barcelona, the last being the summer of 1934. The civil war and Franco's victory meant that the strongly anti-Franco Picasso would never again set foot on Spanish soil. ∎

Picasso and pals hang out on Carrer de la Mercè, where the artist lived for a while.

"Factory at Horta del Ebro" (1909)

Carrer de Montcada

Museu Picasso

www.museupicasso.bcn.es

🅰 Map p. 118

✉ Carrer de Montcada 15–23

☎ 93 319 63 10

🕐 Closed Mon.

$ $$ with temporary exhibitions

🚇 Metro: Línies 1 & 4 (Urquinaona)

MORE THAN 700 YEARS OLD, THIS UNUSUALLY STRAIGHT medieval street has been prime real estate several times. It all started when Count-King Ramon Berenguer IV ceded land to Guillem Ramon de Montcada in the mid-12th century. Montcada had an instinct for business and created a road linking Vilanova de Mar with the commercial area north of Carrer de la Princesa. By the early 14th century it was flanked with fine mansions. Decline came in the 19th and 20th centuries, but the past decade has witnessed a revival, and its mansions now house grand museums, galleries, and sophisticated bars.

The northern end was marked by the small Romanesque **Capella d'En Marcús** (open for Mass—check times posted by the door), on the corner of Carrer dels Carders and Placeta d'En Marcús. The main body of the street was cut off from this wayside chapel when Carrer de la Princesa was built in 1853.

Back in 1166, when the chapel was built, Carrer dels Carders was the main road out of town, having left the eastern city gate (where Plaça del Àngel is today) well behind. The chapel was part of a larger complex financed by a prominent citizen, one Bernat Marcús, but the pilgrims' hostel, hospital, poorhouse, and cemetery have long since disappeared. In the 14th century the "runners' fraternity," or postmen, would call in here for blessing before setting out; their patron saint remains the image of the Mare de Déu (Mother of God) housed here. A simple structure in the sober Lombard style (see p. 38), the chapel has suffered much over the centuries. It was restored in 1980.

MUSEU PICASSO

South across Carrer de la Princesa lies, what is for most, the star attraction of the street—the Museu Picasso. The collection concentrates above all on Picasso's early years, roughly until the time he left Barcelona, but important additions over the years have broadened the display, which is frequently complemented by temporary exhibitions —either on Picasso or other artists.

The museum spreads across five principal mansions dating from medieval times, and a couple of other buildings. These and other residences along Carrer de Montcada make the street one of the most important living documents of civic Gothic construction in Barcelona. (Exploration of the Barri Gòtic, see pp. 57–84, will occasionally reveal similar houses.) Although Gothic at heart, most of these buildings underwent changes with time, with baroque and even neoclassic alterations and additions being usual. What these stout stone houses tend to have in common is an internal courtyard off the street, with a grand external staircase sweeping up to the first floor (second floor to Americans), where the master of the house resided. The first floor (ground floor) was reserved for stables, kitchens, storehouses, and the like.

Thus, on entering the Museu Picasso by Palau Meca (*Carver de*

Montcada 19), this is what you see, with stores and other conveniences occupying the first floor. Ticket in hand, you head up the stairs to view the collection, which begins through a door to the right. You may wish to buy a guide in the first-floor bookstore before beginning.

After a bibliographical introduction, in **Room 2** you are immersed in the mist-bound world of La Coruña, the northwestern coastal town where Picasso lived from the age of 10 to 14. In the small countryside scenes and images of local people (especially in a couple of portraits) you see an already accomplished artist. The "Home amb Boina" ("Man with Cap," 1895) reveals a sensitivity to light and a capacity to lend life to his subjects.

Room 3, which covers the years 1895-97 in Barcelona, contains three small portraits of Picasso's father, one of which demonstrates that Picasso already had a sure hand and was dabbling in ideas beyond the norms of acad-

Formerly one of the top addresses in Barcelona, Carrer de Montcada has made a comeback as a museum alley.

Right: A self-portrait of Pablo Picasso acclaimed by many as the 20th-century's greatest artist.

The courtyard of the Museu Picasso—one of the world's most important collections of Picasso's work

emic painting, in this case the use of monochrome. The contemplative "Retrat de la Mare" ("Portrait of Picasso's Mother") is outstanding. This tranquil portrait shows a mastery of draftsmanship and a will to capture the human essence of his models, often family members during this period. A series of mischievous self-portraits, including one of him wearing a wig, is amusing.

The following room, related to the same period, is full of small scenes of Barcelona, almost all of them done with oil on wood. **Room 5** displays seven nude studies done at art school. They give an insight into Picasso's formal training and amply demonstrate—if proof is necessary—his ability.

In **Room 6**, Picasso moves outdoors with day-to-day scenes of Barcelona in the late 19th century. "La Ona" ("The Wave") is an absorbing work in which the young artist manages to capture a sense of movement and liquid. Others are less generic, with curious snapshots of La Barceloneta and its beach as they were more than a century ago.

The ample **Room 7** embraces a wider sampling of the artist's early years. Among the various country and seaside scenes (mostly oils on wood) done in and around his native Málaga and Barcelona are some Madrid scenes and two key works. "Tia Pepa" ("Aunt Pepa") is possibly his most striking early portrait of a family member. His ability to capture a certain world-weariness in his aunt's eyes is remarkable. "La Primera Comunió" ("The First Communion," 1896) is one of the artist's earliest grand canvases. It is an utterly conventional religious and moral work typically in vogue at the time. For any doubters who might be tempted to see the artist's much later works as childish squiggles that anyone could do, this is formidable evidence of his academic training and capacity.

In the next room comes the still more important "Ciència i Caritat" ("Science and Charity," 1897), in which Picasso's father poses as a doctor at the bedside of a sick woman. Again, the artist marches to the beat of somebody else's drum, but the painting shows that he could have easily been a successful society artist had he so chosen. In the same room, you can inspect some of his preparatory sketches for the final work. Also in here is an assortment of scenes from Madrid and Horta de Sant Joan, plus a copy he did of Velazquez's 1652 portrait of King Philip IV.

Next up in **Room 9** is a curious mix of material done in Barcelona from 1899 to 1900. The view of "Carrer de la Riera de Sant Joan" (1900), a lane where he had a studio, reveals a world of change in the young artist's approach. Looking through the window onto a busy street, the viewer is invited to immerse himself in the activity. Here Picasso displays some liking of the abstract: The carefully accurate recording that dominates many (but by no means all) of his more youthful works is absent here. Minimal but sure brushstrokes render human figures, a cart, and buildings across the way. The image is positive and light. Other scenes from Barcelona figure here, along with various portraits, that by now have left academic rigor behind in favor of a more playful style. They include one of his sister Lola and a brooding image of his close friend Carles Casagemas.

Room 10 is dominated by works from Picasso's first sojourn in Paris in 1900-01. The artist's penchant for louche nightlife is all too evident and, although his use of color is quite different and the element of caricature is not as predominant, these paintings remind one irresistibly of Toulouse-Lautrec, another aficionado of nightclubs. This is especially the case with "La Fi del Nùmero" ("Curtain Call," 1901). In "Margot" and "La Nana" ("The Dwarf"), ugliness and beauty are easily confounded, if only through a joyous summer splurge of color.

Back in Barcelona, Picasso embarked on the first of his many "periods," in this case the Blue Period, which lasted from 1901 until 1904. **Room 11** and two

Order tapas and a glass of *cava* in El Xampanyet, a classic Barcelona champagne bar on Carrer de Montcada.

Elegant stone
walls of a Gothic
courtyard front
the Museu
Barbier-Mueller
d'Art Precolombì.

Museu Tèxtil i
d'Indumentària

www.museutextil.bcn.es

Map p. 118

Carrer de Montcada
12–14

93 319 76 03

Closed from 3 p.m.
Sun. & Mon.

$

Metro: Línia 4
(Jaume I)

annexes are dedicated largely to
paintings from this time, whose
melancholy may have been due in
part to the suicide of Casagemas
(1880–1901). Themes range from
still lifes, such as "La Copa Blava"
("The Blue Glass," 1902), and eerie
moonlit scenes like "Terrats de
Barcelona" ("Barcelona Rooftops,"
1902) to diverse portraits. Among
the more unsettling of the latter is
"El Foll" ("The Madman," 1904).
One painting, "Retrat de la Senyora
Canals" ("Portrait of Mrs. Canals,"
1905), actually belongs to the suc-
ceeding stage in Picasso's career,
variously known as the Pink or
Rose Period. It is the only work
from this period in the museum.

Rooms 12–14 are mostly dedicated to paintings Picasso carried
out during his final stay of any
duration in Barcelona, in 1917.
By now he is well down the cubist
road, although several of these
paintings in no way fit the category.
Here, all is a whirl of experimentation, with Picasso disembodying,
distorting, and moving about elements in many ways.

Opposite Rooms 11–14 you
pass a display on the five mansions
that constitute the museum and
enter the Sala Neoclàssica, the grand
salon that lends insight into the
lifestyle members of Barcelona's elite
led in the 19th century. You then
loop through the Sala Sabartés, dedicated to Picasso's personal secretary,
Jaume Sabartés.

The following three rooms
(15–17) are devoted mainly to
two principal themes. The first and
foremost is Picasso's re-examination
of Velázquez's masterpiece, "Las
Meninas." Through a deforming
and sometimes cubist prism,
Picasso re-creates in seemingly
unending diversity this classic of
Spanish art, and then takes it apart
to section out single portraits of
each figure in the original. The
other theme is "Pichones"
("Pigeons"), a celebration of
Mediterranean light. You may
not like these birds in real life
(Barcelona is full of them), but
in Picasso's breezy rendition they
appear in a much kinder light. Both
series were largely done in 1957.

Finally head along the gallery
of the Gothic courtyard to a
display of 41 ceramic pieces and a
handful of paintings from the final
years of Picasso's life. Temporary
exhibitions are held in Palau Mauri
and Palau Finestrelles.

OTHER MUSEUMS &
GALLERIES

After a visual assault of this type
most of us need a break. So you
may want to save the two museums
across the road for another time.
On the other hand, they are much
smaller and can be visited quite
quickly, should you wish. Both are
again housed in fine Gothic-
baroque mansions.

The Museu Tèxtil i
d'Indumentària is dedicated to
textiles and clothing. Here you can
see several fragments of garments

from Egypt, dating from the 3rd to the 12th centuries, followed by Spanish and Italian medieval church vestments and other clothing. The big bows on the men's shoes indicate a progression to the baroque, followed by an extensive collection of men's and women's dress from the period of the French kings Louis XV and Louis XVI in the 18th century.

The emphasis on French fashion continues after the Revolution (1789), with exhibits reverting to more strictly Spanish models only from the mid-19th century on. You can trace fashion trends right up to the present.

Visiting the **Museu Barbier-Mueller d'Art Precolombì** next door involves a significant change of pace. On view in this restored Gothic structure is a limited but exquisite collection of pre-Columbian art—mostly statuary and ceramics—from South America, especially Nicaragua, Panama, Costa Rica, and Peru. The museum has almost 6,000 pieces.

Heading south toward Passeig del Born, Carrer de Montcada is lined with more grand mansions, many that have been turned into art galleries. If you can, look inside **Galeria Maeght** in Palau dels Cervelló, at No. 25, and **Palau Dalmases,** at No. 20, two of the finer examples.

Bubbly, baroque, & Basque

Wandering down Carrer de Montcada in the evening can be as rewarding as cruising its museums by day. Try the bar in **El Xampanyet**, at No. 22, where you can wash away the day's cares with a glass or two of *cava*, the Catalan version of champagne. It is the standard tipple in this, one of the city's oldest and best-known cava bars. Pick out a couple of the many tapas (bar snacks) on display and soak up the atmosphere.

Later on in the evening (don't turn up before 10 p.m.) the baroque **Palau Dalmases** next door is another world altogether. Drop by for a high-priced glass of wine or a cocktail and, with luck, live classical music in what feels like an 18th-century salon.

Too refined (or pricey)? Saunter on to the **Centre Cultural Euskal Etxea** (Placeta de Montcada 1) for a rowdy taste of the Basque Country with its exquisite tapas, cider, and white wine (txacoli). ■

Exquisite Egyptian textiles are on display in the Museu Tèxtil i d'Indumentària.

Museu Barbier-Mueller d'Art Precolombì

www.barbier-mueller.ch

🗺 Map p. 118

✉ Carrer de Montcada 12–14

☎ 93 310 45 16

🕐 Closed from 3 p.m. Sun., & Mon.

💲 $

🚇 Metro: Línia 4 (Jaume I)

Tapas and cider at the Centre Cultural Euskal Etxea offer a taste of the Basque Country.

El Born

CLOSED OFF AT ITS WESTERN END BY THE APSE OF THE mighty Església de Santa Maria del Mar and at the other by the former Mercat del Born produce market, broad Passeig del Born (Borne in Spanish) has a special place in the hearts of folk from Barcelona. An old saying affirms: *"Roda el món i torna al Born"* (Go around the world and come back to the Born). Once the fulcrum of the city's commercial life, in recent years it has experienced a comeback as a popular haunt for hedonistic barhoppers.

Església de Santa Maria del Mar

- Map p. 118
- Plaça de Santa Maria del Mar
- Closed 1:30–4:30 p.m.
- Metro: Línia 4 (Jaume I)

In the 13th century, what is now a long pedestrian-only island flanked by two traffic lanes was a grand square in the middle of Vilanova de Mar. Much of Barcelona's foreign-trade deals were executed here and the square became a natural pole of attraction. El Born, as the square and its immediate surrounds are more simply known, literally means "limit" or "barrier," and refers to a space cordoned off for tournaments (thus the word came also to mean tournament). Try to imagine the long square surrounded by tribunes for the city's gentry raised above crowds of onlooking commoners, their attention fixed on the colorful spectacle of the joust, with banners fluttering and the clash of lances against shields and armor. El Born was the city's main site for weapons practice and tournaments of all sorts since at least the 14th century; the first documented joust took place in 1372.

But El Born was not the exclusive preserve of dashing knights: All manner of popular festivals and processions took place here. In later years, trade fairs (especially of silver and glassware) were held regularly. From the end of the 15th century, the Inquisition chose El Born as the stage for its autos-da-fé, the gruesome punishments, including burning at the stake, meted out to heretics by the

Holy Office. Non-religious public executions also took place here until 1723. From then on, the prime function of the square was as a market; **Mercat del Born,** a fine metal structure, was raised in 1876 and remained in use until 1971. The excavated site is scheduled to become a cultural center (see p. 135).

Most of the housing that flanks Passeig del Born dates to the 19th and, in some cases, 18th century. Only No. 17, heavily restored, survives from the 14th century. Once dedicated to all manner of activities (Carrer dels Sombrerers was Milliners' Street, Carrer de la Vidrieria was Glassmakers' Street, and so on), the narrow streets woven around El Born have been revived since the mid-1990s by a growing battalion of bars, chic little restaurants, and bijou stores.

Bulging out into the western extreme of Passeig del Born is the apse of the single most majestic example of Catalan Gothic in Barcelona, **Església de Santa Maria del Mar** (Church of St. Mary of the Sea). Earliest evidence of the existence of a church on this site dates from 998. Legend has it that the remains of Santa Eulàlia (see p. 63) lay in a church here after her supposed martyrdom in the twilight years of the Roman Empire. Although more likely fiction than fact, the story has made the present church a symbol of Catalan nationalist identity, so much so that even the Spanish royal family has on at least one occasion been politely told that it could not celebrate a wedding here!

By the time this architectural gem of gray Montjuïc stone was completed (in the record time of 54 years from 1329), its surrounding parish (El Born) had become one of the most important in Barcelona. Many writers have asserted that, had they not seen the Catedral beforehand, they would have taken this for the city's main place of worship.

Flanking the entrance on the broad, unfussy west face of the church are statues of Saints Peter and Paul, while above them is a 15th-century rose window, the principal source of light into the central nave. Around the sides stout buttresses hold up the structure.

The church's splendor becomes truly apparent once you are inside. Gutted during the civil war, the interior is devoid of embellishment; the central choir stalls and virtually all its works of art were destroyed, but to some this only serves to

Intriguing narrow lanes and curious corners characterize La Ribera.

emphasize the exquisite harmony of line and magnitude. Alongside the wide nave run two aisles, and between them slender octagonal pillars rise up between arches to the filigree delicacy of the vaults. Nowhere is this lace work more finely executed than in the narrow arcade that carves its way around the inside of the apse. You are drawn to look upward as if in contemplation of the Almighty, but unlike in many claustrophobic northern Gothic churches, the generous, open width of the Catalan version invites you to look around as well. It is an earthy, human touch. The windows along the sides of the church feature captivating stained glass dating from the 18th, and in some instances from the 15th, century. How they survived arson attacks in 1909 and 1936 is anyone's guess.

To see the church's interior thrown into illuminated relief, take the opportunity to hear Mass or attend one of the occasional classical music concerts that are staged here at night.

The irregular little square in front of the church, **Plaça de**

Santa Maria del Mar's stained glass survived sacking in 1714 and arson in 1936.

The Wise Men bring candy to children on the eve of Epiphany.

Santa Maria del Mar, and the nearby alleys (home to a couple of wine bars) form the best-preserved corner of the bustling medieval commercial quarter that once occupied much of El Born. The square boasts a restored Gothic fountain (facing Carrer de l'Argenteria, the former Silversmiths' Street), while lanes like Carrer dels Caputxers (Hoodmakers' Street) and Carrer dels Canvis Vells (New and Old Money Changers' Streets) have remained largely unchanged, retaining features in their higgledy-piggledy style such as the upper floors jutting out on heavy timber barbicans, a typical medieval space-creating trick in Spain and beyond.

Opposite the south flank of Santa Maria del Mar is the **Fossar de les Moreres,** site of a cemetery located on what had in early medieval times been a hillock covered in mulberry bushes. The cemetery was closed in 1816, but the site has enormous resonance for Catalans. Heroes who died in the defense of Barcelona during the siege of 1714 were buried here, and a flame constantly burns in their memory. ■

The magic of kings

Although the white-bearded, vermilion-clad girth of Santa Claus is making inroads into the end-of-year consciousness of people the world over, for Spanish children Christmas is a bit of a bore. In Spain, the December date marks Christ's birth and is a time for quiet family meals. The gifts don't come, quite logically, until the visit of the Three Wise Men (known to the Catalans as Els Reis Mags, the Wizard Kings) on the eve of January 6 (the Epiphany). The fun happens when the kings arrive by boat in Port Vell and then embark on a long parade starting in La Ribera on Avinguda del Marques de l'Argentera (a couple of minutes from Santa Maria del Mar) and usually finishing up in Montjuïc. They are greeted by throngs of children, who in turn are bombarded by volleys of candy along the whole route. It's all over by about 10 p.m., when it's time to go home and open presents. They say naughty children will get *carbó* (coal lumps), but these days the coal lumps tend to be huge sugary lollipops available in pastry shops weeks ahead of the big day. ■

Parc de la Ciutadella

Gaudí assisted with the design of the Cascada in the Parc de la Ciutadella, one of his earliest assignments.

CENTRAL BARCELONA'S MAIN GREEN LUNG, CENTURY-OLD Parc de la Ciutadella, is laden with heavy symbolism for Catalans—and home to several attractions. As the stage for the 1888 Universal Exhibition, it also has some interesting *modernista* morsels.

In the 1880s, the Ajuntament (City Hall), industrialists, and businessmen of Barcelona were in high spirits. The city was in the vanguard of a slow process of industrialization in an otherwise pitifully backward Spain. Transatlantic trade was booming and many Catalan families were doing nicely out of cash crops harvested largely by slave labor in Cuba. That Cuba and Spain's other remaining colonies would be lost in ignominious battle to the United States in 1898 could hardly be predicted when, in 1885, the Ajuntament determined to hold a Universal Exhibition in 1888.

The site chosen was the gaping hole left behind after the demolition of the notorious and much hated Ciutadella, the fortress that had kept watch over Barcelona, and in which its more rebellious citizens had frequently been jailed and executed, since defeat in the siege of 1714. A model of the fort, built under Spain's Philip V after he marched into the city on September 11 and so ended the War of the Spanish Succession, is on display in the Museu Militar in Montjuïc (see p. 200).

Work to turn the area into a public park began in 1872 and progressed slowly. Then came the decision of 1885 and the city set about with feverish activity to erect the necessary pavilions and other facilities, of which a few still stand. Entering by the main entrance off Passeig de Picasso, you soon arrive at a cluster of buildings from the original Ciutadella. A small chapel and school stand close by one another, the latter having once

Parc de la Ciutadella

Map p. 118

Parlament de Catalunya

www.parlament-cat.net

🄰 Map p. 118

✉ Plaça d'Armes, Parc de la Ciutadella

☎ 93 304 66 45

🕐 Open 1st Fri. of month 4–6 p.m. for special tours in Catalan

🚇 Metro: Linies 1 (Arc de Triomf) & 4 (Barceloneta)

A model mammoth watches over rowers enjoying a pleasant afternoon on the Estany (lake).

served as the Governor's Palace. Immediately east is the landscaped **Plaça d'Armes,** its oval pool overlooked by **"El Desconsol"** ("Disconsolate," 1907), by *modernista* sculptor Josep Llimona.

Behind stands evidence of what may be interpreted as a nice sense of irony on the part of the Catalans: **Parlament de Catalunya,** housed in the Ciutadella's arsenal. Between 1939 and 1980, it was a barracks, but the regional parliament returned when Catalunya's autonomy statute came into effect.

A symbol of Catalan identity, the Parlament is on occasion open for visits. You will be led up the sweeping Escala d'Honor (Stairway of Honor) and on through several solemn halls to the Saló de Sessions, the semi-circular auditorium where parliament sits.

While strolling around the southern end of the park, you could take time out to observe some live works of art at the **Zoo de Barcelona**. The zoo contains

a surprising variety of animal life and makes a handy diversion for those with children. Around 7,000 animals represent about 400 species, ranging from elephants to giant anteaters to black-tailed prairie dogs, from Cuban flamingos to Humboldt penguins. On the less furry side, you can recoil in horror at the boa constrictor and crocodiles, or enjoy the dolphin show.

Directly north of Plaça d'Armes spreads the pleasant **Estany,** or artificial lake. Sitting by the water or having a picnic here makes for a pleasant diversion. You can also rent rowboats. Facing the lake on the north side is the park's most lavish object, the immense **Cascada** (Waterfall) by the Passeig de Pujades entrance. A creation of Josep Fontsère, the man behind the park, it took six years to build and was completed in 1881. Fontsère was assisted by Antoni Gaudí, making this one of Gaudí's earliest contributions to Barcelona's

urban landscape. With its high central arch, flanking staircases, and overcrowded company of neo-baroque statues, it was not universally appreciated, but with gallons of water crashing down it is an impressive sight.

Although most of what was hastily built for the 1888 Universal Exhibition was not designed to last, a few quite sturdy buildings were created and have survived. The most intriguing of these is the **Castell dels Tres Dragons** at the top end of the park on the Passeig de Picasso side, a medieval-style caprice that sprang from the mind of Domènech i Montaner. Conceived as a café-restaurant for the exhibition, it was a clear statement of intent by the architect. The use of unclad brick on an iron frame, with plenty of exposed wrought iron (door frames and the like) became a standard weapon in the *modernistas'* armory. The building creates the impression, quite intentionally, of being a fairy tale castle with an Islamic air. Its battlements, faced by entirely fictitious coats of arms, are topped by ceramic crowns.

Today the building serves as the **Museu de Zoologia** *(Tel 93 319 69 12; closed Mon.)*. Visiting is a bit reminiscent of school trips of yore, but children may get a kick out of the old-fashioned displays. The main collection, ranging from crustaceans in specimen jars to stuffed animals, is on the second floor. The first floor is used for temporary exhibitions. Next door is **L'Hivernacle,** a small hothouse that has a delightfully pleasant eatery.

Then comes another museum, the **Museu de Geologia** *(Tel 93 319 68 95, closed Mon.)*, with its exposition of rocks, minerals, and fossils. Next to it is **L'Umbracle,** a mini-botanical garden.

A block southwest of the Parc de la Ciutadella, the hulk of the once-busy Mercat del Born (closed 1971) might seem to have nothing to do with the park. But there is a close link, actually. Beneath the roof, a network of cobbled streets was unearthed that was until the early 18th century a lively medieval neighborhood. It was part of Barcelona that was swept away to make room for the giant Ciutadella fortress.

There are plans to construct a cultural center around the site, allowing the market building and excavated site to be preserved. The former market (*Tel. 93 319 02 22; closed Mon.-Fri.*) is open to those curious to get a glimpse of what the city looked like before the fortress was built. ■

The classic *modernista* **Castell dels Tres Dragons combines modern building materials with medieval fantasy.**

Parc Zoològic
www.zoobarcelona.com
Map p. 118
Plaça d'Armes, Parc de la Ciutadella
93 225 67 80
Closed Mon.
$$
Metro: Línia 4 (Barceloneta)

To market, to market

The ride back into the centuries often requires considerable powers of imagination. When you wander into the square of streets that surrounds the **Mercat de Santa Caterina** (St. Catherine's Market), a bustling market with a long history and sparkling new clothes, you might notice a small glassed-over corner of ancient foundations. They are all that remain of the 15th-century Monestir de Santa Caterina, a powerful Dominican monastery. Fruit gardens and fields of crops that the monks tended were spread out all around it. The monastery was torn down in 1838 to make way for a market, which in turn was swept away in 1999 to be replaced by its bright successor in 2005. Local architect Enric Miralles (1955-2000) designed the new location, with its wavy roof scintillating in bright color. Propped up by tufts of twisting gray steel bamboo-like trunks, the roof is lined with timber on the underside. All around, the densely packed housing is a strange mix of old and new, pulsating with the life of a melting pot of locals, Latin Americans, and North African migrants.

Modernista entrance to La Boqueria

Most Barcelona *barris* (quarters) have their own market. They all tend to be open Monday through Saturday, although some close for a few hours from 2 p.m. The best known and most central produce market is the historic **Mercat de la Boqueria,** on La Rambla (see p. 90). Its name comes from *boc* (goat), because goat meat was sold around here outside the then city walls from the 13th century on. Simply wandering between the fish and seafood stands, the fruit and vegetable sections, and all the other food stands and bars is a heady experience. Although some parts remain open until well into the evening, the best time to come is the morning.

Not far from Mercat de la Boqueria at Carrer del Comte d'Urgell 1 is another fine neighborhood market and one of Barcelona's biggest, **Mercat de Sant Antoni** (St. Anthony's Market). Built in 1882, it is a classic example of the wrought-iron construction so much in vogue at the end of the 19th century. On Sunday mornings, vendors specializing in old maps, stamps, books, and cards replace the fishmongers and fruiterers. In the surrounding streets, others sell clothes and leather goods—largely of indifferent quality, but you might find a bargain.

The city's biggest flea market is **Els Encants Vells** (*Closed Tues., Thurs., & Sun., metro Glòries*), literally meaning "old charms." Also known as Fira de Bellcaire, or Bellcaire Fair, it has been doing business next to the Plaça de les Glòries Catalanes traffic interchange since 1928. Street vendors endeavor to sell every conceivable kind of item, from antique furniture to ancient magazines. Clearly a lot of it is junk, but it's fun just to wander around.

Several specialist markets enliven the squares of the **Barri Gòtic.** In Plaça de Sant Josep Oriol, an arts and crafts market takes place on Thursdays and Fridays, while on neighboring Plaça del Pi you'll occasionally get the chance to sample all sorts of local food and produce, ranging from tasty cheeses to delicious honeys. On Thursdays an antiques market sets up along Avinguda de la Catedral, while a coin and stamp collectors' market brings an unusually congenial air to Plaça Reial on Sunday mornings.

In the weeks running up to Christmas a market sets up directly in front of the Catedral. You can buy figurines to make your own nativity scene. ∎

Barcelona's markets draw crowds looking for bargains, edible or otherwise.

Mercat de la Boqueria is a hive of colorful activity and tempting fresh produce.

More places to visit in La Ribera

ARC DE TRIOMF

The hastily prepared Universal Exhibition of 1888 needed (at least the city fathers believed) a suitably grand and welcoming entrance. And so the architect Josep Vilaseca (1848–1910) set about creating this highly unusual triumphal arch. Eschewing classical models and the use of stone, Vilaseca turned instead to the Islamic traditions implanted in Spain centuries before and made his arch of brick. His grand idea of flanking the arch with towers was scrapped. Nevertheless, a flurry of Catalan sculptors came together to decorate the arch.

🅰 Map p. 118 ✉ Passeig de Lluís Companys 🚇 Metro: Línia 1 (Arc de Triomf)

ESGLÈSIA DE SANT PERE DE LES PUELLES

One of the earliest churches to be raised in what was in the early Middle Ages countryside beyond the innermost line of city walls, St.

Josep Vilaseca's curious Mudéjar-style Arc de Triomf greeted visitors to Barcelona's 1888 Universal Exhibition.

Peter of the Maidens was one of the most important convents in Barcelona. The Greek-cross floor plan has been preserved, along with a few Romanesque and Gothic traces, such as the 12th-century dome. It has not been the luckiest of locations. Sacked in 985 by a marauding Muslim force that massacred or sent into slavery the nuns they found inside the site has been damaged several times since. Opening hours are somewhat erratic.

🅰 Map p. 118 ✉ Plaça de Sant Pere 🚇 Metro: Línia 1 (Arc de Triomf)

LA LLOTJA

The western end of Plaça del Palau is closed off by the formidable 18th-century neoclass facade of La Llotja. It was here that the likes Picasso and Miró went to art school as you sters (see p. 122). Picasso's father taught he too in the Acadèmia de Belles Artes de Sant Jordi, which occupied part of the building from 1847 until the 1980s. Perhaps more si nificantly for Barcelona, it was the home of the city's stock exchange one way or anothe since the late 14th century to the late 20th c tury. La Llotja was the first such trading ho on the Iberian Peninsula. The medieval inte or of Gran Saló, made up of three aisles sep rated by lofty rounded arcades, is where trading went on. Until disputes about the building's ownership are resolved, it remain tightly shut.

🅰 Map p. 118 ✉ Consolat de Mar 2–4 🚇 Metro: Línia 4 (Barceloneta)

MUSEU DE LA XOCOLATA

Some would say divine inspiration led the town to install a museum dedicated to choc late on the site of the former Convent de Sa Agustí. Displays trace the history of this fu damental foodstuff, but the place abounds i the sticky stuff too. Visitors see what pre-Columbian societies did with cacao and ho it arrived in Europe in the 16th century. Audiovisual displays provide more material And what's a chocolate museum without chocolate? The Sala Barcelona contains cho late models of anything from literary figure to city sights. You can see machines used fo making chocolate, too. In the Obrador (wor shop), you might be lucky enough to catch chocolate tasting classes.

www.museuxocolata.com 🅰 Map p. 118 ✉ Plaça de Pons i Clerch s/n ☎ 93 268 78 🕐 Open 10 a.m.–7 p.m., Mon. & Wed.–Sat. 10 a.m.–3 p.m. Sun. 💲 $ 🚇 Metro: Línies (Arc de Triomf) & 4 (Jaume 1) ∎

A long one of the city's most fashionable boulevards are arrayed some of Barcelona's more intriguing *modernista* mansions. And lovers of contemporary art can expect a visual treat in the Fundació Antoni Tàpies.

Passeig de Gràcia

Rooftop detail of Gaudí's Casa Batlló

Passeig de Gràcia

LINED BY CHIC STORES, CROWDED TAPAS BARS, CAFÉS, AND HIGH-RENT offices, Passeig de Gràcia is one of the most sought-after addresses in town. Starting at Plaça de Catalunya, it links the old city with Gràcia, a separate village until the Eixample filled up the intervening countryside in the last decade of the 19th century. The *modernisme* (art nouveau) theme starts with the street itself, which boasts a series of elegant wrought-iron street lamps erected in 1906. Most Barcelonians think Gaudí designed the lamps and the badly maintained benches below them, but they are in fact the work of a lesser-known colleague, Pere Falqués Urpí (1850–1916).

Office workers and shoppers stroll the Passeig de Gràcia.

It is little wonder that some of Barcelona's wealthiest and showiest families should have acquired property here around the turn of the 20th century and sought to outdo one another by taking on the biggest names in architecture.

These were boom times in the housing construction business. By the 1850s it had become clear the old city could no longer contain its burgeoning population, so the city walls were knocked down and competitions held for urban expansion plans. The winner was Ildefons Cerdà, whose idea for the Eixample (Extension) entailed a grid pattern of streets spreading inland from the old city. Blocks at regular intervals were to be set aside as parks, but property speculation meant that these areas were sold off as building plots.

Into the building-boom atmosphere stepped a gallery of the most daring architects the city had ever seen. And just as they had no fear of convention or of deploying all their imagination, so their well-lined patrons seemed addicted to a limitless eclecticism.

Gaudí's two contributions alone, the wavy La Pedrera and dragon-backed Casa Batlló, demonstrate the impossibility of pinning down *modernistas* to any set of standard rules. Contributions by his most outstanding contemporaries, Puig i Cadafalch and Domènech i Montaner, created a series of wildly discordant houses.

The latter designed another building just off Passeig de Gràcia, destined to become home to the Fundació Antoni Tàpies. Tàpies is one of Barcelona's most celebrated

0   500 meters
0   500 yards

PLAÇA DE LESSEPS

Mercat Lesseps

JARDINS MENÉNDEZ PELAYO

TRAVESSERA   DE   DALT

VIA   AUGUSTA

JARDINS DE MORAGAS

Casa Vicenç

CARRER DE LES CAROLINES

Fontana

PLAÇA DE ROVIRA I TRIAS

Mercat Galvany

CARRER   DELS   MADRAZO

GRÀCIA

PLAÇA DE CARDONA

PLAÇA DEL DIAMONT

Església de Sant Josep

A DE ICESC A

TRAVESSERA   DE   GRÀCIA

Mercat Llibertat

PLAÇA DE LA LLIBERTAT

PLAÇA DEL SOL

PLAÇA DE LA VIRREINA

PLAÇA DE RIUS I TAULET (PLAÇA DEL RELLOTGE)

TRAVESSERA   DE   GRÀCIA

Mercat Abaceria Central

AVINGUDA

Casa Sayrach

DIAGONAL

Hotel Casa Fuster

JARDINS DE SALVADOR ESPRIU

CARRER   DE   PARÍS

CARRER DE CÒRSEGA

PLAÇA DE JOAN CARLES I

CARRER   DE   CÒRSEGA

tal

Hospital Clínic i Provincial

CARRER DEL ROSSELLÓ   Diagonal

Casa Comalat

Palau Baró de Quadras

Casa de les Punxes

CARRER   DE   PROVENÇA

DIAGONAL

Parc Bombers

Casa Enrico Batlló

La Pedrera (Casa Milà)

Casa Thomas

Verdaguer

Mercat Porvenir-Ninot

CARRER   DE   MALLORCA

Fundació Antoni Tàpies

Casa Viuda Marfà

Palau Montaner

PLAÇA MOSSÈN JACINT VERDAGUER

C.   DE   VALÈNCIA

Museu Egipci

Fundació de Francisco Godia

Casa Batlló

Casa Amatller

Passeig de Gràcia

CARRER   D'ARAGÓ

Esc. Univ. de Treball Social

Casa Lleó Morera (Manzana de la Discordia)

CARRER   DEL   CONSELL   DE   CENT

Girona

Tetuan

Universitat Central

L'EIXAMPLE

PLAÇA DE TETUAN

LANES

PLAÇA DE LA UNIVERSITAT

GRAN   VIA   DE   LES   CORTS   CATALANES

Casas Rocamora

Universitat

RONDA   DE   LA   UNIVERSITAT

Casa Pascual i Pons

CARRER   DE   CASP

Casa Calvet

Catalunya

PLAÇA DE CATALUNYA

Casas Cabot

Sant Antoni

Catalunya

PLAÇA D'URQUINAONA

RONDA   DE   SANT

Urquinaona

contemporary artists, and it seems appropriate that the core body of his work should hang in a building that reminds us of the glory days of architectural creativity in Barcelona.

After seeing the cream of the crop, architecture enthusiasts can put together any number of itineraries, especially in the Eixample, in an effort to slake their art nouveau thirst. ∎

Area of map detail

Resembling some
bizarre aquatic
creature, the
Casa Batlló
facade is one of
Gaudí's most
outlandish
creations.

Manzana de la Discordia

IN THE YEARS 1898 TO 1906 THREE MANSIONS ON ONE
block of Passeig de Gràcia (between Carrer del Consell de Cent and
Carrer d'Aragó) were given *modernista* overhauls in what seems in
retrospect like a divine contest between the three greatest names
in *modernisme:* Gaudí, Domènech i Montaner, and Puig i Cadafalch.

Casa Batlló

🅰 Map pp. 140–41

✉ Passeig de Gràcia
43

☎ 93 216 03 06

💲 $$$

🚇 Metro: Línies 2, 3,
& 4 (Passeig de
Gràcia)

The results are so utterly disparate
that this block came to be known as
Manzana de la Discordia. Happily
for lovers of puns, the word *man-
zana* in Spanish means both block
and apple. In Greek myth, Eris
(Discord) threw the Apple of
Discord onto Mt. Olympus with
orders that it be given to the most
beautiful goddess. The jealousies
unleashed led to the Trojan War.

The disappointing aspect of a
visit to these buildings is that you
can't see inside them, and although
this situation has changed on
occasion, don't hold your breath.

By far the most extraordinary
house is Gaudí's **Casa Batlló**
(completed in 1906) at No. 43. He
retained the original structure of
the 1877 building but completely
recast the exterior and interior

design. As always, Gaudí avoided
straight lines and right angles. The
facade undulates and shimmers
with its *trencadís* coat, while the
second floor (the main floor in
Barcelona mansions) is fronted by
what seems to be a series of melting
cavern entrances. The stone and
glasswork are of a singular beauty.

Balconies resembling jawbones
of prehistoric beasts (some liken
them to Carnival masks) jut out
from the upper floors. Finally, the
six-story building is capped by
what is doubtlessly the strangest
roof in all of Barcelona. Said to rep-
resent St. George and the dragon,
its tiles do indeed appear to be the
scales of a mythological beast. It is
capped by a tower with the custom-
ary four-arm cross that appears on
Gaudí constructions elsewhere.

The entrance halls are pleasingly simple, with vaguely rippling ceilings and curvaceous balustrades. Everything, from the elevator doors and balconies on the stairwell down to the tiniest details, received his full attention. The rooms on the main floor, with their swirling ceilings and blob-like windowpanes, are remarkable.

Walk to the rear terrace and then catch the lift up to the roof. You will notice the blue tile decor lightens in tone as you head up. Apart from a behind-the-scenes look at the extraordinary roof, the views are great.

The other two objects of discord may not speak to your fantasy the way Casa Batlló does, but they are fine, original buildings. Puig i Cadafalch completed the remake of **Casa Amatller,** next door to Casa Batlló, in 1900 and it is possibly his most exuberant creation. The facade is largely inspired by religious and civic Catalan Gothic, but with playful touches, such as the twin entrance of differently sized and shaped doorways, dripping with sculptures that include St. George and the dragon, and a woman in classic art nouveau style.

Topping the building is a gabled conceit straight out of Amsterdam, coated in ceramics that exude a mildly metallic sheen. Inside, you are unlikely to get past the pillared entrance hall (where Ruta del Modernisme tickets are on sale; see sidebar), but this at least gives you some idea of the internal decoration, rich in vividly colored tiles, fine timberwork, and good stained glass.

On the corner of the block at No. 35 is Domènech i Montaner's curious **Casa Lleó Morera** (1905). Topped by fanciful battlements, the facade is most pleasing for the mixed shapes in its windows and bulging balconies. The first floor facade has been restored after

having suffered at the hands of 1940s shopkeepers. In the lobby and on the second floor, cheerful primary colors dominate the floral-motif mosaics. The closest you can get now are some displays of furniture in the MNAC (see p. 190). ■

Puig i Cadafalch's
Casa Amatller

You can no longer go inside Casa Lleó Morera.

Ruta del Modernisme ticket

Rather than absorbing the inconvenience and expense of paying for individual *modernista* sights around town, it is worth investing in a Ruta del Modernisme ticket (Tel 93 488 01 39), available at Casa Amatller (Closed Sun. p.m.) The ticket, valid for a year, is a pretty good value because it gives you up to half-price admission to Palau de la Música, La Pedrera, the Sagrada Família, Fundació Antoni Tàpies, Casa-Museu Gaudí (in Park Güell), Museu de Zoologia, MNAC, Casa Batlló, Tramvia Blau, and more. ■

Fundació Antoni Tàpies

Fundació Antoni Tàpies

www.fundaciotapies.org

- Map pp. 140–41
- Carrer d'Aragó 255
- 93 487 03 15
- Closed Mon.
- $
- Metro: Línies 2, 3, & 4 (Passeig de Gràcia)

The grand space at the center of the Fundació Antoni Tàpies is a *modernista* relic.

IN 1984 BARCELONA'S SIGNAL AVANT-GARDE ARTIST, ANTONI Tàpies, launched this foundation not only as a place to exhibit key examples of his own work but as a research center and exhibition space for the promotion of contemporary art.

Before rushing inside, those with an interest in architecture will want to take some time to study the outside of this early Domènech i Montaner creation. Built in 1880 to house the publishing company Editorial Montaner i Simón, the edifice is an important precursor of *modernisme*. In its time, the use of brick and an eclectic mix of styles was innovative, and today helps make the facade a kind of curtain between what lies within and the outside world.

The interior has been substantially reordered to cope with the Fundació's requirements, but a few original elements remain. In the center of the top floor yawns an huge rectangular gap creating a sense of light and space below. Domènech i Montaner opted to use slender pillars of iron rather than stone, another novelty at the time.

For most of the year the collection here is limited. About a dozen large pieces, representative of the past 30 years of the artist's career, hang on the upstairs floor. What you see is largely what you imagine. Tàpies has for many years tended to mix up materials and paints to create physical effects, frequently working on wood rather than canvas. "Amari" ("Wardrobe," 1973) is a stack of clothes tumbling out of a closet. "Terra Sobre Tela" ("Earth on Canvas," 1983) is literally a pile of mud on canvas. More works hang in the basement, mostly from the 1940s and 1950s, when Tàpies was in a playful painting mood.

Those unfamiliar with Tàpies' work may not necessarily appreciate it; those who do will get more joy if they visit the gallery from July through September, when the two lower floors are hung with many more of his works. During the remainder of the year, these floors will be decked with temporary exhibitions by other artists. These shows can be hit or miss affairs in terms of quality and artistic interest. ■

La Pedrera (Casa Milà)

ONE OF GAUDÍ'S LESS CHARITABLE COLLEAGUES WAS ONCE heard to say, "If I had designed Casa Milà I wouldn't sleep easy at night." The building that came to be known as La Pedrera (stone quarry) elicited a range of responses, with cartoonists depicting it variously as a bizarre fortress, with cannon poking out of every opening, and as a science-fiction port for extraordinary flying machines.

The building, with its strange, undulating facade, is considered by most critics to be more significant still than Casa Batlló (although for sheer weirdness the latter makes a greater initial visual impact.) Most significantly, the latter project involved renovation of an existing building, while the existing constructions on the corner of Passeig de Gràcia and Carrer de Provença were bulldozed to make way for La Pedrera. The new block was commissioned in 1906 by the wealthy businessman Pedro Milà i Camps, who once remarked that he was less likely to run out of cash for the costly project than of patience for the time it was taking to finish (work finally ended in 1910.)

Gaudí closely directed every element of construction and decoration and was profoundly disappointed when the owner rejected the crowning glory, which was to be a massive bronze sculptural group depicting the Virgin of the Rosary flanked by archangels Gabriel and Michael. After the events of the Setmana Tràgica in 1909 (see p. 34), in which many churches had been attacked and religious images destroyed, Senyor Milà didn't want to attract such trouble to his house. Gaudí bailed out of the project in its last stages over a contractual misunderstanding in which his chosen interior decorator was replaced by another.

The gray stone (from the Garraf and Penedès areas) used to create the facade flows around the corner

Barcelona satirists never tired of poking fun at Gaudí's curiously undulating residence.

La Pedrera (Casa Milà)

www.caixacatalunya.es

🅰 Map pp. 140–41

✉ Carrer de Provença 261-265

☎ 90 240 09 73

💲 $$

🅼 Metro: Línies 3 & 5 (Diagonal)

Fanciful chimney pots atop La Pedrera look like science-fiction warriors.

of the intersection like a wave in continuous motion. The eye is so caught up in this movement that the serried ranks of windows, buried deep in the folds of the stone, appear almost as after-thoughts. Like drifts of algae on the wave's surface, ribbons of inter-woven wrought iron are draped in front of many of them to form balconies. Across the top is spread the inscription in Gaudí's fanciful script: *"Ave Gratia Plena Dominus Tecum"* (Hail, Full of Grace; the Lord is with You), the archangel Gabriel's words when he appeared to the Virgin Mary.

At ground level, Gaudí's deliberately uneven pillars extend the erratic, sinuous surface to the pavement. When the building was complete municipal inspectors told Gaudí that, since some pillars jutted out farther than others, they were in contravention of city ordinances. He suggested that, if they insisted, he could remove the pillars, but since they supported the building he would not be held responsible for the results. He was not bothered again on the subject.

Champagne on the roof

There is no shortage of distractions on the long, hot summer nights in Barcelona. One of the more surreal options is heading up to the hauntingly illu-minated La Pedrera roof to sip a flute of champagne to the accompaniment of soothing live music (Fri. & Sat. 9 p.m.–midnight mid-June–July).

Two separate and unconnected entrances lead into the building, one on the street corner (now leading into the store) and the other on Carrer de Provença, by which you enter the building proper. The motion-filled design continues in the internal layout, consisting of two separate internal courtyards, one circular and the other a long oval. The apartments and offices of the building swirl around them like river water around boulders. The internal facades are more sober affairs, but the external stairways seem to ripple upward.

Access is available only to the top floor, the attic, and the two first-floor patios. Sometimes you will also come across temporary art exhibitions on the first floor.

You will be guided to an elevator. Get out at the **Pis de la Pedrera** (alternatively, you can walk down the stairs from the attic.) This top-floor apartment has been beautifully restored and furnished in much the way it probably was early in the 20th century. As is to be expected with Gaudí, the interior of the house is almost as curvaceous as the exterior. Where possible, he eliminates the straight line in the ceilings, walls, and doors. The succession of rooms—kitchen, bedrooms, dining area, bathrooms, and so on—take you right around a circuit of the larger of the internal courtyards. Some of the decorative details and furnishings, along with the wrought-iron balconies, were actually designed by one of Gaudí's right-hand men, fellow architect Josep Maria Jujol. The view down Passeig de Gràcia, combined with the simple elegance of the furnishings, is enough to make your heart jump and say, "I want to live here!"

Unfortunately that isn't an option. So the only thing to do is move up to the next floor, the remarkable brickwork attic of the building. Fascinating in itself for its rib cage of parabolic arches, the attic has been turned into the **Espai Gaudí,** a museum-style review of all the master's work. Models of his buildings are interspersed with photographs and videos about the man, his life, and his constructions. You can also see examples of the lead-and-string structural models he used to solve load-bearing and engineering conundrums in a way that allowed him to pursue his ideal of mimicking the wonders of nature. These models hang upside down; by placing a mirror under them you see an image of the sought-after structure.

Access to the rooftop is from the attic and little can prepare you for the bizarre sight that awaits you (not even a prior visit to the Palau Güell). It is not hard to see why some saw La Pedrera as a fortress, for the array of chimney pots and other structures looks like a brigade of soldiers or robots recently disembarked from the imagination of George Lucas. The great squat structures might be watchtowers, while others, dotted with curious openings, seem like space-age pillboxes. More slender types, clustered together in groups and each topped with a menacing helmet, are the troopers manning this fantastical roof. They look like so many pieces ready to move on an intergalactic board game. If you can drag your eyes away from these strange objects for a moment, enjoy the magnificent views across central Barcelona. ■

You won't find any straight lines along the curvaceous stairwell inside La Pedrera.

More *modernisme* walk

The inevitable theme of any stroll around the Eixample will be modernisme. This is a short tour of some striking examples of the style (of which there are hundreds in the city) beyond the key sights mentioned in this and other chapters. Often you cannot even get inside the entrance halls, but simply observing the exteriors reiterates just how eclectic were the tastes and fantasy of this brief but exuberant period.

Gaudí's **Casa Calvet,** at Carrer de Casp 48, is curious above all for its restraint. The architect completed the building in 1899, only a year before he finished the much more fanciful Palau Güell (see pp. 92–93). The house has a baroque flavor, particularly in the wavy crest that tops the facade and in the two sets of protruding wrought-iron balconies.

Around the corner, Josep Vilaseca designed

- See area map pp. 140–41
- Carrer de Casp 48
- 2.7 miles (4.25 km)
- 2 hours
- Avinguda Diagonal 423

NOT TO BE MISSED
- Casa Viuda Marfà
- Palacio Montaner
- Casa de les Punxes
- Casa Comalat
- Casa Fuster

two contiguous buildings, the **Cases Cabot,** for the same family. They were his first fully *modernista* constructions. The outstanding element is the doorway to the one on the left (Carrer de Roger de Llúria 8–10), its tympanum's oriental flavor made singular by the dense floral ornament. The hallway is also worth inspecting for its modernista decor. From here walk down to Ronda de Sant Pere, turn right, and head for Plaça de Catalunya.

Soaring up across from the northeast corner of Plaça de Catalunya is the impressive bulk of **Casa Pascual i Pons ❶,** at Passeig de Gràcia 2–4. Designed by Enric Sagnier Villavecchia (1858–1931), this stone palace is an airy burst of Gothic-inspired modernisme, finished in 1891. The tracery on the second-floor windows, trefoil decoration on the top-floor windows, the towers, and other elements are all medieval throwbacks.

Across Carrer de Casp at Passeig de Gràcia 6–14 is another well-known Barcelona facade, equally inspired by the Gothic but with a heavy French leaning and not completed until 1920 by the brothers Joaquim (1854–1938) and Bonaventura Bassegoda Amigó (1862–1940). The **Cases Rocamora** stand out for their conical tower and the crowning elements of the window galleries that jut out from the facade.

Manuel Comas i Thos (born 1855) reached farther back into the Middle Ages for his **Casa Viuda Marfà** , at Passeig de Gràcia 66, finished in 1905. What most attract the eye are the neo-Romanesque arches that mark the entrance and the neo-Gothic gallery above.

A block farther north, Josep Vilaseca completed the elegant facade of **Casa Enrico Batlló,** now part of the Condes de Barcelona Hotel, at Passeig de Gràcia 75 in

Left: Casa Batlló's ornate roof line

Right: Casa de les Punxes's witch's-hat towers

Below: Fine decoration on the Palacio Montaner

MORE MODERNISME WALK

1896. His use of brick, wrought iron, and ceramic ornament (the latter on the top floor) are all signs that Vilaseca was moving toward modernisme.

Domènech i Montaner was busy in Carrer de Mallorca (turn to the right), having a hand in his cousin's **Palau Montaner** ❸ at No. 278 and **Casa Thomas** at Nos. 291–293. The former has a Florentine Renaissance ring about it and seems quite out of place, standing apart and with just three stories, although the use of ceramic decor on the top floor facade and floral ornament elsewhere are clear signs of modernista handiwork. Domènech i Montaner created the first and second floors of Casa Thomas in 1898. Fourteen years later the upper floors and towers were added, respecting but not imitating the original architect's style.

Possibly the best known of Puig i Cadafalch's works in Barcelona is **Casa de les Punxes** ④, at Avinguda Diagonal 416–420, named for the conical points that crown the six towers. The whole looks like a combination of northern European mansion and Loire Valley château and features florid ornament in the balconies and the galleries.

Imitation is a form of flattery, and Gaudí gets his in **Casa Comalat,** at Carrer de Còrsega 316. Designed by Salvador Valeri Pupurull (1873–1954), the building's main facade swirls uncomfortably between two stock-standard Eixample blocks. However,

Left: Architectural surprises around L'Eixample include the Casa Comalat. Below: Washing the windows of Domènech i Montaner's Casa Thomas

although the first floor mirrors elements of Gaudí's Casa Batlló, the upper levels are highly original. The interlocking windows form an armored casing that resembles the shell of an armadillo.

Another classic Domènech i Montaner mansion, **Hotel Casa Fuster** ⑤, crowns the top end of Passeig de Gràcia (No. 132). Now a luxury hotel, it bursts with variety in its tower, balconies, galleries, trefoil windows, and broad arches. For more Gaudiesque, you need to tramp a few blocks west along Avinguda Diagonal until you reach **Casa Sayrach** ⑥ at Nos. 423–425, by Manuel Sayrach Carreras (1886–1937). The sinuous mansard level clearly takes its cue from La Pedrera, and every inch inside has been exploited to the full. Finished in 1918, it seems almost like a tribute to the master. ∎

Gràcia

Gràcia

Map pp. 140–41

Metro: Línia 3
(Fontana)

WHILE ON THE LOOKOUT FOR MORE *MODERNISTA* caprices, you may end up in the tangle of narrow streets and charming squares that make up Gràcia. Gaudí completed one of his earliest commissions, the Casa Vicenç, up here back in the 1880s. The area is worth exploring, not for any specific sights but for the atmosphere of what was until the end of the 19th century a separate city. The place retains an air quite apart and, because few tourists come here, the sense of a genuinely Catalan environment is all the stronger.

By the time Barcelona absorbed Gràcia in 1897, it was a busy industrial center and its 60,000 souls appear to have been a feisty bunch. In the 1870s, several uprisings were launched here, and by the 1890s Gràcia was a hotbed of liberal, republican, radical Catalanist, and left-wing activity. In the 1960s and '70s it became *the* place to be for intellectuals and bohemians. That spirit has ebbed, but local house prices reflect that, for many, Gràcia still carries a certain cachet.

Right: Gaudí had not yet abandoned the straight line in Casa Vicenç, but his decorative devices add a distinctive touch.

Below: The fashionable Passeig de Gràcia was once a rural road linking Barcelona to the then separate town of Gràcia.

In 1883, when Gràcia was still a separate entity, Gaudí was asked to build a secluded private residence for a ceramics manufacturer. The result was **Casa Vicenç** *(Carrer de les Carolines 18–24),* which, although it doesn't display the fluidity of Gaudí's better known later works, is eye-catching amid the apartment blocks that surround it. Chessboard–style green and white tiles are a prominent decorative touch, and the wrought-iron fence and window grills are also fine. With its towers, windows, and other openings, the house exudes the air of a mini-castle. Visitors are not permitted inside.

Four blocks south of Casa Vicenç, on the rousingly named **Plaça de la Llibertat** (Liberty Square), is an admirable late 19th-century wrought-iron market **(Mercat Llibertat)** designed by Francesc Berenguer (1866–1914), one of Gaudí's closest assistants; on Berenguer's death Gaudí exclaimed that he had lost his right hand. The heart of the area is, however, on the right side of Carrer Gran de Gràcia, the narrow and often traffic-choked extension of Passeig de Gràcia and the main shopping street.

Among the many squares where locals delight in sitting over coffee, or something stronger, some stand out more than others. **Plaça de Rius i Taulet,** named after the mayor who organized the 1888 Universal Exhibition, is dominated by a clock tower that dates from 1862, hence it is known to most locals as the Plaça del Rellotge (Clock Square). It is a favorite meeting place for revelers, but in the 1870s it was a rallying point for revolutionaries. Several small uprisings began here in that period. This is also the site of the pre-1897 local town hall.

Three blocks north is the liveliest square in Gràcia, **Plaça**

del Sol. Ringed by bars and cafés, it is wonderful for the hedonists but not so good for long-suffering residents, especially during the August Festa Major de Gràcia, when it becomes a focal point for about a week's raucous street partying.

A more tranquil spirit reigns on **Plaça de la Virreina,** three blocks northeast. The square, presided over by the modest 17th-century **Església de Sant Josep,** offers a rare treat: trees. Together with a couple of welcoming cafés, they make it one of the most pleasant spots in Gràcia to read the paper over breakfast. Two blocks west is **Plaça del Diamant,** setting for the eponymous book by Mercè Rodoreda (1909–1983), one of the most popular Catalan novels of the 20th century.

Finally, a few blocks farther to the northeast is **Plaça de Rovira i Trias,** dedicated to Ildefons Cerdà's rival for the Eixample urban expansion plan in the 1860s. Antoni Rovira's plan is laid out in bronze beneath his statue here. Judge for yourself whether he or Cerdà deserved the commission. ■

More places to visit in Passeig de Gràcia

FUNDACIÓ FRANCISCO GODIA

This private foundation was set up in 2000 to display the private collections of a Catalan industrialist, Francisco Godia (1921–1990). Godia's tastes were wide-ranging, but the core of his collection is made up of Romanesque and Gothic art, including paintings and sculpture mostly from Spain. The mid-13th century painting (thought to have been executed in León) depicting the taking down of Christ from the Cross is remarkable for its allegorical density and the brilliance of its color. Godia also collected fine medieval ceramics and paintings from the 19th and 20th centuries. Space isn't sufficient to exhibit the entire collection, so a three–month rotation is employed.

www.fundacionfgodia.org [M] Map pp. 140–41 ✉ Carrer de València 284 ☎ 93 272 31 80 ⏱ Closed Tues. $ $ 🚇 Metro: Línies 2, 3, & 4 (Passeig de Gràcia)

Mummies keep an eye on visitors at the Museu Egipci de Barcelona.

MUSEU EGIPCI DE BARCELONA

This private collection is the only museum in Spain devoted to ancient Egyptian artifacts. It affords an opportunity to voyage briefly to the other side of the Mediterranean. Spread out across two floors, the extensive display gives a taste of the wonders of Egypt and the pharaohs. Just past the ticket desk is a row of stone and basalt figures, followed by the colorful sarcophagus of an eighth-century B.C. noblewoman.

Circling the first floor counterclockwise you will see jewelry (including a striking little gold figurine of the god Osiris), ceramics, alabaster jars, and funerary objects. In among the sarcophagi, death masks, and mummies of humans are several belonging to animals, too. The Egyptians believed that certain animals, such as the cat and the falcon, were the earthly incarnations of the gods. Standing to attention upstairs is an array of statuettes and figurines made of bronze, stone, wood, and other materials.

Other curious items include a large stone sculpture of a baboon, Ptolemaic- and Roman-era coins, and fragments from a tomb. The top floor is taken up by a pleasant café and terrace.

www.fundclos.com [M] Map pp. 140–41 ✉ Carrer de València 284 ☎ 93 488 01 88 ⏱ Closed Sun. after 2 p.m. $ $$ 🚇 Metro: Línies 2, 3, & 4 (Passeig de Gràcia)

MUSEU DEL PERFUM

Tucked on the back of the Regia perfume store in what seems like a 19th-century alchemist's den is this unique ode to odors. Here are more than 9,000 historic perfume bottles and accessories in all shapes and sizes, from ancient times to the most elegant in modern brands.

www.museodelperfume.com [M] Map pp. 140–41 ✉ Passeig de Gràcia 39 ☎ 93 216 01 46 ⏱ Closed 1:30-4:30 p.m., Sat. p.m. & Sun. 🚇 Metro: Línies 2, 3, & 4 (Passeig de Gràcia)

PALAU BARÓ DE QUADRAS

Palau Quadras, in which this curious museum of musical instruments is housed, is a *modernista* folly that merits a visit in its own right. As the overburdened mock-Gothic facade suggests, it is the handiwork of Puig i Cadafalch. Note the square fish figures bearing the whole load. It now is the headquarters for the Casa Asia cultural association.

www.casaasia.es [M] Map pp. 140–41 ✉ Avinguda Diagonal 373 ☎ 93 416 11 57 ⏱ Closed p.m. & Mon. $ $ 🚇 Metro: Línies 3 & 5 (Diagonal)

The genius of Gaudí reaches its pinnacle of grandeur in the mighty Sagrada Família church, and its most extreme flights of fantasy in the whimsy of Park Güell. Images of the two have become the city's icons, known all over the world.

La Sagrada Família to Park Güell

Entrance pavilion at Park Güell

La Sagrada Família to Park Güell

FROM A DISTANCE ITS EIGHT COMPLETED TOWERS MAKE THE SAGRADA Família church look something akin to the superstructure of a science-fiction battleship steaming majestically across the urban sea that surrounds it. For many first-time visitors to the city, it is the one thing they know of Barcelona, and frequently it is their first port of call.

This unique temple is a magnificent, yet-to-be-finished architectural symphony. When construction began in the 1880s, the area around it was mostly open land, for building in the Eixample (Extension)—the grid-plan expansion of the city beyond the confines of the medieval walls—had barely begun. It would be decades before this part of town would

fill up with the housing that you now see. And it will be some decades from now before this most unusual of parish churches is finally completed. Thanks to some surviving drawings, photos, and models, architects have been able to get a reasonable idea of how Antoni Gaudí intended to complete the church. Computer studies have confirmed his daring structural calculations, and private donations keep the cranes and workshops busy.

Heading north from the church, a broad avenue bearing the name of the genius behind the Sagrada Família leads to a lesser known but in many respects equally important example of *modernista* building by one of Gaudí's most esteemed peers, Lluís Domènech i Montaner. If the Sagrada Família was conceived as a thing of beauty for God, the Hospital de la Santa Creu i Sant Pau (Holy Cross and St. Paul's Hospital) was designed as a thing of beauty for the people, at the same time having a practical purpose. Its division into cheerful little pavilions, eclectic style, and finely crafted ceramic and mosaic decoration make it an unusually pleasing setting for modern medical care.

It lies on a slight rise in the city. About a mile (1.6 km) to the west, that rise is much more marked and has long been known to locals as "la Muntanya" (the Mountain). A mountain it isn't, but it is a steep walk up to the 45-acre (20 ha) block bought by Eusebi Güell late in the 19th century to create a garden city residential zone. The climb probably deterred potential buyers, but this didn't stop Gaudí from laying out the gardens in his typically fanciful way. The result was that the citizens of Barcelona inherited this Gaudí gem as a stunning public park. ■

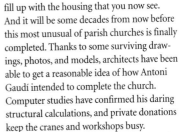

Unfinished it may be, the Sagrada Família is Gaudí's signature piece.

PARK GÜELL

Casa Trias

Sala
Hipòstila

Casa
Museu Gaudí

Area of map detail

EL CARMEL

Hospital
de L'Esperança

Lesseps
(Metro)

TRAVESSERA DE DALT

CARRER DE L'ESCORIAL

PLAÇA DE
LA FONT
CASTELLANA

Camp de
Futbol
de l'Europa

PARC DE
LES AIGÜES

Alfons X

RONDA

C. DE SARDENYA

DE PADILLA

MARE DE DÉU DE MONTSERRAT

DEL

GUINARDÓ

Guinardó

Joanic

JARDINS DEL
PRÍNCEPS DE
GIRONA

C. DE CARTAGENA

DE GAUDÍ

Hospital
de la
Santa Creu i
Sant Pau

TRAVESSERA DE GRÀCIA

C. DE SANT ANTONI MARIA CLARET

PASSEIG DE SANT JOAN

LA SAGRADA
FAMÍLIA

CARRER DE CÒRSEGA

CARRER DE LA INDÚSTRIA

Camp
de L'Arpa

Sagrada
Família

AVINGUDA

Hospital
de Sant Pau

CARRER DE CÒRSEGA

PLAÇA
DE LA
SAGRADA
FAMÍLIA

PLAÇA
DE GAUDÍ

DE PADILLA

CARRER DE PROVENÇA

PLAÇA
MOSSEN JACINT
VERDAGUER

CARRER DE MALLORCA

La Sagrada
Família
(Museu Gaudí)

Encants

C. DE VALÈNCIA

CARRER DE VALÈNCIA

LA DRETA

PLAÇA
DE PABLO
NERUDA

C. D'ARAGÓ

CARRER D'ARAGÓ

AVINGUDA MERIDIANA

Clot

L'EIXAMPLE

SANT JOAN

SARDENYA

DE LA MARINA

Els Encants Vells

Monumental

Plaça Monumental
dels Braus

PLAÇA
DE TETUAN

GRAN VIA DE LES CORTS

PLAÇA DE
LES GLÒRIES
CATALANES

CATALANES

Teatre Nacional
de Catalunya

Glòries

PASSEIG DE

CARRER DE LA MARINA

L'Auditori

AVINGUDA MERIDIANA

Torre
Agbar

AVINGUDA DIAGONAL

EL POBLENOU

Estació
del Nord

PARC ESTACIÓ
DEL NORD

Marina

CARRER DELS ALMOGÀVERS

CARRER DE PERE IV

CARRER DE PALLARS

RAMBLA DEL POBLENOU

Bogatell

Llacuna

Universitat
Pompeu
Fabra

DE LA MARINA

CARRER DEL DOCTOR TRUETA

| 0 | | 500 meters |
| 0 | | 500 yards |

La Sagrada Família

LIKE THE GRAND GOTHIC CATHEDRALS THAT IN PART inspired it, the Sagrada Família church has been more than a century in the making. In spite of repeated setbacks, this dizzying *modernista* temple continues to rise slowly to the heavens, almost 80 years after the death of the man who designed and nurtured it in its early decades—Antoni Gaudí.

La Sagrada Família
www.sagradafamilia.org

🗺 Map p. 157

✉ Plaça de la Sagrada Família

☎ 93 207 30 31

💲 $$

🚇 Metro: Línies 2 & 5 (Sagrada Família)

The long spiral walk down a Passion facade tower

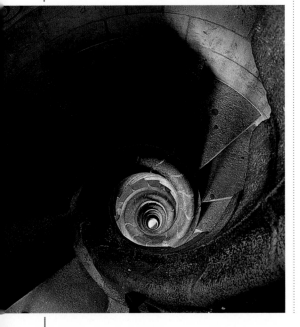

A trip to the Temple Expiatori de la Sagrada Família (Expiatory Temple of the Holy Family) is a visit to a work in progress. Much of the shell is now complete and the most intense work is going on inside the church. Optimistic estimates suggest it may be completed by 2020. Some would argue it should not be completed at all. By the time of Gaudí's death in 1926, one facade (minus three towers), the crypt, and the apse were finished. Lack of funds had slowed construction to a snail's pace, and the political upheavals of the 1930s, civil war, and the difficult years of the 1940s and '50s brought building to a halt.

Since then another facade has been raised, the central nave has been roofed over, and work on the main facade has begun.

The foundation stone of what was initially conceived as a neo-Gothic church was laid in 1882, almost two years before Gaudí took over the project. It was the fruit of a plan by an arch-conservative society dedicated to St. Joseph to turn what it considered Barcelona's increasingly lax citizens back to God.

Gaudí would dedicate much of the rest of his life to this, his most extraordinary creation. Influenced though he may have been by his Gothic predecessors, he sought much of his inspiration in nature. The sinewy, twisting, bulbous forms that inform his planning drafts, models, and completed construction are unique. Although most of his plans and models were destroyed by fire in the civil war, what survived (along with clues provided by some of his other buildings) gave his successors strong hints as to how he might have proceeded.

Gaudí's plans changed as he went ahead, but the final version envisaged a temple 310 feet (95 m) long by 197 feet (60 m) wide, with a central tower 560 feet (170 m) high and another 17 of 329 feet (100 m) or more. It will seat 13,000 people. Twelve of the towers (four on each facade) represent the Apostles (eight have been built), while five others symbolize the four

Evangelists and the Virgin Mary. Soaring above them, the central tower represents Christ. Each of the three facades was planned to tell a story: the Nativity, Passion, and Glory of Christ.

Enter by the **Passion facade,** which architects began to raise in 1954. While it respects largely its designer's original wishes, it is clearly different from the Nativity facade (by which you may also enter) that was mostly built in Gaudí's lifetime.

In 1987 sculptor Josep Maria Subirachs (1927–) started work on the sculptural sequence that depicts the last two days in the life of Christ. His work is designed to be "read" from left to right, describing an "S" from bottom to top and ranging from the Last Supper to end in the top right corner with Christ's burial. His strangely angular, incomplete figures evoke powerfully the most tragic moments in Jesus' life.

At the table of the Last Supper, St. John in his grief rests his head on the table while the other Apostles look on in sadness. To the left of the depiction of Judas's kiss of betrayal is a cryptogram—from its numbers 310 combinations can be made to arrive at 33, Christ's age when he died. In front of the central door is depicted the flagellation of Christ. Other episodes that follow include Christ before Pilate, Peter's denial, and the moment when Veronica wipes Christ's face. Next to her (strangely faceless as she holds out the bloody image of Christ) stand soldiers whose helmets are a deliberate reference to the strange chimney pots of Gaudí's Pedrera (see pp. 145–47). To the left of Christ crucified, the Virgin Mary, Mary Magdalene, and St. John stand in helpless sorrow. To the right yawns open the entrance to his burial place.

Having marveled at the towers from below, you can now go in the right-hand entrance of the Passion facade and take the elevator up the rightmost tower. Follow the signs when you reach the top to climb stairs and ramps in this and the adjacent tower. From up here the views across the city are spectacular. You can take the elevator back down or follow the arrows to walk downstairs, stopping at vantage points along the way.

Once back on solid ground, you enter the church proper. In 2000 the central nave stretching to Carrer de Mallorca was roofed over, and it is now possible to see the uncommon genius of Gaudí. Using photos, models, and computer simulations to test the master's calculations, today's architects have

Resembling the interior of an extraordinary cave, the Nativity facade was nearly complete by the time Gaudí died in 1926.

Captivating detail by Gaudí enhances La Sagrada Família (above).

The towers, four on each facade, represent the 12 Apostles.

Main entrance

Passion facade

Original drawings and computer imaging have enabled modern architects to envisage Gaudí's Glory facade.

Right: View of the city and towers of the Passion facade from the rose window.

erected faithfully the most extraordinary array of pillars to hold up the roof. At their base, they have the appearance of straightforward Doric columns, but they culminate in strangely spherical capitals from which further branches sprout toward the ceiling. Each of these branches, together giving the impression of a high forest canopy, has been designed to share in the load bearing. The tribunes set high above the aisles will be able to host a choir of 1,500.

Most of the nave and transept area is now a busy work site: You can also peer into workshops at the end of the nave along Carrer de Mallorca. The external walls of the nave are lined with spires topped by what look (quite intentionally) like piles of brightly colored wild fruit. Gaudí's plans for the **Glory facade** give it the appearance of a distorted, massive church organ. In it will be represented creation, the virtues, angels announcing the Last Judgment, and the Holy Trinity, with God the Father presiding over

the whole. Work has barely begun on this.

The marked path winds around the nave to the inside of the **Nativity facade.** Step outside to admire it. The busy, swirling, and curvaceous facade stands in stark contrast to the bleak, angular nature of the Passion facade. The joyousness of the one occasion is thus starkly differentiated from the pain of the other. As on the Passion facade, the enormous bulging bell towers soar into the sky, topped by mosaic-bedecked structures representing the symbols of the bishop: the cross, the ring, the miter, and the crosier.

Three portals culminating in acute spires make up the facade, and behind them are four bell towers. Dominating the central portal are the figures of the Holy Family, flanked by the adoring Magi and shepherds. Above them angels announce the birth of Christ. A twisting pinnacle of stone draws one's gaze up to the star that guided

Christ's adorers to Bethlehem. The left door is decorated with sculptures recounting the wedding of Joseph and Mary, the flight to Egypt, and Herod's slaughter of the innocents. Episodes in the young Jesus' life, such as his appearance among the doctors and his presentation in the temple, are depicted around the right door. One of the most striking elements of the whole facade is the luxuriant floral decor. Palms, wheat, a cypress, and other plants are topped by layers of what look like tightly packed dripping stalactites. There are stairs up into the towers, and an elevator that will only take you up.

On either side of the Nativity

A bronze door on the Passion facade is carved with 8,000 letters from a page of the Gospels.

facade's portals are halls designed to be part of a series that will encircle the church. If the church were a courtyard, these halls would be the passageways of the cloister. Gaudí completed the portal dedicated to Our Lady of the Rosary and of Montserrat in the building to the right of the facade. The decoration is particularly fine and symbolically laden. Note the serpent (the devil) handing a terrorist a bomb in representation of the temptation of men to do evil.

The **apse,** its pinnacles appearing from the outside like a dense alpine forest seen through shape-distorting glasses, is not accessible from the inside while construction continues in the transept.

Beneath the church, an extensive **crypt** stretches between the Nativity and Passion facades. It hosts the **Museu Gaudí,** best reached via an entrance just to the right of the Passion facade. On entering you can see drawings for the original project before Gaudí took over. Proceed straight ahead to see photos of various Gaudí works around Spain and the raising of the Nativity facade. You then enter the main aisle by striding beneath a plaster model of the church's central nave. Around you are plans and models of various details and sections of the church. About two-thirds of the way along the aisle to the right, you can look at the workshop where models are still being made. Toward the end of the crypt is a series of Subirach's preparatory sketches for his Passion facade sculptures, as well as a mock-up of the same facade.

Virtually opposite the workshop is a room that leads to a viewing point of the Chapel of El Carmen, where Gaudí lies buried. The Vatican announced its decision in 2000 to investigate the architect's case for beatification. ■

Hospital de la Santa Creu i Sant Pau

ALTHOUGH IT RARELY GETS A MENTION ON TOURIST itineraries of Barcelona, this early 20th-century hospital complex is an extraordinary creation. Domènech y Montaner and, after his death in 1923, his son Pere Domènech Roura, directed the construction of what amounts to a little *modernista* village for the ill. Their aim was to create a new general hospital in which patients would feel soothed by their surroundings.

**Hospital de la
Santa Creu i
Sant Pau**
www.hspau.com
🗺 Map p. 157
✉ Carrer de Sant
Antoni Maria Claret
167–171
☎ 93 291 90 00
🚇 Metro: Línia 5
(Hospital de Sant
Pau)

Started in 1902, it was completed in 1930, by which time the patients of Barcelona's 500-year-old Hospital de la Santa Creu in El Raval (see p. 98) had been transferred here. (Antoni Gaudí died in Santa Creu after being run over by a tram in 1926.)

The main entrance, as was often the case in Domènech i Montaner's projects, was clearly inspired by Gothic models. Grand but not overpowering, it is adorned with statuary, ceramic coats of arms, and several mosaics.

In the grounds you find yourself between two ranks of pavilions set along a central promenade. Each of the pavilions is dedicated to various specialties, but the emphasis is on the human dimension of the buildings. Clad in warm brick, they seem more like imaginative country houses, topped by tiled domes with a vaguely Byzantine look. That Levantine element continues in the domes on the church and of Casa de Convalescència at the eastern end of the compound.

Throughout the hospital, the ceramic and mosaic decoration, designed by artist Francesc Labarta (1887–1963) and executed by the Italian Mario Maragliano (1864–1944), is subtle but constantly pleasing. Particularly beautiful are the glazed tiles that adorn the center of the building at the end of the promenade.

Most of the hospital functions are being moved to new buildings on the site, and the *modernista* part is destined to be used mostly as a university medical facility and for cultural events. It is on the Ruta del Modernisme (see p. 143). ∎

**The *modernista*
facade reflects its
Gothic inspiration.**

Gaudí & Güell

The day the wealthy industrialist Eusebi Güell i Bacigalupi (1846–1918) wandered into the Spanish pavilion at the Paris Universal Exhibition in 1878 was one of the most decisive in Gaudí's career. The young architect had designed a storefront for a Barcelona glove retailer with a stand at the exhibition, and Güell was so impressed by its vitality and originality he sought out its creator upon his return to Barcelona. Güell liked the man as much as the work and soon began to regale Gaudí with commissions of ever increasing importance. It was the beginning of a lifelong and fruitful relationship.

Güell became so confident in the capacity of Gaudí to construct not only sound and original buildings but to express through them their shared Catalanist sentiments, that he commissioned Palau Güell, which was built on Carrer Nou de la Rambla in El Raval between 1886 and 1889 (see pp. 92–93). Here Gaudí began to give freer rein to his architectural expression. The result was a gamble that paid off. One day the two men were observing work to place a great coat of arms on the facade. A couple of passersby looked up and decried the "weird things" being added to the building. Güell, it is said, turned to his protégé and said: "Mr. Gaudí, now I like you even more!"

By the turn of the 20th century, Gaudí was involved in two far more ambitious projects for his benefactor. The first was a church for the Colònia Güell (see p. 238) just outside the city, a self-sufficient village for textile workers, devised in the best traditions of the enlightened magnate. While other architects built the houses, Gaudí set to raising the church. However, he only managed to finish the crypt (1915) before Güell abandoned the project due to lack of funds. The crypt, at Santa Coloma de Cervelló, provides important clues to Gaudí's groundbreaking structural ideas on weight distribution, vaulting, and other dilemmas.

At the same time, Gaudí set about developing Park Güell as a garden city (see pp. 166–67). His patron gave him a free hand in this project and Gaudí gladly accepted it. For 14 years he worked on it, but the land parcels put up for sale failed to attract buyers, and Güell had to admit the idea had been a failure.

While some architects were full of praise

Above: Portrait of Eusebi Güell, Antoni Gaudí, and Torras i Bages by Ricardo Opisso Sala (late 19th–early 20th century)

for Gaudí's unique work, critics abounded too, dubbing Gaudí a *somnia truites*—an omelette dreamer—meaning someone who dreams up crazy things. In one magazine a commentator observed, "Some say that in Park Güell all he is doing is spending money on making monumental omelettes. The fact is, however, that Güell is the one who has to pay for all the eggs!" Well, Gaudí had always insisted that the best way to know a man was to spend his money!

Güell's death was a great personal loss to Gaudí, for whom the patron had also become a friend. By this time he had stopped taking on any projects, preferring to concentrate on La Sagrada Família (see pp. 158–62). ■

During Güell's lifetime, Gaudí was rarely unemployed, with such projects as Park Güell (right) and Colònia Güell (below) to keep him busy.

Park Güell

YOU COULD BE FORGIVEN FOR THINKING, WHEN YOU reach the main entrance to Park Güell, that you have landed up on the set for a Disney fairy tale. The two stone pavilions flanking the wrought-iron gates look like a pair of gingerbread houses topped with generous servings of icing frozen into the most curious shapes.

The original concept behind this and the remaining 50 acres (20 ha) of what is one of the world's most singular public parks was rather more prosaic. The industrialist and Gaudí's patron, Eusebi Güell, who owned the land, yearned to create a garden city that would host some 60 houses for the well to do. He commissioned Gaudí, who set about the work in 1900 with characteristic gusto, employing several outstanding contemporaries (Josep Maria Jujol in particular) to help him. In the ensuing 14 years he managed to trace out the park and its installations. However, only two houses were built before interest in the idea waned, leaving the people of Barcelona with a bizarrely beautiful park in which to stroll and bask in glorious views across the city to the Mediterranean Sea.

The pavilions were designed to house the park's guardians and serve as a reception center for visitors to the residents who never materialized. They are completely in keeping with Gaudí's insistence on the absence of straight lines. Curvaceous ceramic layers culminating in unlikely towers top the rough local stone, and bloated wrought-iron grills protect the windows. The two houses serve as a frame for a grand staircase that one

A great platform with a serpentine bench by Jujol tops the Sala Hipòstila.

Park Güell

www.bcn.es/parcsijardins

⚑ Map p. 157

✉ Carrer d'Olot 7

☎ 93 413 24 00

🚇 Metro: Línia 3
(Lesseps) & a
10-minute walk
following signs

Casa-Museu Gaudí

⚑ Map p. 157

✉ Caretera del Carmel
s/n

☎ 93 219 38 11

🚇 Metro: Línia 3
(Lesseps) & a
10-minute walk
following signs

A playful dragon greets visitors to Park Güell.

might imagine leading to a ballroom above. (One house serves as a shop, and the other has a small display of park history.) Flanked by low walls of *trencadís* ceramics, it is a work of some beauty, a visual spectacle of shattered patterns exuding color.

High up in the middle of the park reigns a ceramic dragon, and beyond it more stairs lead up to the **Sala Hipòstila** (Hypostile Hall), a forest of 86 heavy pillars that supports an enormous platform above. The outer pillars lean inward and direct one's gaze up to the ceramic-covered ceiling above what would have been the garden city's market.

The platform overhead is a broad observation point, overlooking the city below and the shimmering Mediterranean on the horizon. Sparkling ceramic benches, designed by Jujol, resemble one long twisting serpent.

As you head east you reach the rose-colored **Casa-Museu Gaudí,** where he lived off and on from 1906 until he died in 1926. From then until 1960 it was home to an Italian industrialist.

You will guess from its sobriety that this is not a Gaudí design, but it is full of furnishings from other Gaudí houses around the city. The most outlandish are perhaps the dining-room pieces for Casa Batlló (see pp. 142–43); the seats seem to have been cobbled together from wooden elephant ears. On the top floor you can see Gaudí's simple bedroom and office. A devout Catholic, he was also an ascetic, eschewing all but minimal comforts. In the small garden are scattered wrought-iron decorations taken from various Gaudí projects.

Leaving the house, follow the trail uphill, passing stone porticoes that blend into the mountainside. Their clusters of pillars leaning at strange angles and supporting higher levels of the path look like enchanted petrified trees. On the way up you pass the only other house here, **Casa Trias** *(closed to the public).*

Tracks fan out across the park amid the trees planted here in the early stages of the park's development. A clearing by Casa Trias is a tranquil viewing point. ∎

Death in the afternoon

It is a sweltering summer afternoon. A mixed crowd of local aficionados and country people rubs shoulders with hordes of brightly attired tourists to enter the stout-walled arena. Some are connoisseurs, others merely curious. For here will take place one of the oldest blood sports in the world.

The bullfight, or corrida, dates at least from Roman times but is associated particularly with Spain. It is also practiced in Portugal, southern France, and Latin America, although in the former two countries the bull is not killed. The *lidia* (as it is also known) has never been hugely popular in Catalunya but immigration from other parts of Spain after World War II has ensured a sufficient following in Barcelona, always supplemented by curious outsiders.

Traditionally, a torero (bullfighter) is akin to a boxer, seeking fame and fortune through physical prowess and bravura. It is a man's world, although several women trod the arena in the 20th century (often to the disgust of their chauvinist colleagues). All aspire to becoming a matador (killer) and reaching the top by fighting in Madrid's Las Ventas ring.

The corrida is often part of a town festival and staged for a week or so once a year. In bigger cities, fights can be regular weekend fixtures. It begins around 6 p.m., and as a rule three matadors with their *cuadrillas* (teams of toreros) appear to fight six bulls. *Toros bravos* (fighting bulls) are bred especially for this day. Each encounter takes about 20 minutes, but any bull judged to be particularly weak or lacking the necessary aggression will be booed off and replaced by another. The sport is certainly cruel and the bull is bound to lose, but no one should doubt the dangers involved. Matadors frequently wind up in hospital with horrific wounds, although nowadays relatively few are killed.

A whole ritual accompanies the fight. The bull is released from a dark corral into the ring, angry and confused after being penned up for much of the day. Toreros dash about with heavy rose-and-yellow *percale* capes, testing the bull's character and willingness to fight before the matador makes his first appearance.

He then takes on the bull in single combat with a smaller red cape. The "art" is in the daring and finesse of his *faenas* (moves), on

Although not a big part of Catalan culture, the bullfight takes place in Barcelona on summer weekends (left and right). Afterward fans retire to local bars (above).

which whole books have been written. Good maneuvers incite the crowd to scream "Olé!" in encouragement. The matador is followed by picadores, mounted on horseback, who fight off the bull while it charges at the horses. Next come the banderilleros, who rush headlong at the bull and try to lodge short harpoon-like instruments (banderillas) in its withers. All this should serve to wear the bull down for the return of the matador, whose bravado is now fully tested. When he judges the bull can give no more, he steadies himself before his victim for the *estocada* (sword thrust)—the kill.

If the matador has performed to everyone's satisfaction, the judges award him one or both of the bull's ears and sometimes its tail too. If not, he will hear the crowd's disappointment. ∎

More places to visit in La Sagrada Família to Park Güell

PLAÇA MONUMENTAL DELS BRAUS

Barcelona's strangely eclectic bullring was raised in 1915 by the architect Ignasi Mas i Morell (1881–1953). Although *modernisme* was on the ebb, it is clear from this structure that it was far from discredited. Since the 19th century, bullrings had mostly been built in neo-Mudéjar or pseudo-Moorish style, and at first glance you might think this one falls into the same category, with its slim brick casing and ceramic decoration. But openings are uncannily similar to Gaudí's parabolic arches, and ceramics and mosaic are a restrained but still fanciful *modernista* creation. Perhaps the oddest elements are the giant mosaic eggs atop the four main towers. Although the ring was built decades before Salvador Dalí's bizarre Teatre-Museu in Figueres (see pp. 230–32), one can't help feeling that the architect was

Bofill's Teatre Nacional de Catalunya is an adventurous glassy foray into neoclassicism.

precociously surrealistic. In the season, from spring to autumn, tickets are available on the day. In the off-season, visiting acts such as circuses perform here.

🅜 Map p. 157 ✉ Gran Via de les Corts Catalanes 747 ☎ 93 245 58 03 🕒 Closed 2-4 p.m. & p.m. Sun. 🅂 $ 🚇 Metro: Línia 2 (Monumental)

TEATRE NACIONAL DE CATALUNYA & L'AUDITORI

A few blocks southeast of the bullring two rather different arenas of modern culture stand side by side in uneasy competition. The easternmost of the two, the Teatre Nacional de Catalunya, proudly looks south like a cream-colored Parthenon. Lined on either side by smooth columns, the neoclassic theater by Barcelona architect Ricard Bofill opened in 1997. The entire entrance facade and tympanum is a curtain of glass. Upon entering you see the walls of what could be a mini-coliseum, which is the main stage, or Sala Gran.

Beside the aspired-to grandeur of the Teatre Nacional, the city's concert hall, or l'Auditori, completed in 2000, is a strange-looking affair. Designed by Madrid architect Rafael Moneo, it is a game of interlocking rectangular planes. Blocks of reinforced concrete are covered on the outside by panels of russet-red steel and on the inside by oak. The place has two stage halls, the southernmost with a capacity of 2,500 and the other holding about 700 people.

Teatre Nacional de Catalunya
🅜 Map p. 157 ✉ Plaça de les Arts 1 ☎ 93 306 57 06 🚇 Metro: Línies 1 (Glòries) or 2 (Monumental)

L'Auditori
🅜 Map p. 157 ✉ Carrer de Lepant 150 ☎ 93 247 93 00 🕒 Closed 2-4 p.m. & p.m. Sun. 🚇 Metro: Línies 1 (Glòries) or 2 (Monumental)

TORRE AGBAR

It has become the most visible sight on Barcelona's skyline since the Sagrada Família. Jean Nouvel's dazzling cucumber-shaped tower (owned by the city's water authority, Agbar) soars up seemingly out of nothing, barely half a mile northwest of the Teatre Nacional. With the changing light of day, the tower's coating of red and blue panels takes on different hues. This is an innovative addition to Barcelona's already very unusual architectural portfolio.

🅜 Map p. 157 ✉ Avinguda Diagonal 225 🚇 Metro: Línia 1 (Glòries) ∎

Art lovers will be drawn to the Palau Reial, crammed with exquisite ceramics and 1970s designer items. Others may prefer to go to Tibidabo for the views and roller coasters, or opt for the medieval aura of the Pedralbes convent.

Northern Barcelona

Detail from Gaudí's gatehouse at the Finca Güell

Northern Barcelona

FOR THOSE WHO CAN AFFORD TO EVEN THINK ABOUT IT, THE NORTH-western edge of Barcelona, where the plain begins to give way to the chain of hills that effectively cuts the city off from its hinterland, is prime real estate. In less than a century, farming country and villages have been swallowed up by a city whose appetite for land has been nothing short of voracious.

Like a fold in a map, the Avinguda Diagonal, one of the city's great boulevards, cuts a swath across the city and funnels traffic out of Barcelona en route for Tarragona, the west, and ultimately Madrid. It might come as a surprise to find some of the city's unique attractions lying beyond this boundary, seemingly utterly disconnected from the rest of Barcelona.

Indeed, when the Pedralbes convent was raised on a slope northwest of the medieval polis in the 14th century, its founders required precisely that middle distance from the twisted and tangled maritime capital. Its nuns, many from wealthy and powerful families, were far enough away to keep out of trouble but not so far as to relinquish the influence such an institution could exercise over the earthly movers and shakers of the Aragonese Crown. Wandering through the atmospheric interior you discover how nuns lived here down through the centuries—and still do today.

A short way down the road, the Barcelona magnate Eusebi Güell saw fit to raise a grand family palace on the still largely untouched grounds of lower Pedralbes during the early part of the 20th century. Later donated to city hall as a royal residence, it remains cradled by the calming greenery of its gardens and fountains. Inside is a fine collection of Spanish ceramics and a more eclectic gallery dedicated to the decorative arts in Spain down through the centuries.

Farther to the north, the city's highest hill, Tibidabo, not only offers sweeping views of the entire city and surrounding countryside but the allures of a somewhat old-fashioned amusement park, solemnly watched over by the unmistakable hulk of Barcelona's answer to Montmartre's Sacré Coeur, the Temple del Sagrat Cor. You might not like the church artistically (and you won't be alone in that respect), but you can't beat the panoramic vistas from its roof. If they aren't enough, you can always try those from the nearby Torre de Collserola communications tower. ■

Torre de
Collserola   543m ▲
(1,783ft)

Temple del
Sagrat Cor

Parc d'Atraccions
Tibidabo

BV 1418

TIBIDABO

Observatori

Funicular de Tibidabo

Plaça del Funicular

RONDA DE DALT   B20

Museu de
la Ciència

SARRIÀ- SANT GERVASI

AVINGUDA DEL TIBIDABO

PASSEIG DE LA BONANOVA   PASSEIG DE SANT GERVASI

VIA AUGUSTA

Mercat
Tres Torres

CARRETERA DE SANT CUGAT

PARC DEL
TURÓ
DEL PUTGET

RONDA   DEL GENERAL   MITRE

PLAÇA
DE PRAT
DE LA RIBA

A DE LA
MARIA
INA

AVINGUDA   DE   SARRIA

AVINGUDA   DIAGONAL

JARDINS DEL
TURÓ DE
MONTEROLS

Lesseps

Església de
Sant Gregori
Taumaturg

VIA AUGUSTA

TRAVESSERA DE LES CORTS

PLAÇA DE
FRANCESC
MACIÀ

AVINGUDA   DES   J. TARRADELLAS

CARRER DE NUMÀNCIA

Sants-
Estació
ÇA
S PAÏSOS
TALANS

0 _____ 500 meters
0 _____ 500 yards

Area of map detail

Monestir de Santa Maria de Pedralbes

WHEN QUEEN ELISENDA, FOURTH AND LAST WIFE OF THE count-king Jaume II, ordered in 1326 the foundation of the Monestir de Santa Maria de Pedralbes (from the Latin *pedras albas,* or white stones), it was located amid bucolic calm. Seven centuries later, the convent is an island of peace, surrounded by what is now one of the more sought-after locations in suburban Barcelona.

The complex was raised in record time (the church was finished within a year), which explains its remarkable unity of style. Soon thereafter, Clarissine nuns, among them daughters of several powerful Catalan families, took up residence.

A dozen nuns still live here, but they have moved to quarters across the lane from the main entrance into the convent.

The simple, single-nave church (the entrance to which is just off Plaça del Monestir) is a minor gem

Monestir de Pedralbes

- Map pp. 172–73
- Baixada del Monestir 9
- 93 203 92 82
- Closed from 2 p.m. & Mon.
- $
- FGC train (Reina Elisenda) then a 10-minute walk or buses Nos. 22, 64, & 75

of Catalan Gothic, broad, bare and stout. Like so many churches in Barcelona, it was a victim of Anarchist zeal during the first stages of the Spanish Civil War in 1936. An impressive neo-Gothic retable that dominated the altar was destroyed. Untouched, however, was the tomb of Queen Elisenda de Montcada, located in the presbytery. The statue of the queen atop her tomb is presented in full regal splendor, with angels at her head and feet. Alongside the church a typical octagonal bell tower stands watch.

Through the door to the left of the church is the way into the convent itself. You enter a cloister of singular elegance, its two Gothic stories topped by a third added in the 15th century. Cypresses and a tall palm preside over the immaculately kept grounds, in which the baroque well and medieval ablutions fountain are the most notable features.

Visitors follow a counter clockwise route along the lower gallery of the cloister. The first room open off to the right is the **Capella de Sant Miquel** (St. Michael's

Chapel) or abbess' day cell, decorated with frescoes in 1343–46 by Ferrer Bassà, who was credited with having introduced the latest techniques of Italian Gothic painting to Catalunya. Among the scenes depicted are the birth of Christ and his preaching in the temple. At the end of the gallery is the entrance to a grand upstairs hall that served as the Dormidor, or sleeping quarters. For centuries the walls were lined with the nuns' claustrophobic night cells. They have been stripped away and replaced by a modest collection of devotional art collected over the centuries.

There are some curious items in the collection. A stucco relief of hunting scenes (including a knight killing a dragon, which was a creature that people believed in then) is a rare piece of non-religious Gothic art. Among the flood of Flemish art that managed to make way into the convent is a false triptych with a beautiful Florentine *robbiana* (a Renaissance ceramic relief by Andrea della Robbia).

Other interesting objects include a couple of giant medieval

Above: Cloisters house the tiny cells where nuns spent their days in quiet contemplation.

former pharmacy *(botica)* and a series of sparsely furnished day cells, where nuns would pass the time in prayer. Stairs lead up to the next level, with more such cells.

The third gallery of the first floor is taken up by the refectory (restored in the 19th century), where the nuns would take their Spartan meals in silence while listening to readings from the scriptures. "Silentium" is inscribed solemnly around the refectory walls, along with other Latin exhortations such as "Audi tacens" ("Listen and keep quiet.") Meals must have been great fun here.

Behind the refectory is the extensive kitchen. Finally, along the last leg of the cloister, you can inspect the rooms of the 16th-century infirmary. A display of the history and life of the convent and those who lived in it has been set up in these rooms. Beyond it is the *sala capitular* (chapter house), where the nuns met to thrash out issues affecting their community. ■

choir songbooks and several nuns' personal treasure chests, such as ne with Arabic touches that may have come from Granada, the southern Spanish city that was ruled by Muslims for eight centuries. Along this length of the cloister are the

Get thee to a nunnery

Workplace of the mothers superior

It was a common occurrence in medieval times for young girls, whose families had decided they should dedicate their lives to the faith, to be sent to a convent. There their hair was shorn and their civilian clothes replaced by shapeless habits. A year later (assuming they had reached the age of 12) they would take vows of poverty, chastity, and obedience, vows that were considered irrevocable and eternal.

But those vows did not offer equality in return, and a class system intruded at every level. Nuns, seated in tiny day cells around the cloister, spent their days embroidering vestments, painting saints' images, and studying religious texts. Clearly the latter was only for those who could read—meaning the upper classes—and these sisters alone sang in the choirs and attained positions of power in the convent. Empowered by Queen Elisenda's legacy, the mothers superior here maintained close links with the government of Catalunya.

Life for the ordinary nun was well ordered, with a rigorous canonical timetable starting well before dawn and ending after dark. Mealtimes were no less austere. Dishes rarely included meat and from September 8 until Easter the sisters were subjected to a regime of semi-fasting, eating only one full meal a day (except Sundays and holidays). And when they died, they were buried within the walls. ■

Palau Reial de Pedralbes

FOR YEARS, WHENEVER GENERAL FRANCO CAME TO TOWN he stayed in this somewhat overblown neoclassic residence, surrounded by shady gardens and soothing fountains. Until 1926 the land had belonged to the wealthy Güell family, which then put it at the disposal of the Spanish king, Alfonso XIII. The present palace was not finished until 1929, so the monarch, who abdicated in 1931, got precious little use out of it.

In 1883, Eusebi Güell commissioned Gaudí to construct the **Finca Güell**—an entrance gate and pavilions, one destined to be the stables. These can now be admired from Avinguda de Pedralbes, just beyond the present limits of the Palau Reial's gardens. The gate features a fantastical wrought-iron dragon, while the bright little pavilions are all

twisting turrets, sunny brick, and playful ceramics. The one-time stables today house the Càtedra Gaudí, a study center that specializes in the architect's work.

For a few years prior to the civil war, the Palau Reial building was converted into a museum, a vocation not recovered until 1960. The building's interior, a pretentious affair, is nevertheless interesting in

King Alfonso XIII had little time to enjoy the Palau Reial before abdicating in 1931.

Palau Reial de Pedralbes

- Map pp. 172–73
- Avinguda Diagonal 686
- 93 280 16 21
- Closed from 3 p.m. Sun., & Mon.
- $
- Metro: Línia 3 (Palau Reial)

A Museu de Ceràmica tile series depicts a drinker's foibles.

Detail of Palau Reial's facade

its own right and now houses two museums, of which the best is the **Museu de Ceràmica.**

In **Sala** (Room) **2** is a modest collection of ceramics from Muslim Spain, specifically items collected in Seville, Córdoba, Granada, Toledo, and Mallorca. Some of it dates from the tenth century and, while hardly overwhelming, it is worth bearing in mind that the Muslims were largely responsible for bringing the art of ceramics to Spain.

In the next three rooms you'll

find a good collection of material from the Valencian towns of Paterna and Manises, for centuries major centers of ceramic production. The most sophisticated objects are those given a metallic shine. **Salas 6** to **8** feature material from Aragón, among which the blue ceramics are the most refined. Talavera de la Reina, a rather dusty and nondescript city in western Castilla-La Mancha, is still famous for ceramics today, more than 400 years after King Philip II established the industry there. Some of its products fill **Sala 9.**

In **Sala 13,** dedicated to Seville and Úbeda, stand some huge, wonderfully colored urns, one covered with depictions of a bullfight. The next room, a rather narrow corridor, is lined with a series of highly elaborate holy-water holders produced in Manises. **Sala 17** contains tableware (sugar holders, soup bowls, etc.) of fine 18th- and 19th-century porcelain, while in the following room we reach the final extreme with rather cutesy Alcora porcelain animals in lifelike poses—definitely not to everyone's taste.

Signs point you across the central hall and upstairs to the last part of the ceramics collection, which includes works by *modernista* and *noucentista* artists, as well as a room dedicated to ceramics by Picasso and Miró. Other modern creations and the occasional temporary exhibition are on display too.

Back downstairs you enter the **Museu de les Arts Decoratives** via a small bookstore. The collection is a hodgepodge of household furniture and items spanning the 13th century to the present, acquired in Spain and abroad. Starting with the enormous glory-boxes of moneyed future spouses dating from the Romanesque period, you stroll through a series of rooms decked out with beds, desks, finely carved timber chests, and a host of smaller curios.

Standing right out in the area devoted to the 19th-century Imperial style is a sumptuous bed that looks more ornamental than comfortable. The following rooms deal briefly with other 19th-century fashions, Romanticism and *modernisme* in particular, but the most intriguing part of the display, and taking up about half the space, is that dedicated to 20th-century design. From outlandish chairs to old pop-up toasters, outrageous lamps to 1950s cutlery, there are all sorts of oddities here—some enough to make you cringe at fashions of the not-so-distant past. ■

The Finca Güell gatehouse features Gaudí's hallmark parabolic arch.

Tibidabo

**Temple del
Sagrat Cor**

Map pp. 172–73

✉ Plaça de Tibidabo

☎ 93 417 56 86

$ $ (elevator)

🚋 FGC (Avinguda de
Tibidabo) & Tramvia
Blau & Funicular or
Bus: T2 (from Plaça
de Catalunya)

ACCORDING TO THE LATIN VERSION OF THE GOSPEL OF St. Matthew, the devil declared to Christ: *"Haec omnia Tibi dabo si cadens adoraberis me"* (All this I will give you if you will fall down and worship me). At 1,783 feet (543 m), Tibidabo is the highest point overlooking Barcelona and, on a good day, affords views across the city and out to sea, as well as inland to Montserrat. The devil's pact would be a tempting deal.

The hill was developed as a public park in the early 1900s, and a private enterprise ran the Tramvia Blau (Blue Tram) and connecting funicular services that still link the summit with the city proper. Later the Parc d'Atraccions (Amusement Park) and the Temple del Sagrat Cor were added.

The catechist Juan Bosco had already dedicated the hill to the Sacred Heart (Sagrat Cor) so it came as little surprise that the Church should be inspired to build a place of worship here. Enric Sagnier (1858–1931) was entrusted with the task and a year before his

death had completed the eclectic mix that is the **Temple del Sagrat Cor.** Designed to rival Sacré Coeur atop Paris's Montmartre district, the church is far from universally admired. The roughly hewn brownstone crypt is clearly of *modernista* (almost Gaudían) inspiration. Eusebi Arnau, one of the period's most important sculptors, was responsible for some of the statues adorning the crypt.

Inside, the ceramic and mosaic decoration (finished in 1941) has some pleasing aspects. To the right, off the crypt, a door leads into a

Some of the rides are dated, but kids still enjoy the Tibidabo Parc d'Atraccions.

chapel dedicated to the Eucharist. Since June 1966, the chapel has been the scene of the permanent adoration of the Holy Sacrament. Although recruitment of the sufficiently faithful has not always proven easy, the chapel has never been left empty. Day and night at least one person has always been in attendance to worship the Lord. Each day, buses take up worshippers who, if their allotted hour falls during a night shift, sleep over in cells during their free time before being taken back to town the following day.

Stairs sweep up on either side of the crypt to the soaring gray hulk of the bare, neo-Gothic church proper. Some of the stained glass is fetching, but otherwise the building is bereft of significant ornament. From either the crypt or church you can catch an elevator up to the roof, which can be decidedly windy. From there, stairs spiral up to the gold-tinted bronze statue of Christ that crowns the edifice. The other statues around the roof represent the Apostles. From anywhere up here the views across Barcelona and the countryside are spectacular.

For the majority of locals who make the effort to get up to Tibidabo, the main draw is the **Parc d'Atraccions,** the town's only remaining amusement park (one on Montjuïc was shut in the late 1990s). Although it underwent a significant overhaul in the 1980s, the park has a quaintly old-fashioned flavor. It is divided into six levels. A variety of tickets allows you the choice of simply entering and choosing one or two rides or settling in for the day to try everything.

One of the park's big favorites for those who like a fright is the seven-minute trip through the Hotel Krueger, a house of horrors

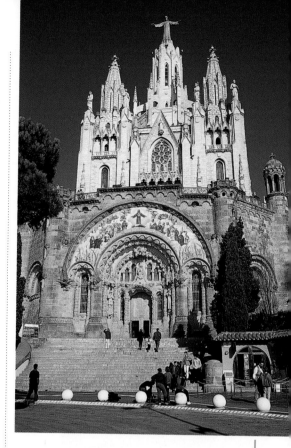

in which everyone from Hannibal Lecter to Dracula attempt to scare the wits out of you. Traditionalists may enjoy a ride on the Muntanya Russa, a rather low-key roller coaster. Especially quaint is the L'Avió (Aeroplane), which simply "flies" around and around in circles. Other attractions include many of the old favorites: miniature trains, water rides, a fine old carousel, *autos de xoc* (dodgem cars), and more. Several shows are also staged, including a puppet performance in the Marionetarium.

Opening hours at the park can vary radically so it is always worth making advance inquiries at the tourist office for the latest details. A number of restaurants and fast-food outlets are dotted about the amusement park. ■

The Temple del Sagrat Cor is an odd mix, with its *modernista* lower half and wedding-cake crown.

Parc d'Atraccions

🅰 Map pp. 172–73

✉ Plaça de Tibidabo

☎ 93 211 79 42

🕐 Closed Mon.–Fri. & a.m. weekends; open daily in Aug.

💲 $$$

🚇 FGC (Avinguda de Tibidabo) & Tramvia Blau & Funicular or Bus: T2 (from Plaça de Catalunya)

More places to visit in Northern Barcelona

CAMP NOU FC BARCELONA

For many citizens of Barcelona, 1899 was a key date in the city's history. It was in that year that Futbol Club Barcelona was formed. During the following century, the red and blue colors of this mighty soccer team have been as much a symbol for the city (and area) as the Catalan flag itself. The club has 110,000 members, almost enough to fill its Camp Nou (New Field) stadium, one of the world's biggest. Built in 1957 and expanded in 1982, it can hold 120,000 spectators.

If you can't see a game, you can drop by the stadium to visit the **Museu del FC Barcelona.** Soccer fans can muse over old trophies, posters, and sports magazines, or seek inspiration in the photo and video sections that celebrate great goals. Also on view are old sports board games, a 19th-century leather football, and the *futbolín* (table soccer) collection. Finally, step outside to gaze across

Futbol Club Barcelona's shield is an icon for local soccer enthusiasts.

the immense playing field. At night the area around the stadium is given over to a different sport as the city's most notorious red-light district.

🗺 Map pp. 172–73 ✉ Carrer d'Aristicles Maillol 12 ☎ 93 496 36 00 (ticket information) 🕐 Closed from 2 p.m. Sun. 💲 $ 🚇 Metro: Línia 5 (Collblanc)

COSMOCAIXA

Among the star attractions of this modern science museum is a 1,000-square meter reproduction of a flooded Amazon rain forest with more than 100 species of plants and animals. This is about as close as you can get to the real thing without hopping aboard a plane for Brazil. The Muro Geològic (Geological Wall) is another original element. Several different strata of rocks from different parts of Spain allow you to understand how such formations came to be through erosion, volcanic activity, glacial movement, and so on. Children love the Toca, Toca! section, in which they come into direct contact with a variety of animals and bugs. Another hall covers matter, recounting everything from the elements of which humans are made to the Big Bang.

🗺 Map pp. 172–73 ✉ Carrer de Teodor Roviralta 55 ☎ 93 212 60 50 🕐 Closed Mon. 💲 $ 🚌 Bus: No. 60 or FGC (Avinguda de Tibidabo) & Tramvia Blau

TOLLE DE COLLSEROLA

Visible from all over Barcelona, this slender communications tower, designed by Norman Foster and erected in the late 1980s, has become one of the city's principal landmarks. At 947 feet (288 m) high, it dominates (along with the Temple del Sagrat Cor) the mountain ridge separating the city from inland Catalunya. The clever design is less of a draw than the elevator ride to the top for bird's-eye views across city and countryside.

The tower is surrounded by the most extensive park in the area, the Parc de Collserola. Joggers, cyclists, and hikers flock here for a little peace and quiet. In the heart of the park is an 18th-century country house where Catalunya's most famous poet, Jacint Verdaguer (1845-1902) passed the last days of his life. It now houses the **Museu-Casa Verdaguer** (closed p.m. & Mon.), most interesting for the house itself, which has changed little since his death.

🗺 Map pp. 172–73 ✉ Camí de Vallvidrera ☎ 93 406 93 54 🕐 Closed Mon. & Tues. 💲 $ 🚇 FGC (Avinguda de Tibidabo) & Tramvia Blau & Funicular or Bus: T2 (from Plaça de Catalunya)

This is a mountain in continual renovation. Where centuries ago were market gardens and a Jewish cemetery now stand grand art galleries and museums, theater space, an Olympic stadium and pool, a fortress, and numerous gardens.

Montjuïc

The futuristic Torre Calatrava on Montjuïc

Montjuïc

THOUSANDS OF YEARS AGO, HOUSEHOLD FIRES BURNED BRIGHT THROUGH the night among the huts of some Celt-Iberian tribe, Barcelona's first inhabitants. At least that's what the archaeologists surmise. When the Romans arrived and founded their town on the plain, Montjuïc became a stage for religious rituals. At its base, it is believed, was the city's first ancient port.

Excepting the inland mountain range that culminates in Tibidabo and closes Barcelona off from the Catalan hinterland, Montjuïc is the city's only significant bump. Its role in the life of Barcelona's citizens has always been dual, as a source of recreation and escape from the urban squeeze below it and as a place of ceremony. A cemetery still occupies its southwestern flank.

In 1929 it was chosen to stage the ritual of the World Exhibition and in 1992 that of the Olympics. Every couple of weekends thousands make the pilgrimage here to see the Espanyol soccer team take on all comers. While fans exhort their team to victory, strollers enjoy the gardens, swimming pools, museums, art galleries, and—a rare thing in Barcelona—fresh air and relative quiet.

That Montjuïc means Jewish Mountain seems demonstrated by the evidence of tombstones found in what appears to have been a Jewish cemetery here. Some of those stones can be seen in the Museu Militar.

Had initial plans for a follow-up to the 1888 Universal Exhibition been acted upon, the show might have taken place in 1907. Sanctioned by the Spanish dictator General Miguel Primo de Rivera as a useful propaganda stunt, it finally occurred in 1929. The result changed this part of town completely.

The Font Màgica gives a splash of color below the majestic Palau Nacional.

Area of map detail

The pompous Palau Nacional was built as the main seat of the exhibition and today houses an excellent art museum. To its north, the grand Plaça d'Espanya traffic circle is flanked on its northwestern side by sober buildings that originally served as hotels for the exhibition. Avinguda de la Reina Maria Cristina was driven between the two and remains cosseted by trade-fair pavilions. Other permanent structures included a sports stadium and the kitsch Poble Espanyol.

Thereafter, the little mountain slipped into decay until the 1992 Olympics sparked a program of regeneration. That momentum has been maintained, and the town's authorities continue to renovate and improve Montjuïc's many gardens. With works of art ranging from Romanesque to Joan Miró, several minor museums, the 18th-century fortress, lovely gardens, and the Olympic sports facilities, there is a lot to attract visitors to the mountain. The Montjuïc Card gets entry into all the area's sites. ■

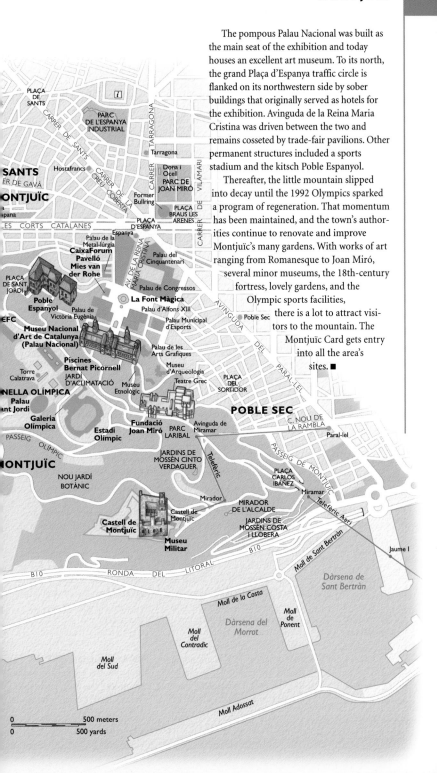

Museu Nacional d'Art de Catalunya (Palau Nacional)

THE *MODERNISTA* ARCHITECT AND CATALAN NATIONALIST
Josep Puig i Cadafalch was entrusted with the original design of the
Palau Nacional, the central pavilion of the World Exhibition. By 1929,
however, the plan was in the hands of other architects just as the
exhibition had become an instrument of dictator General Miguel
Primo de Rivera. What emerged was a mix of neoclassic and neo-
baroque, presumably designed to project an image of Spanish
prowess. It houses the city's most important art displays.

**Museu Nacional
d'Art de
Catalunya (Palau
Nacional)**

www.mnac.es

▲ Map pp. 184–85

✉ Palau Nacional, Parc
de Montjuïc

☎ 93 622 03 76

🕐 Closed from 2:30
p.m. Sun. &
holidays, & Mon.

💲 $$

🚇 Metro: Línies 1 & 3
(Espanya)

The Museu Nacional d'Art de
Catalunya contains a veritable trea-
sure trove of Romanesque frescoes
and other artworks transferred
from churches around northern
Catalunya. There follows an impor-
tant collection of Gothic art, which
covers not only Catalunya but other
regions in Spain. From there the
collections broaden out to the
Renaissance and baroque, both in
and beyond Spain. Two private col-
lections, the Cambò bequest and
the Thyssen-Bornemisza collection
that used to hang in the Monestir
de Santa Maria de Pedralbes (see p.

174) are interspersed among the
rest. From the 19th century on, the
collection again becomes almost
exclusively Catalan, spanning the
likes of Mariá Fortuny, *modernisme*,
and *noucentisme*. Along with paint-
ings and sculpture are displays of
furniture and other applied art.
Photography and coin collections
round out the museum's treasures.

ROMANESQUE ART

First comes the Romanesque collec-
tion, divided into 21 *àmbits* (rooms),
many of them re-creating interiors
of 29 churches from where these

extraordinary works were removed. It is hard to do justice to the collection, but here are some highlights.

Àmbit 5 and **Àmbit 7** contain some of the most extraordinary frescoes of all. The first were removed from the beautiful Església de Sant Climent de Taüll, in northwest Catalunya, while the second came from the nearby Església de Santa Maria de Taüll.

In the case of the former, the main piece is the exquisite decoration from the central apse, in dominating colors of turquoise, ocher, and dull brick red. On high, as is usual for this kind of apse decoration, sits Christ in Majesty in his almond-shaped cocoon. He appears seated on the throne, making the sign of peace and holding a piece of scripture (showing the words "Ego Sum Lux Mundi—I am the Light of the World). In Romanesque iconography Christ is depicted surrounded by the *tetramorph*, the four Evangelists symbolized according to St. Jerome's explanation: the lion of St. Mark, the bull for St. Luke (in this case both are at Christ's feet), the angel for St. Matthew (to the left), and the eagle for St. John (to the right, the saint is holding an eagle.) On either side are seraphim with wings covered in eyes representing the all-seeing God.

Although Romanesque art tended to be rigid and seemingly expressionless, Christ's eyes here are enormously engaging. His depiction is deliberately symmetrical and yet in the folds of his robes there is volume and movement. Below him and the Evangelists, separated by an elaborate dividing line, are various saints and Apostles, as well as Mary, Mother of God.

Mary is the principal figure in the apse of Santa Maria de Taüll. These frescoes are more complete, with large chunks from the walls

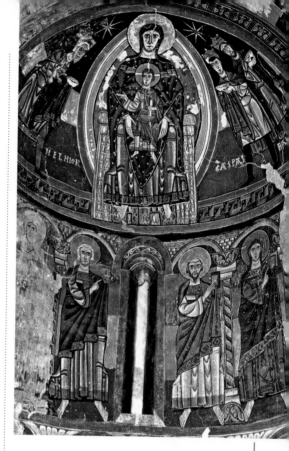

and even one of the columns. Mary is in typical pose with the Christ Child on her lap. Outside the encircling almond stand the Three Wise Men. On the south wall are various episodes from the New Testament.

In **Àmbit 8** is a rare 12th-century wooden crucifix that has retained much of its paint. An altar front in **Àmbit 10** shows the rather nasty martyrdom of four saints, whose equanimity in the face of awful deaths is exemplary (and an inspiration to the faithful). The paintings from the atrium of the immense Església de Sant Vicenç in Cardona occupy **Àmbit 14,** and in the last room, **Àmbit 21,** is the recreated chapter house of the Santa Maria de Sixena monastery in Aragón. The surviving frescoes (not destroyed when the monastery was

This fresco from the Església de Santa Maria de Taüll shows the Three Wise Men visiting the Virgin Mary and Christ Child.

Above: A 13th-century fresco of a Nativity scene
Below: A fresco of the Virgin and Child from the 1100s

Fantastic fountain

On certain evenings, the spectrally lit structure of Palau Nacional seems from its haughty position to be inspecting the broad sweep of Avinguda de la Reina Maria Cristina. A fan of searchlights pierces the night sky from behind the building. An expectant crowd gathers and, suddenly, a strange and colorful spectacle takes place on the terraces below.

La Font Màgica is so corny it's good. In 15-minute bursts for a couple of hours in the evenings (from 7 p.m. Fri.-Sat. Oct.-June; 9.30 p.m. Thurs.-Sun. July-Sept.), this "magic fountain" *performs* a sound-and-light show that can be astonishingly moving. In time with the music, the water changes hue, jets rise and fall, plunge into one another, and ebb away. On the last night of the September Festes de la Mercè they throw in fireworks too. ∎

torched in 1936) recount New and Old Testament episodes, and the genealogy of Christ.

GOTHIC ART

The Gothic collection is more wide-ranging and a good introduction to the period. The first room is devoted to non-religious works, some depicting Jaume I's conquest of Mallorca. Following are rooms with early Gothic works from Navarra, Aragón, Castile, and Catalunya, including remarkable alabaster statuary. In subsequent rooms the development of Gothic painting is traced. Italian painters had an enormous influence on local production, the focus of which shifted to Valencia. By the beginning of the 15th century, artists from Italy, France, and the Low Countries were flocking here (**Àmbit 29**). They brought International Gothic, a pan-western European style that quickly caught on among locals, who spread the word to Catalunya (**Àmbit 30**). Works by the two most outstanding Catalan International Gothic masters, Bernat Martorell and Jaume Huguet, can be seen in **Àmbits 32** and **34**. The latter's "Consagració de Sant Agustí," part of a hagiographic series dedicated to St. Augustine, is extraordinary for its detail and expressiveness.

Almost imperceptibly the collection morphs from the Gothic into the Renaissance. Two of the most striking works are Valencian Pedro Berruguete's (1450-1504) doors for the grand *retablo* sequence in **Àmbit 44.** The scenes appear more akin to sketches Goya might have penned centuries later.

In the following hall is the Cambò bequest, a private, eclectic collection that mixes up Italian Renaissance, Spanish old master, and rococo. A smattering of works by such greats as Veronese (1528-

1588), Titian (1490-1557), Rubens (1577-1640) and even Gainsborough (1727-1788) are among the treasures. In **Àmbit 48** you can enjoy an equally eclectic display, with the works of the Thyssen-Bornemisza collection that used to be in the Monestir de Santa Maria de Pedralbes. Before inspecting before inspecting these, don't miss the El Grecos and Tintoretto hanging in **Àmbit 47.**

You will then pass into the great central hall with bright ceiling frescoes and a café. Concerts are held here occasionally. Head upstairs where you'll find yourself beneath the central dome; check out the views from the restaurant before continuing your way. The next 12 rooms are something of a mishmash, with works ranging from Spain's Golden century, including some by Francisco de Zurbarán

(1598-1664), Claudio Coello (1642-1693), and José de Ribera (1591-1652) among the stars.

From **Àmbit 61** on, the collection fully returns to Catalunya. From here until the end of the main displays, works are concentrated on local painters, sculptors, and other artists from the early 19th to the mid 20th centuries.

After a little Romanticisme, we pass on to Catalan *realisme* (whose greatest exponent was Marià Fortuny) and then on through *anecdotisme, modernisme,* and *noucentisme.* A good deal of the paintings are really only of minor interest, except for those who wish to become more deeply acquainted with these specific periods in Catalan art (see pp. 43-44).

Charging out at you from their centrally placed frame are the cavalry and foot soldiers depicted

The Oval Hall was designed for the 1929 World Exposition. It is still one of the largest indoor areas preserved in Europe.

in Marià Fortuny's grand tableau, *Batalla de Tetuán* (1863), celebrating a grand battle fought out between the Spanish army and Moroccan forces in northern Morocco.

In **Àmbit 65** Joaquim Vayreda (1843-94) dominates with landscapes from around the region.

More significant are the modernistas, of whom you'll find around a dozen paintings each by Ramon Casas (**Àmbit 71**) and Santiago Rusiñol (**Àmbit 72**). Among Casas' most captivating works are grand canvasses reflecting the civil disorders in Barcelona toward the end of the 19th and early in the 20th centuries. *El Garrote Vil* and *La Càrrega*, which depict an execution and police charge respectively, are insightful views into turbulent times. More light-hearted is the painting of the artist himself and his friend and fellow artist Pere Romeu on a bicylce. Rusiñol was probably the more gifted of the two. Among his better works is *Lecció de Piano*.

Modernisme takes on a more tangible feel in the next room, which contains some fanciful furnishings from the modernista Casa Lleó Morera (see p. 143). More furniture and and applied arts in the same vein, including a private chapel, are worth close inspection in **Àmbit 75**. Timber chairs designed by Gaudí for Casa Battlló (see p. 142) and Colònia Güell (see p. 238) are in show in **Àmbit 77**.

Isidre Nonell (see p. 47), whom some like to attribute to a symbolical branch of modernisme but is more typically lumped together with its successor, noucentisme, dominates **Àmbit 82**. The leading light of noucentisme, Joaquim Sunyer, follows in the next rooms, along with the much more abstruse Uruguayan, Joaquim Torres-García (1874-1949). The latter man lived in Barcelona for a long time, but never quite cracked the local market and finally returned home to Montevideo.

Of the final rooms, the most interesting is dedicated to the bronzes of Pau Gargallo (1881–1934), a sculptor who spent most of his life between Barcelona and Paris. His artistic contacts included the *modernistas* and Picasso. His styles ranged from classical to abstract.

For a change of pace, a photographic and coin collection round off a visit to this museum. The former is a mesmerizing stroll down photographic Memory Lane. The emphasis is on Catalan photographers, with one section ranging from the early days to the Civil War period, and the second taking things to the present day. The numismatic collection covers a much longer period—from the Greek colonies in Catalunya thousands of years ago to the introduction of the euro. ■

Churchmen praying is a common theme of the Gothic collection.

Pavelló Mies van der Rohe

IN 1929 THE GERMAN GOVERNMENT ASKED LUDWIG MIES van der Rohe (1886–1969) to design the German Pavilion (Pavelló Alemany) at that year's World Exhibition in Barcelona. The 1920s were a heady time in Germany and Mies van der Rohe was at the forefront of the so-called modern movement, which later gave rise to the International style in architecture and design.

The style sought to reflect a new age by creating "honest," functional buildings bereft of decoration and extraneous additions. Buildings that would exalt space and exploit materials such as concrete, glass, and steel. For Mies van der Rohe, who had worked alongside Walter Gropius and Le Corbusier, Barcelona was too good to pass up.

His design comprised an airy sequence of spaces on a travertine platform, defined by a series of planes: walls of marble, onyx, and frosted glass. It was partially covered by a thin roof, mirrored on the ground by a shallow pool. His steel "Barcelona chairs" were a sensation.

The whole lot was destroyed after the exhibition, but was rebuilt, to the right of the Font Màgica in front of the Palau Nacional, in the 1980s by a society of Mies van der Rohe admirers, who saw it as a key building in the architect's development. It bears its original creator's name and represents a curious architectural anecdote at once out of place and out of time.

Mies van der Rohe left Germany after the rise of the Nazis and went to the United States, where in the following 30 years he was able to fully deploy his talents in such masterpieces as the Seagram Building (designed with Phillip Johnson) in New York City. That cold, austere skyscraper, clad in glass, marble, and bronze, is a perfect demonstration of its builder's adage: "Less is more." He might have said the same about his pavilion. ∎

Pavelló Mies van der Rohe

www.miesbcn.es

- Map pp. 184–85
- Avinguda del Marquès de Comillas
- 93 423 40 16
- $
- Metro: Línies 1 & 3 (Espanya)

Montjuïc Children's Dance Group at Poble Espanyol

Poble Espanyol

IT IS HARD TO CLASSIFY THE COLLECTION OF SPANISH architectural remakes that constitutes this "Spanish Village." Erected in just 13 months for the 1929 World Exhibition as a display of the country's architectural, and hence cultural, diversity, it was destined to be torn down after the fair was over. Luckily for the curious visitors who have passed through since, that decision was rescinded.

Poble Espanyol
www.poble-espanyol.com
🅰 Map pp. 184–85
✉ Avinguda del Marquès de Comillas 13
☎ 93 508 63 00
💲 $$
🚇 Metro: Línies 1 & 3 (Espanya)

A team of two architects, one engineer, and an artist presented an ambitious project for Poble Espanyol in 1927. Not only would many types of architecture from across Spain's regions be reproduced, the village would have its own central square, town hall, church, stores, bars, and eateries (joined much later by a couple of Barcelona's most popular discos).

The main entrance takes you through the stout **Puerta de San Vicente,** a gate in the medieval walls of the Castilian town of Ávila. The original is one of the most complete sets of medieval walls in Europe. Poble Espanyol, too, is in part walled in and blessed with several other gates (only some allow access to the outside.)

Inside Puerta de San Vicente you arrive in Plaza Castellana. The western region of Extremadura inspired the buildings to the right around Calle de la Conquista, all mansions from cities like Cáceres and Plasencia. The exterior of the **Palacio del Maestrazgo** at No. 5 (each building is numbered), is emblazoned with its owners' coat of arms.

Next pass under the arches of **Ayuntamiento of Sangüesa** (No. 26), a town in the northern region of Navarra, and into spacious **Plaza Mayor.** This is the "Main Square," fronted by the thickset **Ayuntamiento** (No. 21), an enlargement of the original in the Aragonese town of Vall-de-Roures. Surrounding the square are buildings from Castilla y León, Madrid, Asturias, Cantabria, and Aragón.

Along Calle del Alcalde de Zalamea and up the graceful Grados de Santiago (Steps of St. James, taken from Santiago de Compostela), you pass a series of houses from the northwestern region of Galicia, but more striking is the Aragonese composite before you. The baroque facade of **Iglesia de las Carmelitas** (No. 57), from Alcañiz, is imposing enough, but soaring behind it is the magnificent **Utebo bell tower** (No. 59). Raised in 1544, it is an exquisite mix of late Gothic and Mudéjar.

The Mudéjars were Muslims left behind in Christian territory as the Reconquista (Reconquest) rolled the Muslims out of Spain. They employed Arab techniques on their new masters' buildings, which are characterized by the use of slender brick, colored tiles, and geometrical decoration. Across Spain the variations on the theme are many, and what you see in this particular case is peculiar to southern Aragón.

Behind the bell tower you arrive in Spain's southernmost region, Andalucía, identifiable by the whitewashed walls, arches, creeping vines, and Tío Pepe sherry ads of **Arcos de la Frontera** (No. 61).

Beyond Plaza de la Hermandad, which lies in the middle of the Andalusian buildings, runs Calle de Levante, lined by specimens from the eastern regions of Spain: Valencia, Murcia, and the Balearic Islands. One building, the bright Renaissance **Casa de Son Berga** (No. 69), represents the latter. More imposing is the Plateresque (a uniquely Spanish and decoratively busy version of Renaissance) frontage of **Casa de los Celdrán** (No. 70), from Murcia.

Calle de Levante leads down to shady Plaça de la Font, where you are closer to home with buildings representing the Catalan provinces. To the right, rose-colored **Puerta de Prades** leads outside the walls toward a Romanesque monastery complex, **Monestir de Sant Miquel** (No. 116), a composite of several Catalan sites.

Back inside the walls, Carrer dels Mercaders, leading past a series of Catalan houses, feeds into Calle del Príncipe de Vergara, surrounded by fine houses from Navarra and the Basque Country. One element that they share is the generous use of timber in balconies and awnings. Calle de los Caballeros, lined by Castilian houses and mansions, is the last stretch that brings you back to where you started. ■

The re-creation of the magnificent Utebo bell tower can be seen from the Plaza Mayor.

Anella Olímpica

The focal point of the 1992 Olympic Games was a stadium rebuilt inside the 1929 World Exhibition exterior.

MORE THAN FOURTEEN YEARS HAVE PASSED AND THEY STILL talk about the 1992 Olympic Games in Barcelona. More than in many other cities where the games have been held, Barcelona took the event to heart with a determination to make them work for the city. Perhaps much of the urban renewal program would have been carried out anyway, but there seems little doubt that the Olympics galvanized Barcelona.

Anella Olímpica
Map pp. 184–85
906 3011 775

Much of the activity took place around the central stadium, a 1929 World Exhibition inheritance that was modernized and around which new facilities and innovative structures were raised. The complex became known as the Anella Olímpica, or Olympic Ring.

At the heart of the ring is the **Estadi Olímpic** (Olympic Stadium), with a capacity of 65,000. This was the venue for the opening and closing ceremonies. The original 1929 exterior, an eclectic mix of styles, was retained but the entire inside was redesigned and reorganized. The original main entrance is topped by two sets of equestrian bronzes.

For the Olympics the entrance was shifted to its present position on Avinguda de l'Estadi. To its left is the slightly bulging pillar atop which burned the Olympic flame. To light it, an archer had to shoot a flaming arrow up into the dish. This was a risky venture, but the authorities were prepared for a miss: The dish was full of inflammable gas, so that the arrow only had to pass within 6.5 feet (2 m) of it to ignite the flame. The archer did indeed miss, but managed to keep within the margin.

For years after the Olympics, the stadium was used only for occasional events. Then in the late 1990s, Espanyol, Barcelona's No. 2 soccer team, moved in while waiting for a new stadium, giving this one a

temporary new lease on life. Every second weekend throughout most of the year the team's supporters, or Espanyolistas, converge on the hill to urge their team to victory.

On the southwest side of the stadium (follow the pedestrian-only area around the stadium's west flank) is the **Galeria Olímpica.** This museum dedicated to the Olympics is an odd affair. As well as the photos and video clips from the Games, the run-up, and the end of the Games, it contains much to do with Cobi, the mascot designed by Javier Mariscal. There is a video, dolls dressed as types of athlete, a life-size Cobi, Cobi bed linen, and even a Cobi bathrobe. No doubt most athletes were thoroughly sick of Cobi by the time it was all over. And if you ever wondered what athletes eat, there are appetizing plastic models of a typical athlete's meal. In all, it's a little strange.

Just west of the stadium sits what could be mistaken for a large UFO atop its landing pad. Actually, it's the shell-like roof of **Palau Sant Jordi,** considered by the

critics the most successful of the new Olympic buildings. Japanese architect Arata Isozaki designed it as a general indoor-sports, concert, and exhibition hall with a seating capacity of 17,000. Completed in 1990, it is now hosts big concerts.

To the north of Palau Sant Jordi are the fine Olympic swimming facilities of the **Piscines Bernat Picornell,** now enjoyed by the citizens of Barcelona. Between the pool and Palau Sant Jordi rises the brilliant white science-fiction telecommunications tower of the Spanish phone company, Telefónica. This slender, graceful structure has become an unmistakable Montjuïc landmark and is now simply known as Torre Calatrava, after its Zurich-based designer, Santiago Calatrava.

Beyond the circular arena west of the Olympic pool is the last of the main Olympic buildings. Created by leading Barcelona architect Ricard Bofill, the bright neoclassic structure houses the **Istitut Nacional d'Educació Física de Catalunya (INEFC),** a sports university. ∎

Galeria Olímpica

www.fundaciobarcelonaolimpica.es

🗺 Map pp. 184–85

✉ Passeig Olímpic s/n

☎ 93 426 06 60

🕐 Closed 2-4 p.m. Mon.-Fri., weekends & holidays

💲 $

🚇 Metro: Línies 1 & 3 (Espanya) & Bus PM

Mobile on Montjuïc

Getting to and around Montjuïc can take some time. Decide on where you want to start, as this will influence how you get into the area in the first place.

The nearest metro stops are Espanya, Paral.lel, and Poble Sec. With map in hand you can walk from these and follow paths up the hill. Bus No. PM does a circle route from Plaça d'Espanya to the Castell de Montjuïc, stopping at most points of interest on the way. A city tourist bus, the Bus Turístic, also gets around the main sights. You need to buy a special ticket (see p. 243 or ask at the tourist office.)

The funicular operates between the aforementioned station and Paral.lel metro stop. At the Montjuïc station it links with the Teleféric chairlift to take you as high as the Castell de Montjuïc and Museu Militar.

The Tren Turístic (one of those little road trains) links Plaça d'Espanya with most sights of interest on Montjuïc, running every half hour daily in summer and otherwise on some weekends (you can get details at the tourist office in the off season). You can rent bicycles for the day at Plaça d'Espanya. ∎

Fundació Joan Miró

IT WAS FITTING THAT THE 20TH CENTURY'S MOST important Barcelona-born artist should, in the latter years of his life, present it with an inestimable gift—a gallery and archive dedicated primarily to his art. Designed by his longtime friend, architect Josep Lluís Sert (1902–1983), the building opened to the public in 1975.

Fundació Joan Miró

www.bcn.fjmiro.es

🅰 Map pp. 184–85

✉ Avinguda Miramar 71–75

☎ 93 443 94 70

🕐 Closed from 2:30 p.m. Sun. & holidays, & Mon.

💲 $$

🚇 Metro: Línies 1 & 3 (Espanya) & Bus (No. 50 or No. 55); or Línia 3 (Paral.lel) & Funicular railway

The foundation's collection is made up of hundreds of Miró's paintings, sculptures, and other works, including thousands of sketches and drafts donated by the artist himself. Only a comparatively small part of this immense store is ever on display, although that portion may grow when new construction at the foundation is completed.

Sert, who had first worked with Miró in 1937 on the Republican Spanish pavilion at the Paris Universal Exhibition, placed an emphasis on light and space. The building's design around an internal courtyard and the bright whiteness of its interior and reinforced concrete exterior are two clear references to the artist's Mediterranean roots. The

organization of exhibition areas, open spaces, and stairways ensures you need never go over territory already covered. Part of the top floor is an open-air walkway dotted with Miró sculptures that nicely breaks the pace of the collection inside.

Fluidity of movement is a theme in the building, as indeed it is with the collection. While the permanent collection retains a simple chronological structure, beginning with Miró's early work on the first floor, the size of the collections is such that works on display are frequently rotated.

THROUGH THE GALLERY

Visitors head first to **temporary exhibitions** displayed in rooms to

Three of the later paintings of Catalan artist Joan Miró, including "The Gold of the Azure"

Below: The artist's sculptures sprinkle the terraces of the Fundació Joan Miró.

the right of the ticket desk before moving around to the beginning of the **permanent collection.**

In the first room of the latter hangs an enormous tapestry done in 1979 for the foundation, along with several of Miró's other later works. You then pass through a **narrow gallery** graced by Alexander Calder's "Font de Mercuri" ("Mercury Fountain"), created by the U.S. sculptor for the Paris exhibition in 1937, into a **vast open space** rising two floors. Here hang a couple of big canvases typical of Miró's later style—all primary colors and symbolic shapes. Some intriguing bronzes are also scattered about. His 1969 "Dona" ("Woman"), is represented as an egg on a crate. A papier-mâché mock-up for statues of a couple of lovers (1975) in Paris's La Défense district marks the end of this room.

From here you turn left into the first room of the core collection. Dedicated to the art collector and Miró's friend, Joan Prat, the room **(Sala Joan Prat)** contains a cross-section of works from the artist's early years and into the 1920s.

"El Pedicur" ("The Pedicure," 1901) is one of the oldest surviving efforts by the artist. Although Miró doesn't display the same precocious genius of Picasso at this early age (he was eight when he drew this), the brightly colored drawing is nonetheless interesting for the cari-

catural traits it displays.

There follow several sketches from the early 1900s of buildings and animals. The 1908 "Serp" ("Snake") is a striking exercise in design. By about 1915 Miró had developed a strong taste for experimentation, with his distorted female nudes and landscapes influenced by the fauvists. One of the most memorable paintings of this period is "Retrat d'una Vaileta" ("Portrait of a Young Girl," 1919), an unsettling portrait of a young blond girl with feline blue eyes.

The beginnings of surrealism in mid-1920s Paris coincided with vast changes in Miró's objectives. He stepped radically away from depiction to a kind of reductionist poetry on paper. Boiled down to the barest bones, the paintings no longer suggest concrete images but invite onlookers to dream. You see this in "Ampolla de Vi" ("Bottle of Wine," 1924), in which the bottle floats in a barely noticeable dreamscape with an insect and serpent. Works of the late 1920s develop the method. "L'Acomodador del Music Hall" ("Music Hall Usher," 1925) and "Arbre en el Vent" ("Tree in the Wind," 1929) convey simple but powerful imagery.

By the 1930s, the woman had become central to Miró's themes. In his bright "Flama en l'Espai i Dona Nua" ("Flame in Space and Nude Woman," 1932), the painter

The end of World War II signified for Miró a new beginning for the world, and his art became characterized by a search for light and harmony featuring women, birds, stars, the sun, and the moon. You pass from these rooms along a corridor toward an **L-shaped hall** dominated by paintings and sculpture from the 1960s and '70s.

Among these works are canvases on a grand scale, made possible by the workshop designed for Miró in Palma de Mallorca by Josep Lluís Sert. In the 1960s, while the underlying themes remained constant, Miró's expressive tools evolved. White and black became fundamental, otherwise dominated by primary colors, and, less frequently, greens. "Personatge davant el Sol" ("Person in front of the Sun," 1968) is a perfect example.

The permanent exhibition closes with a series of photos of Miró and a series of works done from 1944 to 1973, on long-term loan from Gallery K in Switzerland. In the basement are two rooms with works that other artists have given in homage to Miró; they include Henry Moore, Henri Matisse, Max Ernst, and Eduardo Chillida. ■

Miró's art underwent constant change, as does the collection.

moves closer to his mature style, although the human figure of the woman remains instantly recognizable as such.

Miró's progress through the 1930s and '40s continues in the **rooms above** the Sala Joan Prat. Prior to World War II, Miró did etchings to illustrate the books of poets like Paul Eluard. Some of these are on display, as well as some of his paintings from the period. The latter include the bizarre figures of the "Home i Dona davant un Munt d'Excrements" ("Man & Woman Before a Pile of Excrement," 1935).

The enormous Dona i Ocell statue near Plaça d'Espanya

The public face of Joan Miró

The diminutive, taciturn, and introverted Joan Miró got off to a slow and uncertain start in Barcelona. Born in 1893 on Passatge del Crèdit, just off Plaça de Sant Jaume in the heart of the old city, he was not allowed to attend art school and only began to go to classes at La Llotja while he was completing studies in commerce. But business was not for Miró: He fell ill while apprenticed to a store and afterward decided to dedicate all of his time to art.

Although Miró spent most of his adult life elsewhere (chiefly on the island of Mallorca), he never forgot his hometown. Several of his works are scattered about, among them the bright "Dona i Ocell" ("Woman and Bird," 1982) sculpture near Plaça d'Espanya (see p. 201) and a bronze statue, "Dona" ("Woman," 1983), on the first floor of the Ajuntament. There is a ceramic mural at Barcelona's airport (1970) and another Miró design in the pedestrian-only part of La Rambla by Mercat de la Boqueria (see p. 90). ■

Gardens

AT THE END OF THE 19TH CENTURY, WHEN THE IDEA FOR a world exhibition on Montjuïc was first aired, plans were already afoot to breathe new life into the mountain by creating a host of gardens. New gardens were laid out in the late 1990s, and more extensive botanical gardens are planned. For the people of Barcelona, the gardens of Montjuïc represent a rare refuge of peace. Just as driving schools take advantage of the near-empty roads around here, so joggers, strollers, and lovers seek a safe haven in Montjuïc's garden paths.

South across the Passeig Olímpic road from the Estadi Olímpic is the **Jardí Botànic** (Botanical Garden), carved out of what was an old municipal garbage dump. The garden, opened in the mid-1990s, contains some 2,000 species of plants thriving in areas around the world with a climate similar to that of the Mediterranean.

Occupying a privileged position on one of the highest slopes on Montjuïc, the Jardí affords fine views back across the Olympic installations and beyond. The plants and trees on show come from the Eastern Mediterranean, Spain (including the Balearic and Canary Islands), North Africa, Australia, California, Chile, and South Africa. What the display demonstrates is the enormous diversity of plant life in these areas despite the similarity of climate. All the specimens are clearly labeled, and your ticket allows you to come back for a second visit free.

Equally remarkable are the **Jardins de Mossen Costa i Llobera,** stretched out on the south face of Montjuïc and overlooking the busy port and southbound highway. The main feature of the gardens, dedicated to exotic and desert plants, is the cactus, of

Once somewhat downtrodden, Montjuïc's luscious gardens have been lovingly regenerated since the Olympics.

Montjuïc
✉ Font del Gat building, Passeig de Santa Madrona 28
☎ 93 289 28 30

Jardí Botànic
www.jardibotanic.bcn.es
🗺 Map pp. 184–85
✉ Carrer de Font i Quer s/n
☎ 93 426 49 35
💲 $
Ⓜ Metro: Línies 1 & 3 (Espanya) & Bus (PM)

Jardins de Mossen Costa i Llobera
🕐 Open daily

which hundreds of fascinating species are represented.

Higher up, a more conventional garden space adorns **Mirador del Alcalde** (Mayor's Lookout), a pleasant spot with views over the city. It lies south off Carretera de Montjuïc, the road that leads to the Castell and Museu Militar (see p. 200).

Uphill behind the Funicular terminus are the picturesque **Jardins de Mossen Cinto Verdaguer.** Here the specialty is bulbs, and the place is densely packed with almost 20,000 hyacinths, 10,000 tulips, and 12,000 narcissuses, plus various other species. The gardens lie on Camí Baix del Castell, a short walk east of the Fundació Joan Miró (see pp. 194–96). A little farther south are the pleasant Jardins Joan Brossa, with swings and things for children to use.

Within the Anella Olímpica is another simple little garden, the **Jardí d'Aclimatació** (Acclimatization Garden). It grew out of a desire to import a broad range of foreign trees to the city, to be cultivated and observed in a controlled environment. The mixed bag of trees and shrubs comes from as far off as China, Australia, and South Africa.

Cascading down the northeastern side of Montjuïc below the Fundació Joan Miró is shady **Parc Laribal.** With its staircases, pergolas, statues, and fountains, it is a pleasant way to walk up into the heart of Montjuïc. The original idea was to create an atmosphere akin to elements of gardens in the Alhambra in Granada.

Dominating the southwest face of the mountain is **Cementiri del Sud-Oest,** also known as the Cementiri Nou (New Cemetery). Opened in 1883, it is the resting place of several important Catalan figures and laden with tombs and sculptures. To the north is **Fossar de la Pedrera,** once a mass grave and now an extension of the cemetery. Lluís Companys, the Generalitat president executed by the nationalists in 1940, is buried here. There is also a monument to the fallen in the 1936–39 civil war. ■

Created during the Franco period, this sculptural group dancing the sardana graces a Montjuïc park.

Castell de Montjuïc & Museu Militar

WELL MIGHT YOU SHUDDER AS YOU PASS INTO THE central courtyard of Montjuïc castle (really an 18th-century coastal fort), home to a dusty military museum. The yard is lined with artillery, and a stern sign warns in Spanish: "Children! Don't Climb on the Cannons." Although designed to protect Barcelona from naval attack, the fort has often as not been used for more sinister purposes, on occasion even to bombard the rebellious city below. In the wake of the civil war, the nationalists tortured and executed many prisoners here, including the former head of the Generalitat, Lluís Companys, who was executed in October 1940.

Museu Militar

⬛ Map pp. 184–85
✉ Castell de Montjuïc
☎ 93 329 86 13
🕐 Closed Mon.
💲 $
🚇 Metro: Línia 3
   (Paral.lel) then
   Funicular railway &
   Montjuïc Teleféric

The best thing about the fort is climbing up onto the **roof** for the marvelous views over the south end of Barcelona and the sea.

Since you are here, though, you may as well visit the **museum.** Turn left when you reach the courtyard and head for a room marked **Sala** (Room) **2.** The limited art collection includes battle scenes and several portraits of such luminaries as the 1920s dictator Miguel Primo de Rivera and General Franco.

Next door, a stairway leads down past portraits of the masters of Catalan territory (theoretical and otherwise), from Charlemagne to the 19th-century's Queen Isabel II, to a series of **subterranean halls.** These are occupied by a halfhearted display of military hardware, including interminable rows of helmets, swords, armor, old military maps, uniforms, and a diorama of the much-reviled Ciutadella fortress (see pp. 133–35). An equestrian statue of General Franco has been awkwardly placed to one side. At the beginning of the halls are a few other rooms, mostly filled with model soldiers from different epochs and dioramas of castles and forts in Catalunya.

Back upstairs, the **courtyard** is lined with more rooms stuffed with pistols, swords, uniforms, and artillery pieces. Considered by Catalans to be an anachronism in bad taste, there are ideas on the table for turning the military display into a peace museum. **Sala 18** is curious; it is cluttered with tombstones, some dating from the 11th century, from the old Jewish cemetery that once graced this part of Montjuïc. ■

For some, the cannons of the Museu Militar are a Francoist anachronism.

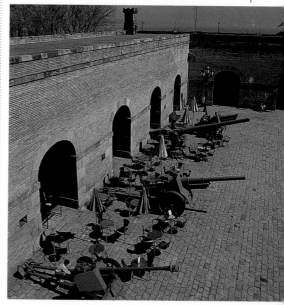

More places to visit in Montjuïc

CAIXAFORUM

Hard to believe that this striking brick structure, the Fàbrica Casaramona, started life as a factory. Beautifully restored, this attractive building was designed by one of the big three of *modernisme,* Puig i Cadafalch. It is owned by one of Spain's leading building societies, La Caixa. Reincarnated as CaixaForum, it has become one of the focal points of the city's contemporary art scene, with revolving exhibitions coming from La Caixa's own art collections and touring shows from abroad. From 1940 to 1993, the building was home to a police cavalry unit. In the courtyard where horses used to drink, there is now a steel tree. There is no single thematic thread behind the exhibitions, of which there can be up to three at a time. In 2005, they ranged from Turner and Venice to Bauhaus de Fiesta. www.fundaciolacaixa.es 🗺 Map p. 185 ✉ Avinguda del Marquès de Comillas 6-8 ☎ 93 476 86 00 🕓 Closed Mon. 💲 Admission depends on exhibition 🚇 Metro: Línies 1 & 3 (Espanya)

MUSEU D'ARQUEOLOGIA DE CATALUNYA

Set low down on the Montjuïc hill, the city's archaeology museum is a mildly interesting detour for those with a special thirst for things ancient. The building itself is one of the few remnants of the 1929 World Exhibition still standing. The collection concentrates largely on finds unearthed in Catalunya and in doing so attempts to trace the remote past of the region. The first rooms cover prehistory with the predictable assortment of Stone Age fragments, ancient skulls, and the like. More interesting is the area (Rooms X to XIII) dedicated to finds from the Balearic Islands, among the most important of which is the jewel-studded bust of the Dama de Ibiza (Lady of Ibiza). Extensive material excavated at Emporion (modern Empúries) is on show (Room XIV and parts of Room XVII), while the sparse collection of Roman finds upstairs comes mainly from Barcelona.

www.mac.es 🗺 Map pp. 184–85 ✉ Passeig de Santa Madrona 39–41 ☎ 93 424 65 77 🕓 Closed from 2:30 p.m. Sun., & Mon. 💲 $ 🚇 Metro: Línia 3 (Espanya or Poble Sec) or Bus (No. 55)

MUSEU ETNOLÒGIC

Apart from a busy calendar of temporary exhibitions, the core of this ethnological museum is the permanent display called Ètnic. It is divided into three parts, the first charting the course of ethnological studies and collections in Barcelona from the 19th century on. Items on display were largely collected by Catalans and come from various regions of Spain and as far off as India and the Philippines. The second part is devoted to objects of daily life from ten peoples, from Catalunya to Nuristan (in Afghanistan). The final stage covers taboos and religions of different cultures around the world.

www.museuetnologic.bcu.eu 🗺 Map pp. 184–85 ✉ Passeig de Santa Madrona ☎ 93 424 64 02 🕓 Closed Mon.& after 2 p.m. Wed., Fri. & Sun. 💲 $ 🚇 Metro: Línia 3 (Espanya or Poble Sec)

PARC DE JOAN MIRO

The uninspiring park behind the empty facade of the former bullring is still known to locals as Parc de l'Escorxador (Abattoir Park). When the bullring was in business, the carcasses ended up in the small abattoir here. The slaughterhouse is long gone, and the bullring is now being converted into a shopping center with offices.

Were it not for a little Miró madness this raggedy open space would not rate a mention. In the northwest corner rises up the bright, spangly "Dona i Ocell" ("Woman and Bird") one of Miró's most famous sculptures. To some, it's just plain phallic. Whatever way you see it, the original plan was for a forest of these sculptures to go up, but the artist's death put a stop to such extravagances.

🗺 Map pp. 184–85 ✉ Carrer de Tarragona 🚇 Metro: Línia 3 (Espanya)

Barcelonians love to explore their city's surrounding area, with good reason. Within easy reach are a former Roman city, grand monasteries, the fascinating work of Dalí, a bizarre mountain range, wine country, and a splendid stretch of coast.

Excursions

Vacationers flock to the Costa Brava.

Excursions

BARCELONA IS IN SOME RESPECTS THE LEAST CATALAN PART OF CATALUNYA, the northeastern-most region of Spain that, although it created a sea empire and long enjoyed at least a degree of independence, never knew nationhood. Yet Catalans are highly conscious of their separate "national" identity, symbolized in the fantastical shapes and monastery of Montserrat, a low but significant mountain range outside Barcelona.

For almost a thousand years, a monastery has stood cradled below the strange, bare peaks of the "serrated mountain." In the days of the Renaixença around the turn of the 19th century, ardent nationalists would set out from Barcelona to hike amid the fantasy-scape above the monastery. They were as much intent on gaining a deeper acquaintance with their region as getting a good few days' exercise. The proximity of these distinctive mountains to the capital and the long medieval tradition of pilgrimage to Montserrat have made the range Catalunya's national symbol.

Long before anyone had thought of raising a monastery there, Barcelona was a secondary town in the Roman territory of Hispania Citerior, whose capital was Tarraco (now Tarragona). Even today you can see parts of what was once the grand circus (where chariot races were staged), an amphitheater, forum, and other key Roman buildings. Although eclipsed by Barcelona in the Middle Ages, Tarragona remained an important center, as its mighty Gothic cathedral indicates.

Stretching across an ever changing landscape between Montserrat and Tarragona lies a remarkably varied array of sights and sensations. Only a short distance out of Barcelona along the highway that eventually leads to Madrid is the Penedès wine and *cava* district. Production of cava (Spanish champagne) is largely the preserve of wineries in this area, which also produces many notable whites and some decent reds.

The rocky coastline of the Costa Brava reaches its most southerly point at the town of Blanes.

Today, a small proportion of the grapes are still produced here by the monks of the greatest Cistercian monastery, the Reial Monestir de Santa Maria de Poblet. Its presence, along with two other once powerful monasteries is testimony to the extent of the power that once lay in the hands of the principal religious orders in medieval Catalunya. Poblet sits amid charming vineyards and gives access to the verdant territory around Prades. And nearby, as if in afterthought, stand the proud medieval walls of Montblanc. Down on the coast, the once tiny fishing town of Sitges is today one of gay Europe's preferred party stops, although it manages to retain a homey feel. The beaches are charming, the summer nightlife wild.

Northward is Girona, with a medieval center that gives a greater sense of completeness than that of Barcelona's. Its steep narrow streets around the cathedral and old Jewish district offer a joyous excursion back in time. Not a great deal farther up the highway toward France you are confronted with a rather more eccentric attraction—Salvador Dalí's museum theater and mausoleum in Figueres.

East of Girona and Figueres, Catalunya meets the Mediterranean with the fortress walls of the Costa Brava (Rugged Coast). Touring

Some of Spain's best wines come from the Penedès vineyards.

here brings you to enchanting coves and tranquil beaches, but can also lead to a breach in the natural defenses and the site of the ancient Greek and Roman cities at Empúries. ■

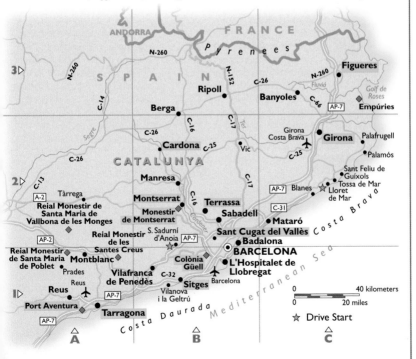

☆ Drive Start

Montserrat

**Montserrat
(Monestir de
Montserrat)**
- 205 B2
- 31 miles (50 km) NW of Barcelona

Visitor information
- Monastery complex
- ☎ 93 877 77 01
- By car: C-58 to exit 12 (past Terrassa), then follow signs. By bus: Julià company (tel 93 317 64 54) from Ronda de l'Universitet 5 in Barcelona at 9:30 a.m. Return at 5 p.m. By train: FGC train (No. R5) from Plaça d'Espanya station to Monistrol & from there rack and pinion "cremallera" train to monastery. The trip takes a little more than an hour.

The Black Virgin of Montserrat

TO SOME, IT IS THE SACRED SITE OF CATALUNYA. TO OTHERS it is the magic mountain, a bizarre platoon of oddly rounded peaks that in the distance look as the name suggests, like the upturned serrated edge of some supernatural saw. On a clear day, from Sant Jeroni, its highest point (4,066 feet/1,236 m), you can gaze clear across Catalunya to the Pyrenees in the north, deep across the inland plains to the southwest, and down to the coast and even the island of Mallorca to the east. There is plenty of walking, but for many the principal object of a visit is the Benedictine monastery that has been cradled in Montserrat's rocky lap for almost a thousand years.

This mountain range, dramatically rising out of the surrounding lowlands, 31 miles (50 km) northwest of Barcelona, seems, because of its abruptness, a great deal higher than it is. Just 6 miles (10 km) long and covering 17 square miles (45 sq km), it is the result of ten million years of geological upheaval and erosion on a conglomerate that once lay beneath the sea. It is frequently much colder here than in Barcelona, and often sea air meets mountain chill to create thick fog.

Archaeological finds in several caves reveal a human presence since neolithic times (about 4000 B.C.). But the real human story begins, at least according to legend, in A.D. 880 when, they say, the Virgin Mary appeared in a cave (known now as Santa Cova, or Holy Cave). The claim caused great excitement, and four small chapels were built in the area before the end of the century.

THE MONASTERY

The Benedictine **Monestir de Montserrat** was founded in 1025 by Oliba, Bishop of Vic and Abbot of the grand monastery of Ripoll. During the 12th and 13th centuries a Romanesque church was built, and the black wooden image of the Virgin now on display was carved. Pilgrims began to make the arduous climb to the nascent monastery, located at an altitude of 2,384 feet (725 m). By the beginning of the 15th century, the complex was an independent abbey and its renown was spreading across Europe.

The Gothic cloister, some of it still standing, was begun in 1476, while the present church, a mix of Gothic and Renaissance, was consecrated in 1592. Disaster struck from 1811 to 1812, however, when Napoleon's troops destroyed much of the monastery, and in 1835 expropriation laws reduced the

Divine voices

Apart from the monks, about 50 boys, or *escolanets*, aged 10 to 14, live in the monastery complex as members of the centuries-old **Escolania**, a kind of boarding school. Selection for entry is a matter of prestige and is judged in large part on musical ability, for the Escolania choir, said to be Europe's oldest music school (founded around 1223), is renowned for its angelic sound. You can hear the escolanets, dressed in medieval armless surplices, daily at 1 p.m. and 7:10 p.m. (1 p.m. only on Sunday) except in July. It is a rare (if brief) treat, as the choir does not perform often outside Montserrat. ∎

inhabitants of what remained to just one monk. Ten years later the Benedictines were back in force and the long process of reconstruction began. In 1881 the Virgin of Montserrat was declared Catalunya's co-patron saint. During the civil war the complex again came close to destruction and 23 monks were killed. Today about 80 monks live and work here.

No matter from which direction you approach the mountain, the unmistakable silhouette begins to work its strange magic from the moment you lay eyes on it. Whether you arrive by road or cable car, you will end up on a single road skirting the buildings until you reach the first of a couple of interlocking squares. From the second of these the path bends back and leads into the broad esplanade, Plaça de Santa Maria, that precedes the basilica. To your left, facing the basilica, are buildings used to house and feed pilgrims and other visitors. To the right an open wall has modern statues of the founders of various monastic institutions. On a clear day you can see the Mediterranean from here.

Before entering the basilica, go down the steps to visit the **Museu de Montserrat,** an engaging display of art and artifacts *below* the esplanade. There are two main collections of paintings. The first spans the 13th to 18th centuries, mainly with works collected in Italy, including paintings by Tiepolo, Caravaggio, Giordano, Luca, and El Greco. The second collection covers roughly the mid-19th century to the mid-20th century, with a heavy

Monastery buildings huddle beneath the fascinating sugar-loaf formations of the Montserrat—a national symbol for Catalans.

emphasis on Catalan artists, notably Dalí and Picasso. Beyond the Catalans there is an emphasis on French Impressionists such as Monet, Degas, Pissarro, and Sisley. Also taking pride of place is an exhibition on iconography dedicated to Montserrat's Black Virgin, affectionately known to Catalans as La Moreneta (the Little Dark One). A separate display, the Espai Audiovisual, takes you on a journey through the monastery's history and the life of a monk.

Back on Plaça de Santa Maria, you will notice to the left two flanks of the original Gothic **cloister** tucked into the side of the modern basilica. Along with the 14th-century octagonal, flat-roofed **bell tower** (largely obscured by more recent building), it is one of the oldest remnants of the medieval basilica. A modern five-door arcade leads to the courtyard. Go right, before walking into the courtyard proper, and you will see a well-worn **Romanesque doorway,** all that remains of the earliest buildings here. The marble floor of the **courtyard,** laid out in 1952, was inspired by the Campidoglio in Rome. The **facade** of the basilica might be stylistically confusing, until you realize that the sculptures (including Christ and the Apostles) and other decorative elements were completed at the beginning of the 20th century as an overlay to the baroque original. To the right, before entering the basilica itself, is the entrance and walkway to the venerated image of the Virgin Mary. We'll come back to that soon.

Inside, the **basilica** is in dazzling shape since its restoration in the 1990s. It dates from the second half of the 16th century and is a mix of late Gothic and Renaissance. The broad nave is typical of grand Catalan churches, with Gothic vaulting, whereas the classical

arches are a Renaissance touch.

For pilgrims, the high point of a visit is to file past the Romanesque black bust of the Mare de Déu (Mother of God). Return to the courtyard and look for the sign to the **Cambril de la Mare de Déu** (Chamber of the Mother of God), a pre-*modernista* rearrangement of the area in the apse in which the young Antoni Gaudí had a hand.

THE HERMITAGES
The compact mountains are crisscrossed by trails, some of which lead to a handful of the 13 hermitages built by solitary monks in precariously remote locations above the monastery. They are largely in ruins, but add interest to the range of possible **walks,** many of them easily accessible to anyone of average fitness. The monastery tourist

Cambril de la Mare de Déu

🕐 Closed 10:30 a.m.– 12:15 p.m.

MONESTIR DE MONTSERRAT

information office has a basic brochure detailing five such walks. To make things easier, catch the **Funicular de Sant Joan** for the first 822 feet (250 m) up from the monastery *(departures every 20 minutes; the last one down leaves at 7 p.m.)*. Several walks are possible from here, including one of a little more than an hour to the highest peak, **Sant Jeroni.** Along the way you can enjoy fine views of some of the more bizarrely shaped peaks in the range and then drop down into woods. When you reach the little 19th-century **Capella de Sant Jeroni,** turn sharp left to rejoin the trail. The last stretch to the top (and some superb views) is the only steep bit and it's brief. ■

The Funicular de Sant Joan

The Escolania (School of Music)

Black Virgin

Cable car terminus

Basilica facade

Basilica

hic cloister
a de Santa Maria

Inner courtyard

eu de Montserrat

Plaça de la Creu

Right: The restored interior is a mix of late Gothic and Renaissance.

Wine & monasteries drive

Barely an hour out of downtown Barcelona by car (or train), you can be in the heart of Catalunya's winemaking area, the Penedès. In addition to *cava*, the local version of champagne, vintners here also produce a fine range of quality non-sparkling whites and the occasional red. After thus treating with Bacchus, you may minister to the soul. A tour of three once powerful Cistercian monasteries allows you to marvel at fine Gothic construction and enjoy the varied countryside.

Heading west from Barcelona, follow the signs for the AP-7 tollway toward Tarragona and Lleida. Take exit 27 for **Sant Sadurní d' Anoia,** a town of little grace but one emblematic in the wine business. Here you will find the *modernista* cellars (designed by Puig i Cadafalch) of the Codorníu label and their direct opponents, Freixenet. They are the two biggest names in cava production in Spain, although in Sant Sadurní alone another 20 or so wineries operate. You can visit **Codorníu** (*Tel 93 818 32 32, www.codorniu.es*) and **Freixenet** (*Tel 93 891 70 00, www.webfreixenet.com*) for tours of their installations and tastings.

Back on the AP-7, the next stop is **Vilafranca del Penedès** ❶, in a sense the area's wine capital, 8 miles (13 km) to the southwest. Wine lovers should go to the tourist office (*Plaça de la Vila, tel 93 892 03 58*) for tips on interesting wineries to visit all over the Penedès. In the town itself you could head a block north to Plaça de Jaume I to visit the mostly Gothic **Basilica de Santa Maria** and, opposite, the combined **Museu de Vilafranca** and **Museu del Vi** (Wine Museum). (*Closed 2–4 p.m. & from 2 p.m. Sun. & Mon.*)

> ⓜ See map p. 205
> ▶ Barcelona
> ↔ 102 miles (163 km)
> ⊕ Full day
> ▶ Montblanc
>
> **NOT TO BE MISSED**
> - Wine-tasting in the Penedès area
> - Reial Monestir de les Santes Creus
> - Reial Monestir de Santa Maria de Poblet
> - Montblanc

The museums are housed in an impressive Gothic building. A tour of the wine museum usually culminates in a free tasting. One tip you may get from the Vilafranca tourist office is to head for the **Caves Romagosa Torné wine cellars** (*Tel 93 899 13 53*) at Finca La

Right: A huge wood-and-stone wine press forms the centerpiece of the Museu del Vi in Vilafranca de Penedès.

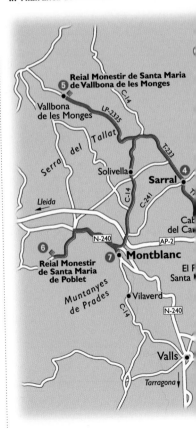

The grand monastery of Santa Maria de Poblet.

Serra on the BP-2121 road from Vilafranca to Sant Martí Sarroca. Whether or not you drop in here for the wines, continue to **Sant Martí Sarroca ➋**. Seated on a hill just outside the new part of town are two marvelous little Romanesque gems, a church and a castle. Anyone feeling hungry could try one of the small restaurants serving good Catalan cuisine located off the road up the hill.

A drive of about 19 miles (30 km) west cross-country takes you to the first of three extraordinary testaments to the power of medieval faith. **Reial Monestir de les Santes Creus ➌,** or Royal Monastery of the Holy Crosses (*Closed 1:30–3 p.m. & Mon.*), suffered greatly during the 19th century and then in the civil war but remains a magnificent place. Founded in the 12th century by Cistercian monks from France, the structures show all the influence of that order's building style—transitional between Romanesque and Gothic, austere and imposing. Their churches —and the one here is no exception—boasted a tall central nave and aisles, and it is often claimed the Cistercians were responsible for the spread of the pointed Gothic arch across Europe. The White Monks, as they were also called, eschewed external decoration but oth-

erwise the style of this and other monasteries of the order in Catalunya reflects French taste. The contrast with the broader, plain Catalan Gothic you see in the great churches of Barcelona and elsewhere (such as Girona) couldn't be clearer.

After passing a huddle of houses you arrive before a grand baroque portal that in turn leads into a somber, elongated square. Right before you, poised theatrically on a slight rise, is the mixed Romanesque and Gothic facade of the church that occupies the left wing of the complex. The entrance lies to the right of the building and from the ticket desk you emerge into an exquisite Gothic cloister. The delicacy of the stonework complements the warmth of the sandstone. A peculiar element is the pavilion, with its fountain, jutting from one side.

Nuns still live in the partly dilapidated Reial Monestir de Santa Maria de Vallbona de les Monges, deep in the heart of Catalunya.

The grapes of the lush green vineyards around the Reial Monestir de Santa Maria de Poblet end up in quality Torres wines.

into the garden. Off to the right of the cloister is the fine *sala capitular* (chapter house) and, above it, the monks' dormitory. Pass through to the second, older, and more disheveled cloister, off which you can view the royal apartments, where the count-kings of the Crown of Aragón frequently stayed for Holy Week. In the stark church lie buried Count-Kings Pere II and Jaume II.

From Santes Creus, head north for El Pont d'Armentera and then west 4 miles (6 km) to El Pla de Santa Maria. From here you follow the TP-2311 country road northwest to **Sarral** ❹, a quiet rural town where you could stop to stretch your legs before proceeding 6 miles (8 km) northwest until you hit the C-14 road. Turn left onto this and within 0.6 mile (1 km) you will see a signpost to

Vallbona de les Monges heading right (west). By now you are in the roasted ruddy hills of the **Serra del Tallat.** A 5-mile (8 km) drive brings you to one of those dusty, neglected country towns that signal you are far away from the general tourist trail, which is probably just how the Cistercian nuns of **Reial Monestir de Santa Maria de Vallbona de les Monges** ❺ *(Closed 1:30–4:30 p.m. & Mon.)* prefer things. In its heyday, this was the most important Cistercian nunnery in Catalunya, and its political influence was immense. Although in need of restorative care, the convent is still home to a handful of nuns today. Two wings of the cloister can be seen up close and the lofty church leaves its own haunting impression. During the civil war it was all but burned to a cinder. You will have to join a guided tour here that will almost certainly be in Catalan.

Head back to the C-14 road and follow it south to Montblanc, where you will return

Reial Monestir de Santa Maria de Poblet, the most powerful in Catalunya, still houses a magnificent pantheon of count-kings.

presently. Six miles (8 km) west of this walled town stands the most impressive of the Cistercian monasteries, **Reial Monestir de Santa Maria de Poblet** ⑥ *(Closed 12:30–3 p.m.).* Aloof and self-sufficient behind the forbidding perimeter of its magnificent defensive walls, by the mid-19th century the whole site had been pillaged and left to its fate. Only in 1940, when four dedicated Italian Cistercians returned, did the arduous process of restoration begin.

Founded in the 12th century by Ramon Berenguer IV in territory recently reconquered from the Muslims and donated to the Cistercians, the monastery grew rapidly to be the most important in Catalunya. This was the count-kings' spiritual center and pantheon. Contrary to the Cistercians' original rules, which forbade the accumulation of wealth, the abbots of Poblet came to be the masters of considerable territory and counselors to the count-kings. After the monks were unceremoniously evicted under expropriation laws in 1835, locals ransacked the place, destroying its immense library and carrying off other treasures.

You enter the monastery complex by the stout **Porta Reial** (Royal Gate), where you wait for the compulsory one-hour guided tour (in Catalan or Spanish) to begin. You will be led through a Romanesque door into the extraordinary Gothic cloister, easily the most striking among the cloisters of the three

Bubbling along nicely

Way back in 1498, Javier Codorníu purchased land in the Penedès area outside Barcelona with the intention of planting grapevines. The business was a success, and for centuries Javier's successors have made wine here. In 1872 they bottled the first ever batch of *cava*, a frothy, energetic, champagne-style wine.

Other winemakers such as Freixenet realized the Codorníu family was on to something, and soon everyone in the region was making bubbly. Today, the small area around Sant Sadurní d'Anoia accounts for 85 percent of national production. The method is the same used in the French Champagne district, but the French producers became indignant at the free and easy use of the term "champagne." And so the Catalans chose the word *cava*, which simply means "cellar." ∎

monasteries with its pavilion, fountain, rows of arches and vaults, and fine decoration. From here you are taken into the rear of the church, which houses a breathtaking array of alabaster: the immense *retablo* (altarpiece) and **Panteón dels Reis** (Pantheon of the Kings) made up of sarcophagi of count-kings including Jaume I the Conqueror and Pere III. Afterward, you are led upstairs to the dormitory and around the top of the cloister before heading through a series of halls and dependencies, including the onetime wine cellars. Nowadays, about 30 monks in residence raise grapes on a 30-acre (12 ha) property. The vineyards and nearby **Prades** hills give the countryside a special lilt; those with time could do worse than tour around the area.

When you are done at Poblet, head back to **Montblanc 7,** an intriguing town surrounded almost completely by its 1.25 miles (2 km) of hefty 15th-century walls. Of the original 28 towers, 17 remain.

Inside the town gates, make for **Església de Santa Maria la Major,** a Gothic church with an elegant Plateresque (early

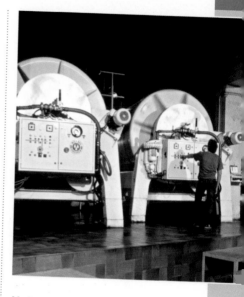

Modern presses at the Freixenet winery

Spanish Renaissance) entrance. Also worth a peek is the simple Romanesque **Església de Sant Miquel.**

From Montblanc you can pick up the AP-2 motorway for the trip back to Barcelona. ∎

Wine lovers pour into Sant Sadurní d'Anoia to taste champagne at the annual *cava* fair.

Sitges

Sitges, barely a half hour south of Barcelona, is a charming town with pleasant beaches, and lots of great bars and restaurants.

Sitges

🗺 205 B1

✉ 19 miles (31 km) SW of Barcelona

🚗 By car: C-32 to exit 27.
By train: Rodalies train from Barcelona Sants station to Sitges. The trip takes about 30 minutes.

Visitor information

✉ Carrer de Sínia Morera 1

☎ 93 894 42 51

UNTIL THE FINAL DECADES OF THE 18TH CENTURY, SITGES barely figured on the map. The cosmopolitan seaside resort town of today was little more than a fortified fishing village, some 12 hours' ride by coach-and-four from Barcelona. The sudden influx of wealth that came when Catalan merchants were finally permitted by Madrid, from 1778 onward, to trade directly with the American colonies was responsible for its early development into a cheerfully self-satisfied bourgeois outpost. Then in the 1890s the *modernista* artist Santiago Rusiñol, a cofounder of Els Quatre Gats, moved in, attracting the bohemian art world with him and setting the trend that would lead Sitges to where it is today.

Although in summer the population quadruples with the influx of well-heeled vacationers and hedonists, Sitges somehow manages to retain a relaxed small-town air. The area around the train station is lamentable, but development is controlled and the narrow streets near the waterfront make for pleasant wandering.

The main city **beach** is kept silky clean and is reason enough for a trip down from Barcelona. As you approach its eastern end you will pass a brilliant white statue of the 16th-century painter **El Greco.**

You may be wondering what on Earth the Cretan master, who spent most of his working life in the central Spanish city of Toledo, has to do with Sitges. Nothing really, except that Rusiñol thought so highly of the artist that he hauled two of his paintings here (see p. 218) amid much public to-do in early 1894, and thus hoped to revive interest in his idol.

In front of you, dominating the bluff of land that jabs defiantly into the Mediterranean, is 17th-century **Església de Sant Bartomeu i Santa Tecla.** Inside are several baroque altars and an organ that dates to 1697. The church underwent considerable modification in the 19th century. A stroll around its seaward flank brings you to the most charming, albeit tiny, corner of town.

THREE MUSEUMS

Two buildings confront you on the little square. The one on the right is the **Museu Maricel,** formerly a 14th-century hospice that now contains an eclectic collection of paintings, objets d'art, and other bits and pieces. Charles Deering, an American collector, purchased the building toward the end of the 19th century and began to fill it with his expanding collection. Then he had the building renovated, and across the lane built another edifice, similar in style, which became known as **Palau Maricel de Terra** (*only open in summer*). The two are connected by a lofty covered walkway.

As with the other museums in Sitges, this one is as interesting for the building as for the content. Nevertheless the collection, on view as a museum since 1970, is a curious mix. The first floor is filled with wooden religious sculptures ranging from the 12th to the 15th centuries, some fine ceramics, and furniture of various epochs. One of the most striking items is the 14th-century Gothic fresco cycle depicting the martyrdom of St. Bartholomew (Sant Bartomeu in Catalan). It was transferred here from Belmonte de Calatayud, in Aragón. There are a number of modernista and noucentista statues in the glassed-in alcove that looks out over the sea, and on the third floor an eclectic mix of furnishings, porcelain (in particular in Room XIV), household items, and a pewter collection are on display.

On the top floor is the museum's **pinacoteca** (art gallery). The paintings hanging here include a half-dozen by Rusiñol. Also represented is his buddy, Ramon Casas, with one canvas. The noucentista Joaquim Sunyer has a couple of pieces here too. Out in a back room is a collection of model sailing boats and seagoing paraphernalia. The main reason for visiting the Palau Maricel de Terra, however, is to wander around the mansion.

You can get more insight into Rusiñol by visiting the **Museu Cau Ferrat,** next door to the Museu Maricel. Rusiñol bought two fishermens' houses and renovated them to his tastes to create what would for years thereafter be his home, studio, and private museum. Its doors were thrown open to the public in 1932, a year after the artist's death. The house alone is worth the entry price. The first floor is richly decorated with exquisite ceramic tiles. It contains the kitchen, an expansive fireplace, the artist's bedroom, and a hodgepodge of his collections. These

At the heart of what was a tiny village, Museu Maricel looks out over the Mediterranean.

Museu Maricel & Museu Cau Ferrat

✉ Carrer de Fonollar s/n

☎ 93 894 03 64

🕐 Closed Mon., & Sun. p.m. (except in summer)

💲 $$ for all three museums

Museu Romàntic

✉ Carrer de Sant Gaudenci 1

☎ 93 894 03 64

🕐 Closed Mon., & Sun. p.m. (except in summer)

💲 $$ (all three museums)

Magdalena Penitent" ("Mary Magdalen Repentant"), and some copies of Italian masters by Rusiñol, including a couple of Giottos and Botticelli's "Birth of Venus." Of his originals, one of the best known is the rather sad "La Morfinòmana" ("The Morphine Addict").

The third in Sitges' trio of museums is the **Museu Romàntic,** a few blocks in from the waterfront. Guided visits (obligatory) take about 40 minutes and start on the hour in various languages. Can Llopis was built late in the 18th century by the wealthy Falç and Llopis families, grown rich on the production of *malvasia,* a sweet malmsey. The tour takes you through the refurbished 19th-century drawing rooms, ballroom, bedrooms (have a look inside the wardrobe off one of them), and so on. The spitoons liberally sprinkled around the house were for the benefit of tobacco chewers.

On the top floor is a rather disconcerting collection of several hundred dolls, the oldest of which was made in the late 18th century. Most of them are distressingly ugly. You can also see a series of dioramas made in the 1950s to depict typical scenes in the life of the wealthy and not so well off in 19th-century Sitges. ■

An eclectic display of period pieces, painting, and sculpture fills the Sala Gòtica in the Museu Maricel.

A drink is never far away in the narrow streets of central Sitges.

range from porcelain, some of it dating to the 14th century, to a series of paintings by Rusiñol and his pals, including four early works by Picasso.

Upstairs, the wrought-iron pieces that Rusiñol started collecting at the beginning of his artistic career dominate. They range from elaborate candelabras to an incredible assortment of keys. Tucked in among all the ironwork are the two El Grecos mentioned earlier, "Les Llàgrimes de Sant Pere" ("St. Peter's Tears") and "Santa

Down on Sin Street

Not everyone in Sitges comes to town for culture. The real activity for beautiful night owls after a hard day on the beach and slipping from late lunches to even later dinners begins around midnight. Head down to Sin Street (Calle del Pecado). During the day this short and unprepossessing lane goes by the name of Carrer del ler de Maig and has an air about it that reflects the hungover state of its nocturnal patrons. At night, and continuing well into the wee hours, a dozen disco bars thump and bump to the latest summer rhythms, all washed down with rather pricey drinks. There is a prominent gay scene but straights mingle in well and those with stamina have a choice of clubs (mixed and gay) in and around town where they can groove on from 4 a.m. until…whenever. ■

Tarragona

YOU WOULD NEVER KNOW IT TODAY, BUT IN ROMAN TIMES Barcelona was a bit of a backwater. The real power lay in Tarraco, capital of the Roman province of Hispania Citerior (subsequently Tarraconensis), a jurisdiction that covered two-thirds of the Iberian Peninsula, from Galicia in the northwest to Almería in the south.

Modern Tarragona is a more modest affair, but plenty of evidence of its splendor as a Roman city remains, together with an awe-inspiring cathedral of more recent manufacture. The Scipio brothers founded Tarraco as a military camp when they landed in 218 B.C. to carry the Second Punic War into Carthaginian-held territory. The camp was built alongside the Celt-Iberian settlement of Kesse, of which nothing remains. As the Romans consolidated their grip over the peninsula, Tarraco grew rapidly in importance as the provincial capital.

The end for the Romans came with the arrival of the Visigoths in A.D. 476, who were followed by the Muslims in 717. The latter razed the city, which remained largely abandoned until Christians returned to repopulate it at the end of the 11th century. Although an important port, it has played second fiddle to Barcelona ever since.

Second fiddle or no, Tarragona boasts the most extensive Roman remains in Catalunya, as well as the region's grandest cathedral. The bulk of the old city rests high above the shoreline, which is characterized at its northeastern end by a broad sandy beach, **Platja del Miracle,** the first of several strands on the way out of town.

To begin reconnaissance of Roman Tarraco, head for Plaça del Rei in the heart of the old town, or Part Alta (High Town). Two museums launch you into the ancient city and lie at what was the seaward, southeastern end of the provincial forum. This immense piazza (a few remains can be seen in Plaça del Fòrum) was the central meeting place for people from all over the province. To the northeast, where the cathedral now stands, was the temple to Jupiter.

The **Museu Nacional Arqueològic de Tarragona (MNAT)** is the first port of call. Here are collected the best of the artifacts found in excavations around and beyond the city, discoveries that continue to be made today. The best known item on display is the extraordinary "Mosaic dels Peixos" ("Fish Mosaic"), which once decorated the floor of a Roman villa outside the city and

now hangs on the wall by the stairs leading to the top floor. Judging by the 47 creatures depicted, the Mediterranean was a great deal more abundant in sea life than today. When you enter the museum, head downstairs to the basement, where you will see that the building bestrides part of what was the Roman defensive wall. On display around it are tombstones, columns, and statues, along with a limited collection of coins minted here and an audiovisual program recounting the history of the city.

The first floor is split into two parts. The main area is dominated by hefty pieces of statuary and architectural decoration, including

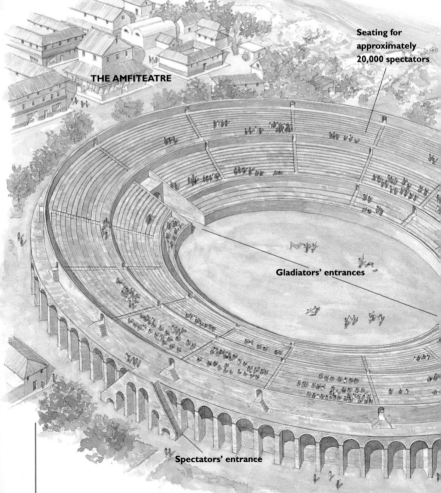

THE AMFITEATRE

Seating for approximately 20,000 spectators

Gladiators' entrances

Spectators' entrance

columns, friezes, and two fine medallions depicting Jupiter. In the other area some mosaics retain spectacularly vivid color, notably the one of Medusa. More mosaics are on view on the next floor, as well as objects of daily life, ranging from amphorae, the Romans' standard storage vessel, through to bronzeware, ceramics, glass, and some interesting statuary, including one of a phallus (representative of the fertility deity Priapus). The top floor has more mosaics and statuary. Throughout the museum are handy returnable booklets in several languages.

Facing the museum on the same square is the entrance to the **Museu d'Història de Tarragona,** which administers several Roman sites across the city. What you enter here are the **Pretori i Circ Romans** (Roman Pretorium and Circus). The former, also known as the Torre de Pilat (Pilate's Tower), was built in the first century. Whether or not, as legend suggests, Pontius Pilate came from Tarragona will probably

never be known. The tower was modified in later centuries and by the 12th century was known as the Castell del Rei (King's Castle). During Roman times, the 987-foot-long (300 m) circus was used for events ranging from chariot races (especially of *quadrigas,* chariots drawn by four horses) to the sacrificing of Christians to wild animals, a spectacle that was later transferred to the amphitheater. Stretching to the Ajuntament (town hall) building on Plaça de la Font, the circus could accommodate up to 23,000 cheering and jeering spectators.

On entering you will be directed to the elevator to the top of the tower (with wonderful views) from which you work your way downstairs. One level down is the **Sala Gòtica,** a medieval room that replaced the earlier Roman structure. The five broad arches are reminiscent of Barcelona's Saló del Tinell (see pp. 69–70). A long staircase leads down to a bare, high-ceilinged space dominated by the remains of a pillar from the imperial temple that dominated

Elliptical in shape

Spectators' entrance

Museu Nacional Arqueològic de Tarragona

www.mnat.es

✉ Plaça del Rei 5

☎ 977 23 62 09

🕐 Closed Mon., & p.m. Sun. & holidays

💲 $

the forum and stood some 53 feet (16 m) tall. Next door is the **Volta Superior,** or upper vault, which was part of the gallery that extended around the original forum.

The most intriguing part of the visit starts on the first floor. You first enter the **Volta Inferior** of the forum. This vaulted gallery was part of a structural support to level the enormous surface upon which the forum rested. From here turn back the other way and then right into the 306-foot-long (93 m) **Volta Longitudinal** of the Roman circus. It also served a structural purpose for the circus' upper levels. From one of the side rooms you can see some of the original spectator seating. After retracing your steps, proceed outside through what was a monumental gateway to the next covered section. You are now at the point where the Porta Triumphalis was, the gate through which victors exited the arena. Passing under vaults, you walk through what was one of the main arena entrances, claustrophobically enclosed by city walls. Stairs (mostly restored) lead up to what was once the top level at the eastern end. Back down those stairs you can exit into La Rambla Vella.

"Ruta Arqueològica Urbana," a leaflet available at the tourist office, indicates a series of premises along Plaça de la Font and Carrer de Trinquet Vell where, with a little luck, proprietors won't mind you popping in to see other bits and pieces of the circus upon which their properties were subsequently built.

Next head toward the coastline to visit the **Amfiteatre** (see illustration, pp. 220–21), the Roman amphitheater built in the second or third century (part of the Museu d'Història de Tarragona). In this elliptic enclosure locals enjoyed the clash of steel and the spilling of blood as gladiators hacked away at

each other and at wild beasts. In the center of the arena are remains of a Romanesque chapel built over a Visigothic church, raised to commemorate the martyrdom of Bishop Fructuosos and two deacons, burned alive in A.D. 259.

A wander back across the old town brings you to the entrance of the **Passeig Arqueològic,** a walkway along part of the perimeter walls. The inner line is predominantly Roman, while the outer walls were constructed by British military engineers during the War of the Spanish Succession.

Yet another element of the museum are the remains of the **Fòrum Romà** on Carrer de Lleida. Among the ruins several tall columns remain. A basilica where legal disputes were heard once occupied the northern end of this forum, while the hub of life for the populace was the lower southeastern part; the two are now linked by a footbridge. In the latter, a Roman street has been excavated.

Known popularly as the Pont del Diable (Devil's Bridge), the **Aqüeducte Romà** (Roman Aqueduct), 2 miles (3.2 km) from the center of town on the road to Valls, is typically impressive. What you see is a 540-foot-long (164 m) leftover of what was once a 20-mile (32 km) structure that supplied Tarraco with water.

Where once Roman citizens prayed to Jupiter now stands one of the most remarkable cathedrals in Catalunya. Begun in 1171 on the site of the Roman temple (of which a few vestiges remain), the predominantly Gothic **Catedral de Santa Tecla** incorporates some Romanesque elements, along with a few later baroque afterthoughts. Its construction was completed in 1331. The entrance is by the cloister on the northwestern side of the building.

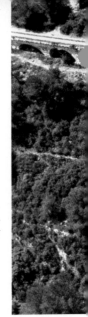

The aqueduct that lies outside Tarragona is proof of the Roman genius for construction.

The facade is an interesting mix. The two lateral doors are Romanesque while the main entrance, flanked by 22 statues of Apostles and prophets and split by a column graced with a statue of the Virgin and Child, is Gothic.

You enter the cathedral through the cloister. The 13th-century marble altar has reliefs recounting scenes of the life of St. Thecla. Four apses, three of them Romanesque and one Gothic, round off the northern end of the church, which is more than 329 feet (100 m) long.

Fine Gothic arches line the four sides of the cloister, mounted on a total of 276 columns, whose capitals were mostly completed in Romanesque style and depict all sorts of scenes, from the biblical to the comic. One of the most famous illustrates the tale of a procession of rats celebrating a cat's funeral. The only hitch is that the said cat comes back to life!

Rooms off the cloister house the **Museu Diocesà,** which contains a host of religious art and some Roman artifacts. ∎

Catedral de Santa Tecla

✉ Plaça de la Seu
☎ 977 23 86 85
🕐 Closed Sun. & holidays
💲 $

One for the kids

It is entirely conceivable that children's patience with Roman ruins and grand churches will be limited. One method for preventing explosion might be the promise of a trip to **Port Aventura,** the Catalan answer to Disneyland. This is one of Europe's biggest amusement park complexes. In 2005, a spine-chilling ride was added; the Hurakan Condor drops its passengers almost 12,000 feet (86 m) in just three seconds. Other thrills range from a virtual submarine tour to a Wild West scenario. Or head to the Caribe Aquatic Park for water rides. The park lies 4.5 miles (7 km) west of Tarragona and is accessible by train.

www.portaventura.es 🔺 205 A1
✉ 64 miles (103 km) SW of Barcelona ☎ 90 40 30 60
🕐 Closed Mon.–Fri. Nov.–Easter
💲 $$$$$ ∎

Girona

Tightly packed lanes border the Riu Onyar.

Girona

⬜ 205 C2

✉ 57 miles (91 km) NE of Barcelona

Visitor information

✉ Rambla de la Llibertat 1

☎ 972 22 65 75

🚗 By car: AP–7 E to exit 7. By train: Barcelona Sants station to Girona. Trip takes about 1.5 hours.

Museu d'Història dels Jueus de Girona (Centre de Bonastruc Ça Porta)

✉ Carrer de la Força 8

☎ 972 21 67 61

🕐 Closed from 3 p.m. Sun.

$ $

EXCAVATIONS HAVE REVEALED THAT AS EARLY AS THE FIFTH century B.C. a settlement existed at the junction of the Onyar and Ter Rivers. Phoenicians, Celts, and Celt-Iberians, to whom it was known as Geru Undar, later occupied it. It was only natural that the Romans should eventually waltz into what they called Gerunda, through which they laid the Via Augusta, the imperial road between Rome and Cádiz, in southeastern Spain. Conquered briefly by the Muslims in the eighth century, Girona was incorporated early on into the Count of Barcelona's territories. The city prospered in medieval times, but in later centuries Girona became a backwater: A feisty backwater, as its fierce resistance to Napoleon in two long sieges in 1808 and 1809 demonstrated.

Stacked up against the right bank of the Riu Onyar, Girona's old city has a magical quality about it. Peppered with small boutiques and charming restaurants, the narrow, twisting lanes, serpentine stairs, and closely huddled houses make it a wonderful place to discover at leisure.

Sooner or later you will end up walking along Carrer de la Força, which in Roman times followed the course of the Via Augusta through town. By the Middle Ages it was the main street of the Jewish quarter. Strung to either side was a web of narrow alleys, some of which (such as Carrer de Sant Lorenç) still exist. To become acquainted with the history of the Jewish community here, visit the **Museu d'Història dels Jueus de Girona,** in the much-restored Centre de Bonastruc Ça Porta. The house gives you an idea of how the better-off members of this community lived. Apart from explanatory panels and the like, little is on display except for a series of tombstones with inscriptions (the Jews buried their dead a few miles out of town at a place called

Bou d'Or). Upstairs, however, interesting temporary exhibitions are frequently staged.

A little farther north along Carrer de la Força, you arrive in Plaça de la Catedral. Among the fine buildings around the square are the **Pia Almoina** (constructed over the 13th to the 15th centuries as an almshouse), which is now home to an architects' society, and the 15th-century Casa Pastas, host to the city courts.

To your right, a grand 17th-century staircase sweeps regally up to the baroque facade (finished in 1733) of the **Catedral de Santa Maria.** Entry is off Plaça dels Apòstols through a Gothic doorway to the side of the church. Inside you are confronted by an enormous space of great austerity. Here the Gothic masters pushed the Catalan trend of creating broad, single-nave churches to its extreme; it is the widest Gothic nave in Europe.

Opposite the entrance, a shop gives access to the cathedral's cloister—a jewel of Romanesque architecture left over from the Gothic structure's predecessor—and its museum. The trapezoid shape of the cloister is unique, and the decoration of the capitals on the rows of columns that encircle the garden is exceptional. On the south side friezes depict biblical episodes, including the stories of Cain and Abel, and Abraham and Isaac, along with another of the taking down of Jesus from the Cross. From the cloister you can see the 13th-century Torre de Carlemany bell tower.

In the museum, or Treasury, reached from the shop, you pass through several rooms full of religious works of art, silverware, and so on, but the real treat is waiting for you at the end—the early 12th-century Tapís de la Creació (Creation Tapestry), rich in color and

iconography. Pick up an explanatory booklet when you buy your admission ticket. Also significant is the 975 Beatus codex, a rare illuminated tome on display in the first room of the Treasury.

On exiting the church you can submerge yourself in more art in the **Museu d'Art,** housed in the Palau Episcopal (Bishop's Residence) next door to the cathedral. The second floor is the main area of interest, with a varied collection of paintings, frescoes, sculpture, and architectural touches such as columns and capitals. The first four rooms are dedicated to the Romanesque period. Here the single most curious item is a column that once adorned a Girona street: A fanciful medieval lioness is scampering up it. The next four rooms are dominated by Gothic art and the last of them, a grand hall, is bedecked with enormous *retablos* (or *retables),* grand iconographic sequences that were painted on wood and placed behind altars. The most important of these are the "Retaule de Sant Miquel" (St. Michael) by Lluís Borrassà (1416)

The Museu del Cinema traces the history of the moving image from the camera obscura to Hollywood.

Catedral de Santa Maria
www.lacatedraldegirona.com
✉ Plaça de la Catedral
☎ 972 21 44 26
🕐 Closed Sun. Oct.–June & Mon.
💲 $

Museu d'Art
www.museuart.com
✉ Plaça de la Catedral 12
☎ 972 20 38 34
🕐 Closed Mon.
💲 $

and, opposite, the "Retaule de Púbol" by Bernat Martorell (1437). Both are masterpieces of the International Gothic style.

A couple of rooms on the second and third floors are given over to a collection of 16th-century paintings by minor artists, with nothing of particular note. The third floor also gives access to a onetime medieval prison—a large single room that, given the usual standards of the time, really wasn't too bad. The upper floors contain limited collections of art spanning the 17th to the 20th centuries, including a couple of canvases by Santiago Rusiñol in Room 17 on the fifth floor.

Back down in Plaça de la Catedral, follow the main street to the brooding twin towers that make up the **Portal de Sobreportes.** Since the third century (plenty of changes were made between then and the 15th century) this has been the main gate into the old city. As if in defiance, the immense Gothic apse of the **Església de Sant Feliu** juts out in front of the gate. You can walk around its left flank in the hope of getting inside the church *(often closed),* the second in importance after the cathedral. The nave has 13th-century Romanesque arches but 14th- to 16th-century Gothic upper levels. The northernmost chapel hosts the splendid

Modernista **design came to Girona, too, here in the form of the Casa Teixidor, with its landmark witches'-hat roof.**

Museu del Cinema
www.museudelcinema.org
✉ Casa de les Aigües, Carrer Sèquia 1
☎ 972 41 27 77
🕐 Closed 3 p.m. Sun.

Girona's Jewish quarter

Although the first Jews to reach Catalunya arrived after the destruction of Jerusalem, the earliest written records of their presence in Girona date from the late ninth century. At this time, they enjoyed the direct protection of the Catalano-Aragonese count-kings in return for financial aid. Girona's town authorities had no jurisdiction in the Jewish quarter, or *Call,* and this caused friction. However, until the 11th century it appears Jews and Christians got along well enough, but then tension began to mount. Their privileged status and economic power frequently made the Jews the object of popular ire, particularly in 1391, when the Call was sacked. The authorities passed decrees virtually shutting the district off from the

Carrer de la Força was the medieval main street.

rest of the city, ostensibly to protect the Jewish population. Even in the toughest times, the community, which never exceeded a thousand, produced some of the Middle Ages' greatest Jewish thinkers, foremost among them Moshe ben Nahman (aka Nahmanides or Bonastruc de Porta), the Grand Rabbi of Catalunya in the early 13th century and author of the Iberian Peninsula's most ancient Cabbalistic poetry. He and others brought enormous intellectual prestige to Girona, attracting learned confreres, Jewish and Christian, from around Europe to debate issues of theology and science. It all ended with the 1492 order by the united Spain's Catholic Monarchs to expel all Jews who did not convert to Christianity (see pp. 74–75). ■

alabaster Gothic sculpture of "Crist Jacent" ("Recumbent Christ"), executed by Aloi de Montbrai (active in the 15th century).

A stroll down the street north from the Portal de Sobreportes will lead you to two little Romanesque gems, the **Capella de Sant Nicolau** (a diminutive 12th-century chapel) and the **Monestir de Sant Pere de Galligants** (a monastery built in the 11th and 12th centuries). The latter contains a modest archaeology museum (with artifacts ranging from Roman coins to Jewish tombstones) and a pretty cloister.

Circling back into the old town across the Galligants River you again approach the old city. A couple of paths lead you on pleasant walks along the medieval city walls. But before embarking on these, there is one other stop worth making. On Carrer de Ferran el Católic are the so-called **Banys Àrabs,** or Arab Baths. Although it was modeled on Muslim and Roman bathhouses, with a changing room *(apodyterium),* a cold bath *(frigidarium),* a warm bath *(tepidarium),* a hot bath *(caldarium),* and a kind of steam bath known as the *hypocaust,* this public bathhouse was built in the 12th century. The frigidarium, with its octagonal shallow pool and slender columns, is particularly appealing.

Down in the new town is a modern museum for the modern age—the **Museu del Cinema.** This is a fascinating trip down film-making memory lane, put together from the vast collections of a Catalan cinephile, Tomàs Mallol (born 1923).

The display begins on the fourth floor (take the elevator) and continues on the third. Several shadow puppets dating from the 18th and 19th centuries get the

ball rolling, while ensuing rooms explain the history of the camera obscura, the first attempt to project images onto a flat surface, and subsequent developments in the popular entertainment business, such as the magic lantern. The floor ends with the arrival of the first clunky still cameras of the late 19th century.

The third floor, progressing from still to moving pictures, is crowded with projectors, cameras, and other equipment from the 1920s on. Some of the earliest TVs (from the 1930s), looking like old-fashioned wirelesses with a small round screen in the middle, are among the more intriguing items. On several, you can see some of the earliest golden moments of the Silver Screen. ■

Light floods through the domed lantern into the octagonal pool at the heart of the impressive 12th century Banys Àrabs (Arab Baths), built not by Arabs, but by Christians.

Banys Àrabs
- ✉ Carrer de Ferran el Católic
- ☎ 972 21 32 62
- ⏱ Closed from 2 p.m. Sun. & from 2 p.m. Mon.
- 💲 $

Delirium Dalí

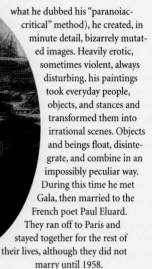

When Salvador Dalí (1904–1989) found himself surrounded by flames in his fantasy castle-mansion, the Castell de Púbol, south of Figueres, in 1984, he must have thought all the psychedelic weirdness of his most nightmarish paintings was coming true. Ever since, a fire extinguisher has stood by the bed in his blue bedroom, although no one has slept there since the painter's death in 1989.

Dalí acquired the mansion for his headstrong Russian wife, Gala, subject of his obsessions and many of his later paintings. They had previously spent much of their time in his Port Lligat home on the north Catalan coast. The parties they threw in the 1960s and '70s were legendary, as apparently was Gala's appetite for young men.

It had all begun modestly enough. As a young artist born in Figueres, Dalí came to the attention of Barcelona critics and was sent to study at Madrid's Escuela de Bellas Artes de San Fernando, where he met the likes of poet Federico García Lorca (1898–1936) and experimental film director Luis Buñuel (1900–1983). With the latter he would later make two key surrealist films, *Un Chien Andalou (An Andalusian Dog)* and *L'Âge d'Or (The Golden Age)*.

Dalí was good and his range was broad. Classic portraiture with a touch of the unreal, a few stabs at Cubism, sunny urban and country scenes were all accomplished with skill. The deceptively simple but engaging "Noia a la Finestra" of 1925 is a memorable work. But he did not really find his voice until the late 1920s when, influenced by Freud's teachings on the erotic and subconscious, he joined the Surrealist movement in Paris and embarked on the most fecund period of his artistic life. Inducing hallucinatory states in himself (by

what he dubbed his "paranoiac-critical" method), he created, in minute detail, bizarrely mutated images. Heavily erotic, sometimes violent, always disturbing, his paintings took everyday people, objects, and stances and transformed them into irrational scenes. Objects and beings float, disintegrate, and combine in an impossibly peculiar way. During this time he met Gala, then married to the French poet Paul Eluard. They ran off to Paris and stayed together for the rest of their lives, although they did not marry until 1958.

Dalí's work had always displayed tendencies toward the unreal.

Expelled from the Surrealist movement because of his thirst for commercial interests, Dalí and Gala moved to the United States for most of the 1940s. The French surrealist poet André Breton coined the anagram Avida Dollars (meaning "avid for dollars") from Dalí's name. It was apt, but probably left its target indifferent. Dalí's art was popular in the United States, and he began a campaign of purposeful eccentricity with the aim of attracting publicity and money. It seems to have worked. Moving around a lot, he worked on movie sets (including scenes from Alfred Hitchcock's *Spellbound)* and in theater, wrote a couple of books, and generally sold his name to all comers. Meantime, he abandoned the hallucinogenic painting and returned to more classic lines, or what he liked to refer to as his "mystical and nuclear stage."

By the 1960s (having returned to Europe in 1948) he was painting big canvases, often with religious themes. Even after the death of Gala in 1979 and the 1984 fire, he continued to paint, although he spent his last five years as a recluse in the Torre Galatea, which he bought along with the former theater in Figueres. He converted the theater into a museum of his work and chose it for his burial place. ■

The courtyard of the Dali Museum in Figueres

Dalí, pictured here at his easel, churned out an extraordinary quantity of art.

Figueres

ITS CREATOR DESCRIBED IT AS A "GIGANTIC SURREALIST
object." Others might settle for just plain strange. Whatever you may
think, a visit to the Teatre-Museu Dalí in the drab northern Catalan
town of Figueres, where Salvador Dalí began and ended his days, is a
unique artistic experience.

Figueres

🗺 205 C3

✉ 80 miles (128 km)
NE of Barcelona

**Visitor
information**

✉ Plaça del Sol

☎ 972 50 31 55

🚗 By car: AP-7 E
to exit 4.
By train: Barcelona
Sants to Girona.
The trip takes
2–2.5 hours.

One doesn't even need to go inside
to realize that this former
municipal theater, which Dalí
transformed between 1961 and
1974, is off the wall; just look at the
walls. Wine red, they are topped
with a series of androgynous
statues and what look like huge
eggs, a recurring theme in some of
Dalí's more nightmarish art.

Upon entering the building, you
have before you a circular **courtyard** that was once the theater

stalls, and you will hardly fail to
notice the Cadillac that squats in
the middle. It is said to have once
belonged to the gangster Al
Capone. Be that as it may, it is a
strange beast indeed. Near the front
passenger door you can insert coins
to trigger a rain shower *inside* the
car, hence the title of this "work,"
"Taxi Plujós" ("Rainy Taxi").
Suspended above this scene is a
small fishing boat; why it should be
there is anyone's guess.

somehow disquieting "Port Alguer" (a view of the Sardinian town of Alghero). Several portraits of Gala (see pp. 228–29) are also on view. Stairs to the right take you down to the crypt where Dalí is buried. Back upstairs you continue up another flight on the right of the stage to enjoy one of Dalí's games: The "furnishings" of the Sala Mae West make up her portrait. Climb the staircase and you will see how the sofa becomes her lips, the fireplace her nose, two paintings her eyes, and the curtains her hair.

The surrounding rooms and galleries above the courtyard are jammed in seemingly disorderly fashion with paintings and drawings by Dalí (such as his extensive series of lithographs on mythological themes) and others. Should you follow the layout of the museum you will likely end up in the **Torre Galatea** (named after his beloved Gala and in which Dalí spent the last years of his life as a recluse) in the last stages of your

Teatre-Museu Dalí

www.salvador-dali.org

✉ Plaça de Gala i Salvador Dalí 5

☎ 972 67 75 00

🕐 Closed Mon. Oct.–June

💲 $$

Visitors relax outside the museum dedicated to Dalí, a native of Figueres.

In the so-called **Sala de les Peixateries** (Fish Shop Room) off the courtyard, you can wonder at Dalí's "Autoretrat Tou amb Tall de Bacon Fregit" ("Soft Self-Portrait with Fried Bacon"), in which you can barely make out what appears to be a melted plastic death mask. His extremely unflattering "Retrat de Picasso" ("Portrait of Picasso") reveals all the bile Dalí apparently felt well up inside him at the mere mention of his rival's name.

Behind the courtyard is the former stage, now topped by a geodesic dome and dominated by a Dalían set (he contributed his skills to the theater on many occasions). Off to the left is the **Sala del Tresor** (Treasure Room), in which you will find some of Dalí's earlier works, like the bright, crisp, and

Dalí fever continues beyond his museum—Figueres cafés also adopt his distorted themes.

Museu de l'Empordà
- ✉ La Rambla 2
- ☎ 972 50 23 05
- 🕐 Closed 1–4 p.m. Tues.–Sat.; 1:30–5 p.m. Sun. June–Sept., & Mon.
- 💲 $

The Museu del Joguet, with a collection of more than 3,500 toys, offers an antidote to Dalí weirdness.

tour. These rooms are dominated by the artist's later work, including "stereoscopic" paintings (works in repetition to be viewed simultaneously), mostly of Gala and himself. A separate entrance leads to Dalí Joies, the Owen Cheatham collection of 37 jewels in gold and precious stones designed by Dalí with his usual brio.

OTHER ATTRACTIONS

A handful of items remain to be explored in this otherwise uninspiring town. Back in 1876, a local collector founded the **Museu de l'Empordà** (the northeastern part of Catalunya). It houses a collection of locally found artifacts from Celt-Iberian, Greek, and Roman times. You can expect to come across the usual kinds of

things: personal effects, black-and-red Greek ceramics, and glass. The display continues with odds and ends ranging from column capitals taken from the Monestir de Sant Pere de Rodes (a monastery set in a majestic position overlooking the northern Catalan coast) to minor paintings from the storerooms of Madrid's Prado gallery. Other sections are devoted to Catalan art from the mid-19th century to the early 20th century (Antoni Tàpies is among those represented) and strictly local painters.

A few doors down, the **Museu del Joguet** is for many a great deal more captivating. With some 3,500 pieces, it's one of Europe's biggest toy museums. Housed in a late 18th-century mansion, the collection has a bit of everything: toy animals, soldiers, cardboard horses, planes, trains, cars, puppets, dolls, teddy bears, and tricycles, plus all sorts of other stuff. Mixed in with old photos of kids playing, this is a trip back down through the years. A few of the toys belonged to such personalities as Joan Miró, Federico García Lorca, and Dalí himself.

To the north of town a small group of soldiers remains stationed in the **Castell de Sant Ferran,** an enormous star-shaped fortress built from 1750 to 1763 as a late

reaction to the loss of territory known as "Catalunya Norte" (of which the main city is Perpignan) to the French by the Pyrenees Treaty of 1659. Built about a half mile (1 km) north of central Figueres according to the criteria of the famed French military engineer Sébastien Le Prestre de Vauban (1633–1707), it was the second largest such fortification in Europe. Its walls are more than 5 miles (3 km) long, and it was said to be capable of resisting siege by a force of 8,000 soldiers and 500 horses for up to two years. They needn't have bothered. On the two occasions when the French invaded Spain (in 1793 during the French Revolution and again in 1808 under Napoleon) the fortress was surrendered without a shot— clearly it could not defend itself without a little help from the soldiers inside! Since then it has been a barracks, a training ground, and a prison, but never has it been tested in siege. The Republican government held its last meeting here in early 1939, shortly before fleeing to France and thus signaling the end of the 1936–39 civil war.

Although the fort is still army property, it can be visited (with or without a guide). Special two-hour visits including a ride in Zodiac in the huge subterranean cistern are another option. ■

Museu del Joguet
www.mjc-figueres.net
✉ Carrer Sant Pere 1
☎ 972 50 45 85
🕐 Closed 1–4 p.m. & from 1 p.m. Sun.
💲 $

Castell de Sant Ferran
wwww.grn.es/santferran figueres
✉ Cami al Castell de Sant Ferran
☎ 972 50 60 94
💲 $

Along the Costa Brava drive

Although speculators do their best to spoil things, the beauty of the Costa Brava (Rugged Coast) remains largely intact. To some the name conjures up images of budget package tourism, crowded beaches, and English-style pubs full to bursting with lobster-red revelers ferried in from northern climes. Apart from some infamous exceptions, the truth is thankfully rather different. What follows takes in the best of the coast from Barcelona most of the way to the French border. It would be a stretch to do in one day, but any given spot can easily be reached by car from Barcelona (taking the AP-7 tollway and cutting in to the coast at the appropriate point), with several stops along the way. Consider spending a night on the coast before returning to the big city.

From Barcelona, take the C-32 northeast and where it turns inland at Malgrat de Mar, follow the signs along the coast road for Lloret and Tossa. **Lloret de Mar** is mentioned only in passing, for that is exactly what you will want to do. Just 39 miles (62 km) northeast of Barcelona, this sprawling mass of dormitory hotels, poor restaurants, and loud bars is the epicenter of the package tour. Hotels and apartment blocks creep up the hills behind what is, admittedly, a good beach. If anything, this marks only the beginning of the Costa Brava—and the end of its more lurid dimension. Our first stop is 8 miles (13 km) of winding road farther along, at **Tossa de Mar ❶**.

⛰	See map p. 205
➤	Barcelona
↔	131 miles (210 km)
🕐	Full day/two days
➤	Cap de Creus

NOT TO BE MISSED

- Tamariu
- Empúries
- Parc Natural dels Aiguamolls de l'Empordà
- Cadaqués' pretty harborside restaurants

There's no shortage of summertime visitors here either, but the atmosphere is altogether different. Excavations show there has been a settlement here at least since Roman times and the *vila vella* (old town), with its twisting lanes and freshly painted houses, is a joy to explore. Up on a rocky, pine-stubbled promontory that closes off the southern end of the wide sandy beach, Platja Gran, a medieval watchtower stands guard over the coast and what remains of the 12th-to 14th-century city walls. Within them is a smattering of charming stone houses and a handful of bars and restaurants. The views and sunsets from up here are magical. In summer, glass-bottom pleasure boats set out from Platja Gran for tours of otherwise hard-to-reach beaches up and down the coast.

Leaving Tossa behind, the GI-682 road contorts itself on a series of winding climbs, mild switchbacks, and cliff-side spurts along

Capped at one end by a high promontory, Tossa de Mar is a delightful seaside village.

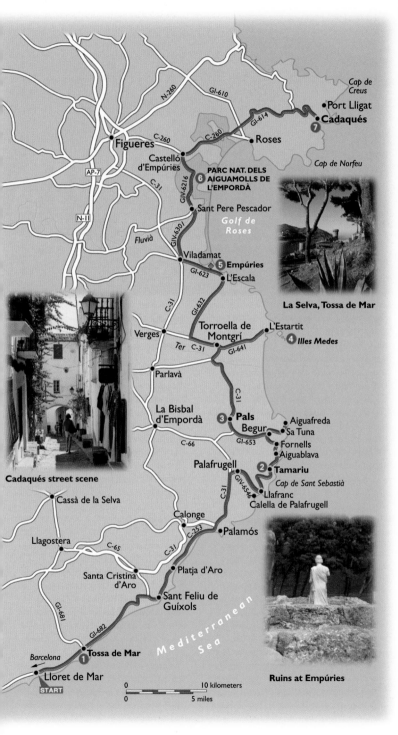

Cap de
Creus

● Port Lligat
⑦ **Cadaqués**

N-260
GI-610
GI-614
Roses
C-260

Cap de Norfeu

Figueres
C-260
Castelló
d'Empúries
AP-7
⑥ **PARC NAT. DELS
AIGUAMOLLS DE
L'EMPORDÀ**

GIV-6216
● Sant Pere Pescador
*Golf de
Roses*

N-II
GIV-6301
Fluvià

Viladamat
⑤ **Empúries**
GI-623
L'Escala

C-31
GI-632
Verges
**Torroella de
Montgrí**
L'Estartit
④ *Illes Medes*

Ter
C-31
GI-641

Parlavà

La Bisbal
d'Empordà
③ **Pals**
Begur
● Aiguafreda
● Sa Tuna

C-66
GI-653
● Fornells
● Aiguablava

Palafrugell
② **Tamariu**
GIV-6546
Cap de Sant Sebastià

C-31
Llafranc
Calella de Palafrugell

● Cassà de la Selva

Calonge
C-253
Palamós

Llagostera
C-65
C-31

Santa Cristina
d'Aro
Platja d'Aro

GI-681
GI-682
Sant Feliu de
Guíxols

Barcelona
① **Tossa de Mar**
*Mediterranean
Sea*

● Lloret de Mar
START

0   10 kilometers
0   5 miles

La Selva, Tossa de Mar

Cadaqués street scene

Ruins at Empúries

one of the most majestic stretches of the Costa Brava. The 13 miles (21 km) from Tossa to **Sant Feliu de Guíxols** is admirable, and along the way you'll see below you several tempting inlets and pretty little beaches. Development is taking place but hopefully the steep terrain will hold it in check.

From Sant Feliu, not an unpleasant seaside town, the GI-682 coast road leads northeast to a couple of popular beaches. Among them is **Platja d'Aro,** a lively little resort that attracts foreigners and Spaniards alike.

Continue north to Palamós, exiting it northward along the C-31 inland highway

Salvador Dalí chose the quiet fishing harbor of Port Lligat, just north of Cadaqués, to build his coastal hideaway.

(there's no choice). The next stop is **Pala-frugell,** not in itself an objective but the hub from which three delightfully restrained beaches are reached. They are, from south to north, **Calella de Palafrugell, Llafranc,** and **Tamariu ➋.** The latter is the quietest, a lovely beach with limpid water backed largely by thick woods and a few low-key hotels and restaurants. Calella, with its waterfront houses, restaurants, and fishing boats, has something

Diving the Illes Medes

The marine nature reserve of the Illes Medes is made up of seven tiny islets off the flat, arching coast town of L'Estartit. With nearly 1,400 species of animal and plant life and a labyrinth of underwater tunnels and caves, the isles have become one of Spain's favorite diving and snorkeling spots. Even close to the surface and by the rocks you can see all sorts of algae, fish, crabs, and octopuses. The deeper you go the more interesting things get, with lobsters, eels, grouper, and other fish at between 32 feet (10 m) and 49 feet (15 m). Deeper still, about the deepest dive possible is

164 feet (50 m), which for most is quite deep enough, you may come across rays.

Other diving options on the Costa Brava include the Illes Formigues, rocky islets off the coast between Palamós and Calella de Palafrugell with waters down to 148 feet (45 m), and Els Ullastres, three underwater hills off Llafranc with some sheer walls and depths to 178 feet (54 m).

L'Estartit is full of companies waiting to take you out diving. Exercise some caution, however, as not all are top-notch: Equipment and safety measures could be found wanting. ■

of the feel of a Greek island town. Between them, Llafranc has a fishing harbor and is a little dull compared with its neighbors. From Tamariu, follow signs for **Aiguablava**, a pretty cove, along unnumbered roads. Continue on the GIP-6532 to **Fornells**, another cove, and **Begur,** a bustling town with castle ruins.

From Begur, the GI-653 road heads west to meet the GI-650, which you follow for a few miles north to **Pals ③**, with its Gothic defensive walls and handful of centuries-old mansions. From Pals, continue on to **Torroella de Montgrí,** distinguished mainly for the castle ruins (accessible only on foot) that lie high up on a ridge above the town. From here divers may want to take the GI-641 east for 4 miles (6 km) to **L'Estartit,** to join groups diving off the **Illes Medes ④** (see box opposite).

Otherwise, head north for 7.5 miles (12 km) on the GI-632 to **L'Escala,** a pleasant seaside spot from where you can walk a couple of miles (or drive around the back) to the ancient site of **Empúries ⑤**. This was a trading post and among the first of the Greek coastal settlements in Spain. The Greeks and indigenous Celt-Iberian tribes rubbed along in peace until the Romans landed in 218 B.C., beginning a long campaign to conquer the entire Iberian Peninsula. Today you can make out the Greek and Roman parts of the town—the latter is farther from the waterfront and reveals more detail, such as the forum, floor mosaics in private houses, and remains of the landward wall and amphitheater.

From L'Escala, the GI-623 cuts inland to Viladamat and then north via Sant Pere Pescador to **Castelló d'Empúries.** This town has a pleasant old center dominated by the grand, Gothic Església de Santa Maria on Plaça de Jacint Verdaguer, retaining a fine Romanesque bell tower from an earlier church. Before Castelló, you may want to take a nature break in the **Parc Natural dels Aiguamolls de l'Empordà ⑥** (*Visitor information, tel 972 45 42 22*). This sanctuary is all that remains of the salt marshes that once lined the entire Golf de Roses (Roses Gulf). Although the best times for bird-watching in the park (there are marked trails and observa

tion points) are the March to May and August to October migration periods, you can usually spot plenty of birds year-round. Of the more than 300 species here, resident and migratory, common birds include herons, terns, glossy ibis, and even the occasional black stork.

Four miles (6 km) east of Castelló d'Empúries a road leads up into the highlands of the Cap de Creus Peninsula and onto the chic coast town of **Cadaqués ⑦**. Along with its neighbor around the next headland, **Port Lligat,** this was long a haunt of the rich and famous and retains a sophisticated air. The steep, narrow cobbled lanes of old Cadaqués are enchanting, as is the walk to Port Lligat, where you can visit Salvador Dalí's old seaside house (*Tel 972 25 10 15, closed Jan.–mid-March*). If time permits, drive out to **Cap de Creus,** Spain's most easterly point. ∎

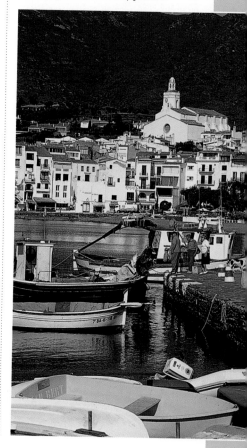

Cadaqués remains one of the classiest of the Costa Brava's resort towns.

More excursions from Barcelona

CARDONA

It is well worth considering taking the 56-mile (90 km) trip to this town near the Pyrenees Mountains to see the mighty 18th-century Castell de Cardona and, within its walls, one of the grandest examples of early Romanesque church building in Catalunya. Protected by the three defensive walls of the hilltop castle—that has been converted into a luxury hotel—the 11th-century Església de Sant Vicenç is splendid. Its nave and two aisles end in three proud apses and, unusually for a Romanesque structure, the ceiling is dominated by a central dome. The old town center also excites curiosity with its uneven lanes and Gothic parish church.

🅰 205 B2 ✉ Avinguda del Rastrillo s/n ☎ 93 869 27 98 🚆 Rodalies train (Línia 4) from Estació de Sants & Plaça de Catalunya to Manresa, then Alsina Graells (Tel 93 265 68 66) bus to Cardona

The Gothic entrance of the church of the Sant Cugat del Vallès monastery

COLÒNIA GÜELL

Only 6 miles (10 km) west of Barcelona, reached via the C-32 and TSV-2002, the sleepy hamlet of Santa Coloma de Cervelló hides one of Gaudí's last and least known projects. Gaudí was to build the church for a Utopian workers' village financed by Eusebi Güell, whose engaging cottages were designed by other architects. Gaudí had finished only the crypt when finances ran dry in 1915. Now used as a chapel, it provides intriguing clues as to what Gaudí's intentions had been for La Sagrada Família. The heavily leaning pillars holding up the ribbed vaulting are reminiscent of an enchanted forest. The long-abandoned factory buildings are being renovated as office space, maintaining the facades and structures.

🅰 205 B1 ☎ 93 630 58 07 🚆 FGC train (Nos. 54, 57 or 58) from Plaça d'Espanya to Colònia Güell station 🕐 Closed 2-3 p.m.; from 3 p.m. Sun. April–Oct. & daily Nov.–March 💲 $–$$

SANT CUGAT DEL VALLÈS

Once a summer getaway for Barcelonians, this town has little to offer except for the grand monastery from which it takes its name. Built near the site of its Visigothic predecessor (parts of which have been excavated), the present structure is interesting above all for the fine Romanesque first floor of its cloister. The upper level is Gothic, as is most of the church. The monastery, supposedly founded personally by St. Benedict, is named after a saint martyred in a Roman fort here in A.D. 303.

🅰 205 B2 ✉ Plaça de Barcelona 17 ☎ 93 675 99 52 🕐 Closed noon–4 p.m. 🚆 FGC train (Nos. S1, S2, S5 or S55) from Plaça de Catalunya

TERRASSA

They say Japanese urban planning students come here to learn how *not* to do things! Amid the high-rise suburbs lies an interesting old town center whose real treasure is a trio of pre-Romanesque churches. The Esglésies de Sant Pere (Churches of St. Peter) are actually dedicated to Sant Pere, Sant Miquel, and Santa Maria. The oldest elements date to the ninth and tenth centuries. Sant Miquel may be the most charming, with its square floor plan and pillars from Visigothic and Roman structures.

🅰 205 B2 ✉ Raval de Montserrat 14 ☎ 93 739 70 19 🕐 Closed 1:30–4 p.m., Sun. p.m. & Mon. 🚆 Rodalies train (Línia 4) from Estació de Sants or Plaça de Catalunya ■

Travelwise

**Barcelona's taxis are
inexpensive by European
standards.**

TRAVELWISE INFORMATION

PLANNING YOUR TRIP

Visiting Barcelona is an enriching and fun exercise. A modern, forward-thinking western city in most respects, it also has two millennia of history behind it and its own sometimes quirky ways. Things generally run efficiently, but often they run *differently* from how you might expect. The city is also bilingual, which on occasion can create confusion (especially if you are making some effort with one of the languages, probably Spanish). Still, so long as you are enjoying yourself, discovering how things are done can be a revealing part of the experience.

WHEN TO GO

The statistics speak for themselves. Year-round, Barcelona's hotels register about 85 percent occupancy. The city is a 365-day destination although clearly some times are busier than others. Peak periods include Easter week, Christmas to New Year, and the summer.

August is a funny month, though. Traditionally the time when most locals take their annual holidays to escape the strangulating heat, the city takes on a strangely empty air as many shops, restaurants, and bars shut down. Banks and public offices work on reduced morning-only timetables. The vacuum is filled to some extent by foreign visitors undeterred by the thought of cooking in the city and by Barcelonians who choose to stay behind to enjoy the summer theater season, Festival de Grec, or the local street festivals. One of the biggest, the Festa Major de Gràcia, takes place in the middle of August. It is a week-long sweaty celebration of food, drink, music, noise, and community, preceded and followed by similar, if less hectic, versions in other barris.

The best time to come is late April through June, when the weather is crisp and bright, and sometimes hot. February's Carnival (at its most raucous in Sitges—see pp. 50–51) already marks the passing of the worst of winter, but March is an unstable month, because you never know if it is going to be cold, wet, or hot!

The coolest and quietest period is from early December to late February (except Christmas and New Year's).

Some, but by no means all, hotels drop prices in slacker periods, but you shouldn't bank on it.

CLIMATE

Extremes of summer heat and humidity aside, Barcelona basks in a moderate Mediterranean climate. The hottest months of the year are July and August, when daytime temperatures reach the mid-90s°F. The city's location on the sea means that humidity can be high but equally (if you're in the right place) you can sometimes benefit from soothing sea breezes. In summer you will need only light clothes (natural fabrics are best). Otherwise come prepared for changes in temperature. Even if it's hot during the day, the nights can cool off considerably, so a sweater and light jacket could come in handy.

Traditionally Barcelona gets a thorough bath in late September and well into October, while November, although cool, can be agreeably dry and sunny. Spring can have its wet moments too, so you should bring an umbrella and possibly a raincoat.

Winters are chilly but not excessively cold. You will want a room with heating and decent winter clothing for the evenings, but you could easily find yourself enjoying crisp, sunny days. Temperatures hardly, if ever, go below freezing, and snow, even a dusting, is a rarity.

WHAT TO TAKE

Barcelonians tend to wear conservatively stylish dress. They don't have the same obsession with the latest fashion that many Italians do, but a certain Mediterranean desire to look good certainly pervades the atmosphere. Many younger people are pretty relaxed, however, and scathing about the middle-class pretensions of *pijos* (spoiled brats with nice clothes and cars).

If you intend to dine out in any style at all or go to concerts, you will want at least one set of casually elegant evening clothes. For tramping those city miles during the day, take a pair of sturdy shoes.

Other useful items include sunglasses (year-round), sunscreen lotion (spring and summer), and, for those sensitive to the sun, a hat. An under-the-clothes money belt or shoulder wallet is a good idea for keeping cash and documents out of sight.

INSURANCE

Comprehensive travel insurance is an essential investment and should cover you for theft, loss of possessions, money, emergency medical treatment, repatriation, and refund of flights and other travel should you be delayed by circumstances beyond your control, such as strikes or illness.

PASSPORTS

You need a valid passport. Keep a photocopy of the details pages in a separate location for ease of replacement in case of loss. Spain is part of the Schengen agreement, under which 16 western European countries have dropped passport controls between them. U.S. and Canadian citizens do not need a visa to enter any Schengen country for up to three months. For longer stays, you will need to consider applying for a residence permit —a nightmarish process.

FURTHER READING

An excellent introduction to the history and art of Barcelona is Robert Hughes' witty and insightful *Barcelona* or *Barcelona The Great Enchantress*. *Homage to Barcelona* by Colm Tóibín (1990) is an excellent personal intro-duction to the city's modern life and artistic and political history. *Homage to Catalonia,* on the other hand, is George Orwell's account of the 1936–39 civil war in Catalunya, moving from the euphoria of the early days in Barcelona to disillusion-ment with the disastrous in-fighting on the Republican side. If you want a good general history of the war, get *The Spanish Civil War* by Hugh Thomas.

HOW TO GET TO BARCELONA

Most U.S. and Canadian citizens will fly to Barcelona. However, the city can be reached by rail from Madrid and other parts of Spain, as well as from France. There are also high-class car-ferry services from Barcelona to Genoa and Civitavecchia near Rome in Italy.

AIRLINES

Iberia
Tel 902-40 05 00 or tel 93 401 33 73, Carrer de la Diputació 258, Barcelona
Air Europa
Tel 902-40 15 01, office at airport only, Barcelona
Spanair
Tel 902-13 14 15, office at airport only, Barcelona

Iberia and, to a lesser extent, Air Europa fly between Spain and North America, but you may well fly with another air-line. You can find local phone numbers for these under Línies Aèries/Líneas Aéreas in the phone book.

All three airlines above have extensive internal flight networks in Spain. Flying within Spain is not particularly cheap, but if time is of the essence you can reach any major city this

way. If flying from elsewhere in Europe, check the various options: regular scheduled flights, charters, and budget airlines (especially out of London). The latter operate on a first come, best served basis and on occasion you can get startlingly low fares.

AIRPORT

El Prat (7.5 miles/12km southwest of Barcelona). Tel 93 298 38 38

Direct flights between North America and Barcelona are available, but you will often find the best deals routing you through other European cities, possibly the Spanish capital Madrid but more than likely major hubs such as London, Paris, Amsterdam, or Frankfurt. Barcelona has one airport, which, while a little small for the volume of traffic it receives, functions relatively smoothly.

Getting into town is easy. The Rodalies (*Cercanías* in Spanish) local train service runs from a station about a five-minute walk along an overpass between terminals A and B. Main stops include Estació Sants and Plaça de Catalunya. Trains run every half hour from 6:13 a.m. to 11:15 p.m. (17 minutes to Sants; 23 minutes to Catalunya). Departures from Sants to the airport are from 5:43 a.m. to 10:16 p.m.; from Catalunya they're six minutes earlier. Tickets available from ticket office or machine at the station.

The A1 Aerobús service runs to Plaça de Catalunya via Estació Sants every 12 minutes from 6 a.m. to midnight. Departures from Plaça de Catalunya are from 5:30 a.m. to 11:30 p.m. The trip takes about 40 minutes, depending on traffic.

A taxi to downtown should not cost more than about 18-20 euros.

BY CAR

The AP-7 tollway takes you into Barcelona from the French border (and proceeds south to Tarragona and beyond along the entire Spanish Mediterranean coast). From Madrid you take the N-II toward Zaragoza, from where you have the choice of continuing along that road (with only one lane in either direction part of the way) or picking up the AP-2 tollway.

BY BOAT

Three days a week a luxury car ferry run by Italy's Grimaldi lines makes the crossing between Barcelona and Genoa. The trip takes about 17 hours and you can book through most local travel agents, online at www1.gnv.it, or (if there is space) by simply turning up at the port (Moll de San Beltran in Barcelona). In Genoa, the ferry terminal is at Via Milano (Ponte Assereto). Grimaldi opened a similar service to/from Civita-vecchia (Rome) in 2005. To book, see www.grimaldi-ferries.com.

BY BUS

Most national bus services arrive and depart from Estació del Nord (tel 90 226 06 06, Carrer d'Alí Bei 80). For travel along the Costa Brava, for instance, or farther afield you generally have no option but to take the bus as both areas are poorly served by train. Many international services depart from Estació d'Auto-busos de Sants, alongside the Estació Sants train station.

BY TRAIN

The main station is Estació Sants, on Plaça dels Països Catalans. Trains fan across Catalunya and the rest of Spain from here, as well as north into France. A bewildering variety of train types and classes confront the traveler moving around Spain, ranging from slow all-stops *regionales* to high-speed *talgos* (and all their subvariants!) For information, call RENFE (the Spanish rail company, generally Spanish speaking only), tel 902-24 02 02. You can book and check timetables at the station or on the Web site (www.renfe.es). For international services, book through selected travel agents or at the station direct.

GETTING AROUND

BY CAR

CAR RENTALS
In Spain:
Avis (Carrer de Corsega 293-295, l'Eixample, tel 90 213 55 31 or 93 237 56 80)
Europcar (Gran Via de les Corts Catalanes 680, tel 90 210 50 30)
Hertz (Carrer d'Arago 382-384, l'Eixample, tel 90 240 24 05)
National/Atesa (Carrer de Muntaner 45, l'Eixample, tel 90 210 01 01 or tel 93 323 07 01)
Pepecar (www.pepecar.com, Plaça de Catalunya, tel 80 721 21 21, bookings online)

A car is handy for making extensive trips beyond Barcelona (especially along the Costa Brava or if you want the liberty to move where and when you want), but not essential, as many day excursions are easily done by local transport. A car in Barcelona itself is more trouble than its worth (and a liability, as rental cars are frequently broken into). It is cheaper to rent a car before you arrive in Barcelona.

DRIVING REGULATIONS & CONVENTIONS
An international driver's license is not required for short-term visitors; your national license will suffice. When driving, carry all car documents (including insurance papers and at least a photocopy of your passport). Do not leave these documents (or anything else if at all possible) in the car when you park.
Barcelona traffic may appear chaotic, but most drivers respect most rules. Take care on pedestrian crossings, as many drivers seem to ignore their existence. Locals also have the habit of moving off at red lights just *before* they turn green—as though the extra 30 seconds will help. Barcelona is full of motorcycles and mopeds. Watch these anarchic beasts, as their riders frequently run red lights and overtake on the right (your blind side). Parking illegally in Barcelona is commonplace, but the parking police can be ruthless. If you get towed away, call the Dipòsit Municipal (car pound), tel 90 236 41 16 (the staff may not speak English) to find out where to pick up the car (there are pounds scattered across town). The longer you leave your car in the pound, the more you will pay to release it—and the fees are high.

In built-up areas, the speed limit is usually 30 mph (50 kph), rising to 60 mph (100 kph) on major roads and 75 mph (120 kph) on *autopistas* and *autovías* (toll and toll-free motorways). Vehicles already on roundabouts have right of way. The blood-alcohol limit is 0.05 percent. Motorcyclists must use headlights at all times. Crash helmets are obligatory on bikes of 125 cc or more.

CAR BREAKDOWN
Rental car companies will have their own emergency contact numbers. If you are driving your own car, your insurers should also have provided you with a number. If not call the RACC (Reial Automòbil Club de Catalunya). Their assistance number is tel 90 210 61 06.

PUBLIC TRANSPORTATION

Barcelona's buses, metro, and suburban trains were integrated into a single ticket system in 2001 under the Autoritat del Transport Metropolità (ATM). The network extends well beyond the city in six zones, but for most people all of interest is within zone 1. A single ride costs 1.15 euros. *Targetes* are multiple-trip transport tickets sold at most city-center metro stations and some newspaper stands. *Targeta* T-10 (6.30 euros) gives you 10 rides. You can catch a combination of metro, bus, and train within 1 hour and 15 minutes from the time you validate each ride on boarding. Targeta T-DIA (4.80 euros) gives unlimited travel for a day. The Targeta T-50/30 is for 50 trips within 30 days and costs 26.25 euros. The T-Mes is a monthly pass for unlimited journeys and costs 40.75 euros.

For public transportation information, you can call tel 010 or tel 93 205 15 15 (for FGC trains only). TMB, the public transit authority, runs four customer service centers: in Estació Sants (the mainline Renfe station) and the metro stops of Universitat, Diagonal, and Sagrada Família.

METRO
Operates: 5 a.m.–midnight Sunday through Thursday; 5 a.m.–2 a.m. Friday, Saturday, and the day before public holidays. The metro has six lines, numbered and color-coded, and it is the simplest way to get around town. Take care of your pockets on the metro, as pickpockets have been known to empty them, especially in a rush-hour crush.

FGC (Ferrocarrils de la Generalitat de Catalunya)
Operates: 5 a.m.–11 or 11:30 p.m. Sunday through Thursday, and 5 a.m.–2 a.m. Friday and Saturday. This is a supplementary suburban train system with a couple of lines through central Barcelona (no main terminal).

Rodalies/Cercanías
Operates: 5 a.m.–11:30 p.m. (some lines close earlier), stopping at Sants, Plaça de Catalunya, Passeig de Gràcia, and some other stations. Run by RENFE, these trains fan out

from the city to towns such as Sitges and Vilafranca del Penedès.

BUS
TMB (daytime service)
Operates: 5 a.m.–11 p.m. (some services start later and end earlier)
TMB Nitbus (night service)
Operates: 11 p.m.–5 a.m. (some services end earlier)

The city is covered by an extensive bus network, although in general the metro is a faster and more convenient way of moving around. The night buses are a clear exception to that rule but operate on limited routes, all of which start or pass through Plaça de Catalunya.

TAXIS
Barcelona's black-and-yellow cabs are reasonably abundant (although locals gripe about how hard it is to get one in the early hours of the morning) and, by European standards, good value. Generally, taxi drivers follow the rules and turn on the meter. Note that the final fare may have extras thrown in (for instance, for large items of luggage and for driving to the airport). Fares go up marginally between 10 p.m. and 6 a.m. on weekends and on holidays. You can hail a cab on the street or pick one up at cab ranks. Look for a green light on the roof, which means the cab is free. Sometimes you'll also see a *lliure* or *libre* sign in the windshield (respectively Catalan and Spanish for "vacant"). You can call a taxi at tel 93 225 00 00, tel 93 330 03 00, tel 93 300 11 00, or tel 93 322 22 22. General information is available at tel 010.

BICYCLE TOURS
You can get on your bike and indulge in one of several two-wheeled tours of the old center of town, La Barceloneta, and Port Olímpic with Un Cotxe

Menys bicycle store (www.bicic letabarcelona.com; tel 93 268 21 05, Carrer de la Espartería 3). They organize daytime rides around town on weekends and nighttime tours, including a meal in La Barceloneta, a few nights a week.

BOAT TOURS
Half-hour boat trips with the Golondrinas service (Tel 93 442 31 06) chug out to the break-water (*rompeolas*) and lighthouse (*faro*) from Moll de les Drassanes in front of the Monument a Colom (3.80 euros). The same people also organize a one-hour return trip to Port Olímpic (9.20 euros) on a glass-bottom catamaran (not that there is all that much to see down there!) Frequency of trips depends on season and demand.

BUS TOURS
The Bus Turístic service covers two circuits (35 stops) linking virtually all the major tourist sights (a third circuit of seven stops is added in the summer.) It is not a tour as such but a handy way of covering the sights. You hop on and off as you please. Tourist offices, TMB offices, and many hotels have leaflets explaining the system. Tickets, available on the bus, are 17 euros for one day's unlimited rides, or 21 euros for two consecutive days. Frequency of buses varies from 5 to 25 minutes, depending on the season, from 9 a.m. to 7:45 p.m. Tickets entitle you to discounts on entry fees to more than 25 attractions, the Tramvia Blau, funiculars, and cable cars, as well as shopping discounts. To join daily city tours (half or full day) contact Julià Tours (tel 93 317 64 54, Ronda de la Universitat 5) or Pullmantur (tel 93 318 02 41, Gran Via de les Corts Catalanes 645).

INDEPENDENT SIGHT-SEEING
Really the best way to enjoy Barcelona is to get around it yourself and at your own pace. The metro and bus systems

make it easy to cover a lot of ground, although inevitably some shoe leather will be involved too. At some specific sights guided tours are obligatory (e.g., Palau Güell), while at others (e.g., La Sagrada Família) they are optional.

WALKING TOURS
A walking tour of the Ciutat Vella (8 euros) starts on Saturday and Sunday mornings at the main tourist office on Plaça de Catalunya (English at 10 a.m.; Spanish & Catalan at noon). For other guide services and tailor-made options, contact the Barcelona Guide Bureau (tel 93 268 24 22) or the tourist office.

PRACTICAL ADVICE

POST OFFICES
Main branch: Plaça d'Antoni López, 08002, tel 902-19 71 97, metro: Línia 4 (Jaume I or Barceloneta), bus: 17, 19, 40, 45. Open: Mon.–Sat. 8:30 a.m.–9:30 p.m.
Local branches: Mon.–Fri. 8:30 a.m.–2 p.m. A handful open Mon.–Fri. 8:30 a.m.–8:30 p.m., Sat. 9:30 a.m.–1 p.m.

Known in Catalan as *Correus* (*Correos* in Spanish), the Spanish postal service has branches across the city, although surprisingly few in central Barcelona. This is partly because, for ordinary mail, you can also purchase stamps from *estancos* (tobacconists). Look for the yellow-on-maroon *tabacos* signs. Anything more complicated (like parcels) will oblige you to make a trip to the post office. Mail forwarded to you at the central post office should be addressed to you at Lista de Correos, 08080 Barcelona. Take your passport along as ID to pick up any mail.

Yellow *bústies/buzones* (mail-boxes) are located at post

offices and sprinkled liberally across town. Addresses in Barcelona can be quite complex, reflecting the location of apartments in various parts of any given building. C/ Carme 14, 3°D Int. probably looks utterly indecipherable. It means 14 Carme Street, 3rd floor, right hand (*dreta/derecha*), interior (where there are several sets of floors, some might be well inside off the street and look onto an internal courtyard).

TELEPHONES

All Spanish phone numbers have nine digits. The first two or three digits (93 in the case of Barcelona) indicate the province but must always be dialed, even if you are calling from next door. Numbers beginning with 6 are mobile phone numbers and suitably expensive. Toll-free numbers start with 900.

To call Spain from the United States, dial 011-34 (international dial out and Spanish country code) and the nine-digit number.

To make a domestic call from telephone booths in Spain you can use coins or (preferably) buy a *tarjeta telefónica* (phone card), available in tobacconists and post offices. When you pick up the receiver, wait for a few seconds and then insert the card; the balance will be displayed on the screen, at which point you can dial your number. Increasingly all sorts of cheap rate (or supposedly cheap rate) cards are available for long-distance calling to destinations outside Spain. These usually function with free-phone dial-in numbers and PIN codes and are only worth considering for international calls.

To make an international call from Spain dial 00, followed by the country code (1 for the United States and Canada), the area code (omitting the initial 0 if there is one), and the number. The easiest way to make a reverse charges call is to dial

9900 and then the country code, thus connecting you with an operator in the country you are calling.
American long-distance operators include:
AT&T: 990011; Sprint: 990013; and MCI: 990014.
Spanish directory assistance, tel 11818
International assistance, tel 11825

ELECTRICITY

Spanish circuits (mostly) use 220 volts; American appliances need adaptor plugs and those that operate on 110 volts will also need a transformer. These can be bought in Barcelona but are more easily purchased before you leave home.

ETIQUETTE & LOCAL CUSTOMS

It is not a bad idea to learn a few polite phrases in Spanish. No one expects you to know any Catalan and may well reply to you in Spanish even if you say something in Catalan. Remember that many (perhaps more than half) people living in Barcelona are *not* Catalans. *Buenos días* (good day) and *buenas tardes* (good afternoon/evening—used after lunch) are standard greetings when entering and leaving shops. *Hola!* (Hi!) is also common. On leaving, it is customary to say goodbye. In Barcelona most people, Catalans or not, use the Catalan *Adéu!* (¡Adiós!). It may seem strange, given that the above greetings are more or less mandatory, that in Barcelona (and the rest of Spain for that matter) people are less concerned about their pleases and thank-yous. A profusion of *por favors* and *gracias* is a sure sign that you are not a local!

HOLIDAYS

Some of the following public holidays are celebrated in Barcelona or Catalunya alone,

while others are national.
Jan. 1, Jan. 6, Good Friday, Easter Monday, May 1, Pasqua Granda (Monday after Pentecost Sunday), June 24, Aug. 15, Sept. 11, Sept. 24, Oct. 12, Dec. 6, Dec. 8, Dec. 25, & Dec. 26

MEDIA

NEWSPAPERS

Most *quióscos* (newsstands) in central Barcelona sell a broad range of English-language newspapers and magazines. In addition to the *International Herald Tribune*, *Time*, and *Newsweek*, you will find a host of British dailies. Heading the list of Spanish national dailies is the middle ground *El País*, excellent for broad coverage of foreign and local news. *El País* now publishes an abbreviated version, distributed with the *International Herald Tribune*. Others include the right-wing *ABC* and the investigative paper, *El Mundo*. Several important local papers also thrive, including *La Vanguardia* and *El Periódico* (published in Spanish and Catalan editions). The main Catalan nationalist paper is *Avui*. *Expansión* and *Cinco Días* are financial dailies and *Marca* the popular sports newspaper.

RADIO

You can tune into the national network, Radio Nacional de España (RNE), on several stations: RNE 1 (738 AM; 88.3 FM in Barcelona) for current affairs; RNE 3 (98.7 FM) for pop and rock music; RNE 5 (576 AM) for sports and entertainment. Among the most listened to rock and pop stations are 40 Principales (93.9 FM), Onda Cero (89.1 FM), and Cadena 100 (100 FM). The American InRadio program broadcasts in English on 107.6 FM on Monday, Tuesday, Wednesday, and Friday from 9 to 10 p.m.

TELEVISION

Eight standard TV channels are available in Barcelona. TVE1 and La 2 are run by Spain's state television broadcaster, Televisión Española. There are three independent national stations: Antena 3, Tele 5, and Canal Plus (only available if the TV owner subscribes to Canal Plus). The Catalunya regional government station is TV-3. Programs in Catalan are broadcast on Canal 33 and the city's BTV station.

MONEY MATTERS

American Express, La Rambla 74 08002 (tel 93 342 73 11) Metro: Línia 3 [Liceu]).

Barcelona is full of banks, in most of which you can change foreign currency (look for signs saying canvi or cambio, or tables with the day's exchange rates). As a rule, you are better off changing money in the banks but if you need to change money out of banking hours, currency exchanges abound in the center, especially along La Rambla. You should always ask about commission (rates vary from bank to bank) and confirm the day's exchange rate. Note that many currency exchanges advertising "no commission" usually offer an inferior exchange rate. Exchange rates and commission tend to vary for cash and travelers' checks.

The currency of Spain is the euro, as in a dozen other European Union member countries. Euros come in coins of 1, 2, 5, 10, 20, 50 cents and 1 and 2 euros. Bills are 5, 10, 20, 50, 100, 200, and 500 euros.

The best sources of currency with a credit/debit card are ATMs (caixer automàtic/cajero automático), outside many banks. Most major cards (Visa, MasterCard, etc.) will work but you should check with your bank or credit card supplier that your PIN is valid overseas. ATMs offer information in various languages. Cash advances, whether obtained over the counter or by ATM, incur a transaction charge.

OPENING TIMES

Bank opening times tend to vary considerably, but as a rule of thumb you should try to do your banking between 8 a.m. and 2 p.m. Mon.–Fri. Some banks stay open until 4 p.m. (or occasionally later). Virtually all close by 2 p.m. in the hot summer months.

Bar hours are much more flexible, and the distinction between where you have a cup of coffee or settle in for a night's drinking is vague. Many bars aimed at daytime and after-work customers will be closed by 10 p.m. Quite a few in the center stay open later and in many more alcohol-oriented bars it is quite possible to get a coffee too. Restaurants are generally open 1 p.m.–4 p.m. and 9 p.m.–midnight.

Store hours vary considerably, but many open Mon.–Fri. 9 a.m.–8 p.m., closing 1–4 p.m. for lunch. Many open on Saturdays too, sometimes only until 2 p.m.

TIME DIFFERENCES

From the last Sunday of October through the last Sunday of March, Barcelona is one hour ahead of Greenwich Mean Time; for the rest of the year (summer time) it is two hours ahead. If it's midnight in Barcelona, it is 6 p.m. in New York City and 3 p.m. in California.

TIPPING

Spain does not have a big tipping culture, but it's usual to leave a little cash (5 percent is quite sufficient) if service is not included. Locals leave change at bars para el bote (a common tips fund). You can tip hotel porters and maids at the end.

TRAVELERS WITH DISABILITIES

Barcelona is improving quickly for wheelchair-bound visitors, who in general will need to be accompanied. Only line 2 of the metro has elevator access to all stations, along with a few stations on other lines. This situation is being improved, and all lines should be accessible by 2007. An increasing number of buses are adapted to the needs of the disabled. You can book specially adapted taxis by calling Fono Taxi at tel 93 300 11 00. Some museums and other sights have installed ramps to facilitate access for the disabled. A good Web site is www.accessible barcelona.com.

VISITOR INFORMATION

INTERNET SITES

Turisme de Barcelona (www.barcelonaturisme.com) is the city's official tourist office site, with interesting listings and info on what's going on in Barcelona. The official site of the Ajuntament de Barcelona, the city's town hall (www.bcn.es), is full of interesting information on the city, including zoomable maps and a virtual flight over the city. Ciudad Hoy (www.ciu dadhoy.com) is a Spanish-language site. Click on Barcelo nahoy.com for a comprehensive site with links to the white and yellow pages and much more. The Generalitat de Catalunya's site (www.gencat.es) contains some interesting background material on the region in English as well as Catalan and Spanish.

TOURIST OFFICES

Oficina d'Informació de Turisme de Barcelona (main city tourist office), Plaça de Catalunya 17-S (underground), 08002, tel 80 711 72 22 from within the country and tel 34 93 368 97 30 from abroad. Metro: Catalunya. Open daily 9 a.m.–9 p.m. Aside from stacks of city information and a souvenir shop, you can book accommodations and theater tickets. A branch of this office operates in the Ajuntament (Town Hall), Plaça de Sant Jaume. Metro: Jaume I. Open Mon.–Sat.

10 a.m.–8 p.m., Sun. 10 a.m.–2 p.m.

Palau Robert (regional tourist office), Passeig de Gràcia 107, 08008, tel 93 238 40 00. Metro: Diagonal. Open Mon.–Sat. 10 a.m.–7 p.m., Sun. 10 a.m.–2:30 p.m. Information on all of Catalunya.

There are other tourist offices at Estació Sants train station and the airport. A nationwide general tourist information service can be reached at tel 90 130 06 00. In all these cases the staff speak at least some English. The general Barcelona infoline (tel 010), in Catalan and Spanish, can be useful.

EMERGENCIES

CONSULATES

Canadian Consulate, Carrer d'Elisenda de Pinós 10, 08034, tel 93 204 27 00, FGC: Reina Elisenda, bus: 22,64, & 75
United Kingdom Consulate, Avinguda Diagonal 477, 08036, tel 93 366 62 00, metro: Línia 3 (Maria Cristina), bus: 6, 7, 15, 33, 34, & 68
United States Consulate, Passeig de la Reina Elisenda de Montcada 23-25, 08034, tel 93 280 02 95, FGC: Reina Elisenda, bus: 22, 64, & 75

Embassies and consulates in Madrid
Canada (Calle de Núñez de Balboa 35, tel 91 423 32 50)
United Kingdom (Calle de Fernando el Santo 16; Consulate: Paseo de Recoletos 7/9, tel 91 524 97 00)
United States of America (Calle de Serrano 75, tel 91 587 22 00)

CRIME & POLICE

Barcelona is not a particularly dangerous city, but tourists are perennial targets of petty crime. In few American cities could you wander the downtown streets with so little fear of anything serious going awry. But pickpockets thrive. Leave any

valuables you do not immediately need in your hotel (preferably in a safe). Documents, credit cards, and cash you don't intend to spend immediately should be carried in money belts or shoulder wallets worn *under* your clothes. Wear bags, cameras, and the like across your body and keep a hand on them in crowded areas. Be careful of anyone getting unnecessarily close to your personal space, and be wary of people who simply start talking to you in the street, because there is a good chance their pals are hovering nearby to take advantage of your distraction. If you are robbed or lose valuables, you will need a police report for insurance purposes. See Lost Property below.

EMERGENCY PHONE NUMBERS

General emergencies (all services), tel 112
Guàrdia Urbana (local police), tel 092
Policía Nacional (national police), tel 091
Guàrdia Civil (national military police, highway patrol, and other tasks), tel 062
Mossos d'Esquadra (a Catalan force that has largely taken over duties of the Guardia Civil in Catalunya), tel 088
Fire, tel 080
Ambulance, tel 061
Hospital de la Santa Creu i de Sant Pau, tel 93 291 90 00, Carrer de Sant Antoni Maria Claret 167
Hospital Clínic i Provincial, tel 93 277 54 00, Carrer de Villarroel 170

24-hour pharmacies are at Carrer d'Aribau 62 and Passeig de Gràcia 26. Other pharmacies alternate on long shifts (9 a.m.–10 p.m.). Signs indicating the nearest one are posted at closed pharmacies, or you can get the day's list in the listings pages of *El País*.

WHAT TO DO IN A CAR ACCIDENT

Keep calm and alert! For a minor accident you and the other driver involved need to get each other's details (name, passport/ID, car registration, both sides' insurers, and if possible a diagram indicating what happened, along with details of where and when the incident occurred). If you have a rental car, the firm may have provided forms on which to do this, although they will probably be in Spanish. If an amicable agreement on the exchange of this information looks unlikely, at least get the registration number of the other vehicle so that you can report the accident to the police and insurers. Clearly, in a serious accident you will have to await the arrival of an officer of the law anyway.

LOST PROPERTY

Objetos perdidos (Ajuntament), Carrer de la Ciutat 9, 08002. Metro: Línia 4 (Jaume I), tel 010. Open Mon.–Fri. 9 a.m.–2 p.m. If you leave anything in a taxi, tel 93 223 40 12.
In the case of things lost on the metro, try the Centre d'Atenció al Client at the Universitat stop, tel 3 318 70 74.
Airport lost and found, tel 93 298 33 30

Lost credit/debit cards
American Express, tel 900 99 44 26
Visa, tel 90 099 11 24
MasterCard, tel 900 97 12 31
Diners Club, tel 901 10 10 11

If you lose documents, credit cards, or other things, you'll need a a police report for insurance/replacement purposes. Go to the *comisaría* (police station) at Carrer Nou de la Rambla 80, where you should find someone who speaks English. Be ready for long lines.

HOTELS & RESTAURANTS

As long as Barcelona remains flavor of the month for many travelers in Europe, you can expect competition for rooms and restaurant tables (especially on the weekend) to be tough. It is always best to book ahead if you can. Many hotels and restaurants accept all major cards, although cheaper eateries and *pensiones* (small family-run hotels) frequently do not take them at all.

HOTELS

Hotels in Barcelona (listed here by price then in alphabetical order) have multiplied over the past years to meet demand, which has taken some of the pressure off when looking for a room. Nevertheless, reservations are a good idea, and many hotels will require fax confirmation and possibly an acceptable credit card number to hold a room for you. The abbreviations used for credit cards are: AE (American Express), D (Discover), DC (Diners Club), MC (MasterCard), V (Visa). If you leave things too late, you might find yourself lodging a long way from the center.

The hotel building boom has taken some of the upward pressure off room prices too. For many years, inflation was crazy, but it has slowed. Lodging in Barcelona remains cheaper than it can be in many major European cities.

Although the old heart of town and parts of the Eixample are home to a handful of highly colorful hotels, many others are comfortable but surprisingly run-of-the-mill, could-be-anywhere places. We have therefore included a handful of the better pensiones for those looking for good but modest lodgings with a family touch. Rooms may come without private baths—the prices listed are for those with them.

Barcelona is one of the noisiest cities in Europe, but many hotels have off-street rooms where the racket is greatly reduced, and double-glazing and air-conditioning can help. Those who are disturbed by noise should consider bringing earplugs.

Street parking is never easy to find in Barcelona and virtually impossible in the oldest parts of the city (where many streets are pedestrian-only). Many of the better hotels have limited garage space, but in some cases where a hotel is listed as having parking the garage is not actually hotel property but located close by. In the old city in particular, most hotels are reasonably close to public parking. If you plan to have a vehicle, ask about parking when making reservations.

Grading system

Hotels in Spain are officially categorized by the Generalitat into three divisions: Hotels and Hotel-Residencias, Hostals and Hostal-Residencias, and Pensiones. Stars are awarded within each division according to different criteria, so a two-star hotel in the Hotel category is quite different from a two-star hotel in the Pensiones category. Hotels (H) and Hotel-Residencias (HR) are awarded from one to five stars, depending on the number of rooms with full private bathrooms, TV, air-conditioning, and other facilities. Rooms in the hotels listed here have their own bathroom unless otherwise noted.

Hostals (HS) and Hostal-Residencias (HSR) tend to be more modest, and may be family-run. Stars range from one to three. Pensiones (P) get one or two stars and are generally the simplest of establishments; you'll see plenty of these around.

The official star-rating system is not a particularly reliable guide to quality, and room rates are not regulated according to star ratings. Many hotels opt to stay in a lower category for tax purposes. Prices include sales tax (IVA) and in some cases Continental or buffet breakfast (which is often compulsory).

PRICES

HOTELS
An indication of the high-season cost of a double room with breakfast is given by $ signs.

$$$$$	Over $300
$$$$	$225–$300
$$$	$150–$225
$$	$100–$150
$	Under $100

RESTAURANTS
An indication of the cost of a three-course dinner without drinks is given by $ signs.

$$$$$	Over $80
$$$$	$50–$80
$$$	$35–$50
$$	$20–$35
$	Under $20

RESTAURANTS

Restaurants in this directory are listed by price then in alphabetical order. Reservations are generally recommended, particularly Thursday to Saturday. You can often get away with just turning up earlier in the week. Many of the restaurants listed below serve Catalan food and/or a mix of Spanish regional cuisine. Some offer more international and Mediterranean menus. Foreign cuisines are rapidly gaining acceptance in Barcelona, and it has become possible to eat good Japanese, Thai, Indian, and other food. It's still a drop in the ocean compared with London or New York, but the options are there should you feel the need.

Typically, a Catalan meal can consist of a starter, first course, and main course (usually meat or fish). Always ask if the main comes with vegetables (or anything!), the *guarnició,* or whether this has to be ordered separately. The first course may be considered your opportunity for ingesting vegetables. There are no hard-and-fast rules, and you are not obliged to eat more than one course if you do not wish to.

During the day, many restaurants offer a *menú del día*, a set meal consisting of all courses and a drink. Frequently such meals are solid rather than gourmet attractions, but they tend to be good value, and if the budget is looking frayed, you could make lunch your main meal of the day; it is easy to eat for 8 to 12 euros (coffee is usually extra).

Smoking seems to be almost de rigueur in Spain, and few restaurants bother with non-smoking sections. It may seem like a trip into the primitive past, but think of it as adding to local color and have another glass of wine to ease the pain!

Dining hours
Lunch is from 2 p.m. to 4 p.m., although in many establishments you can start earlier (1 p.m.) if hunger pangs have become extreme. You probably won't be eating with many locals though. Dinner is roughly from 9 p.m. to midnight. Some restaurants close their kitchens as early as 11 p.m. and some remain open until 1 a.m. Again, should you feel the need to eat earlier, there is generally no problem in the center of town, where eateries with an eye for the tourist buck (but often shunned by locals) are happy to have you seated at just about anytime you want. If you can, adjust to the local eating timetable, as the atmosphere of taking a meal amid people who live in Barcelona is part of the pleasure.

Closures & holidays
Most restaurants shut for a day or two (often Sunday night and Monday, but there are no hard-and-fast rules) during the week. Some also close at Easter, over Christmas, and for anything from two to four weeks in August. This can change rapidly and radically, especially in the case of the holiday periods, so it is best to be prepared for the occasional closed door (even if not indicated below) in these peak holiday periods.

TIPPING
Service charges are occasionally, but by no means always, included in the check (sales tax, or IVA is always included). Spaniards tend to be somewhat restrained about tipping. If service has not been included and you feel a tip is warranted, about 5 percent is sufficient.

BARRI GÒTIC

During the day, the epicenter of Barcelona overflows with people, both locals, and tourists. At night parts of it become quiet, while others hum with the activity of restaurants and bars. As in other areas of the old city, you need to be aware that some streets are potentially risky during the hours of darkness.

HOTELS

🏨 COLÓN
$$$$ ★★★★
AVINGUDA DE LA CATEDRAL 7, 08002
TEL 93 301 14 04
FAX 93 317 29 15
www.hotelcolon.es
This is perhaps the choice hotel in the Barri Gòtic. The views alone, which extend across the square to the Catedral, are worth the cost. If you are fortunate enough to get one of the top-floor rooms with a terrace, you will be in heaven. However, if you end up with one of the back rooms you'll be looking onto nothing much at all. Decor varies from room to room.
🛈 146 🚇 Metro: Línia 4 (Jaume I) 🅿 🛗 🌐 All major cards

SOMETHING SPECIAL

🏨 NERI
Broad stone arches, carefully chosen timber furnishings, and the latest in design touches (like flat-screen plasma TVs) make this a stunning central option in a centuries-old mansion. Each room offers an individual color scheme and decor. Have a relaxing snooze on the sun deck when sight-seeing becomes too much.
$$$$ ★★★★
CARRER DE SANT SEVER 5, 08002
TEL 93 304 06 55
FAX 93 304 03 37
www.hotelneri.com
🛈 22 🚇 Metro: Línia 3 (Liceu) 🛗 🌐 🌐 All major cards

🏨 RACÓ DEL PI
$$$ ★★★
CARRER DEL PI 7, 08002
TEL 93 342 61 90
FAX 93 342 61 91
www.hotelloracodelpi.com
A charming old building on one of the most attractive little streets in this part of town has been carefully modernized to create comfortable rooms with such touches as timber beams in the ceilings, parquet floors, sound-proofing, and free high-speed Internet connections.
🛈 37 🚇 Metro: Línia 3 (Liceu) 🛗 🌐 🌐 All major cards

🏨 SUIZO
$$$ ★★★
PLAÇA DE L'ÀNGEL 12, 08002
TEL 93 310 61 08
FAX 93 310 5 04 61
www.gargallo-hotels.com
Despite the aging exterior, this hotel has modern rooms that are simply and elegantly decorated. The common areas have a touch of old-world charm that is lacking in many more recently built hotels. An impressive buffet breakfast is served.
🛈 50 🚇 Metro: Línia 4 (Jaume I) 🛗 🌐 All major cards

🏨 JARDÍ
$$ ★
PLAÇA DE SANT JOSEP ORIOL 1, 08002
TEL 93 301 59 00
FAX 93 318 36 64
www.hoteljardi@retemail.es

KEY 🏨 Hotel 🍴 Restaurant 🛈 No. of rooms 🛏 No. of seats 🚇 Metro 🅿 Parking 🚫 Closed 🛗 Elevator

The refurbished rooms in this delightfully located hotel make it a popular spot. If street noise bothers you, try to get a room off the square.

[i] 40 🚇 Metro: Línia 3 (Liceu) 🔲 🅢 All major cards

🏨 LEVANTE
$ ★

BAIXADA DE SANT MIQUEL 2, 08002

TEL 93 317 95 65

FAX 93 317 05 26

www.hostallevante.com

This old center is littered with hostels and cheap hotels, but this is one of the brighter ones. A great range of rooms of varying size and quality are available. If a little street noise doesn't bother you, the doubles with balconies are the best.

[i] 50 🚇 Metro: Línia 3 (Liceu) 🔲 🅢 All major cards

RESTAURANTS

SOMETHING SPECIAL

🍴 ELS QUATRE GATS

A century ago this is where the bohemians of the *modernista* art scene hung out. It has been restored to its original appearance, complete with copies of paintings by some of its onetime patrons, and is a fascinating place to wander into even if you don't stay for a meal. Food is traditional Catalan.

$$$

CARRER DE MONTSIÓ 3 BIS, 08002

TEL 93 302 41 40

🍴 180 🚇 Metro: Línia 3 (Liceu or Drassanes), Línia 4 (Jaume I) 🔲 Closed L Sun. & first 2 weeks of Aug. 🅢 All major cards

🍴 PLA
$$$

CARRER DE BELLAFILA 5, 08002

TEL 93 412 65 52

An inviting decor with timber tables and muted lighting

will lure you in here for a romantic dinner of fun fusion. You can expect options from adapted Asian dishes through to cheerful travesties of local faves, such as the cod in green apple sauce. The menu changes regularly.

🍴 60 🚇 Metro: Línia 3 (Liceu) 🔲 Closed L daily 🅢 MC, V

🍴 AGUT
$$

CARRER D'EN GIGNÀS 16, 08002

TEL 93 315 17 09

A classic of Catalan cooking in the labyrinth of alleys at the lower end of the Barri Gòtic, Agut combines a contemporary feel (inspect the art on the walls) with tradition in a homey setting. It offers a variety of meat and seafood, and is known for its *bacallà* (cod).

🍴 85 🚇 Metro: Línia 4 (Jaume I) 🔲 Closed L Sun., & Mon. 🅢 All major credit cards

🍴 CAFÈ DE L'ACADÈMIA
$$

CARRER DE LLEDÓ 1, 08002

TEL 93 319 82 53

A tiny restaurant squeezed into a magnificent 13th-century house that overlooks an equally quaint square, this spot has become a standing favorite with the local left. Hearty traditional meat and venison dishes dominate the menu. Try to book one of the couple of upstairs tables.

🍴 50 🚇 Metro: Línia 4 (Jaume I) 🔲 Closed weekends & 2 weeks in Aug. 🅢 AE, MC, V

🍴 CAN CULLERETES
$$

CARRER D'EN QUINTANA 5, 08002

TEL 93 317 30 22

Founded in 1786, this is Barcelona's oldest restaurant. Although a little stuffy, the steadfastly Catalan menu does not disappoint and the dark, timber decor and old-style,

poker-faced service are a treat in themselves.

🍴 170 🚇 Metro: Línia 3 (Liceu) 🔲 Closed D Sun., Mon., & 3 weeks in July 🅢 MC, V

🍴 COMETACINC
$$

CARRER DEL COMETA 5, 08002

TEL 93 310 15 58

A duplex dining area in medieval obscurity. Just as the cuisine crosses all established boundaries, so the feel of the place is an almost disconcerting mix. A vibrant, urban staff whisk about the designer settings delivering anything from copious salads to Thai options, from couscous to excellent carpaccio.

🍴 75 🚇 Metro: Línia 4 (Jaume I) 🔲 Closed L daily & Tues. 🅢 MC, V

🍴 EL PARAGUAYO
$$

CARRER DEL PARC 1, 08002

TEL 93 302 14 41

For a taste of South America, pop in here and tuck into slabs of succulent meat, served on wooden tablets with slightly spicy or herb gravy and drink the robust house red, of which they give you a free taster when you're seated. The atmosphere is buzzy, and the caramel dessert, *dulce de leche*, satisfies any sweet tooth.

🍴 64 🚇 Metro: Línia 3 (Drassanes) 🔲 Closed Mon. 🅢 All major cards

🍴 LES QUINZE NITS
$$

PLAÇA REIAL 6, 08002

TEL 93 317 30 75

Try to get a window seat on the upper floors of this smart, mid-level restaurant in the heart of the old city. The menu is mixed Catalan-Spanish, with a smattering of that ambiguous genre—Mediterranean. They have a reasonable wine list. The place is good but perhaps does not merit joining the almost inevitable line outside!

🛏 200 🚇 Metro: Línia 3 (Liceu) ⬛ All major cards

🍴 LOS CARACOLES
$$

CARRER DELS ESCUDELLERS 14, 08002

TEL 93 302 31 85

Perennially busy and serving guests since the 19th century, this is a remarkable locale, all timber and wine barrels and garlic hanging on the walls. You wait at the bar for a table out the back, where you will be served all sorts of things ranging from rice specialties to snails.

🛏 230 🚇 Metro: Línia 3 (Drassanes) ⬛ All major cards

🍴 PITARRA
$$

CARRER D'AVINYÓ 56, 08002

TEL 93 301 16 47

Named after a 19th-century playwright who worked here, this is a spacious, mid-level restaurant offering decent quality Catalan dishes. They range across fish, meat, and game. *Civet de porc senglar al perfum de xocolata* (jugged boar with chocolate) is a tempting choice.

🛏 58 🚇 Metro: Línia 3 (Liceu or Drassanes) 🕐 Closed Sun., Aug., Christmas & Boxing Days ⬛ All major cards

🍴 VENUS DELICATESSEN
$$

CARRER D'AVINYÓ 25, 08002

TEL 93 301 15 85

This little candlelit hideaway is a soothing spot to go for a romantic dining experience with places for two at the small marble-top tables. You could skip the main course (which might be anything from moussaka to a walnut salad) and plunge straight into the cheesecake and other desserts. Unusual for a restaurant in Barcelona, this one stays open without a break from noon to midnight.

🛏 30 🚇 Metro: Línies 3 (Liceu or Drassanes) & 4 (Jaume I) 🕐 Closed Sun. & 3 weeks in Nov.

LA RAMBLA & EL RAVAL

Barcelona's most famous boulevard is lined with hotels ranging from cheap student dives through some century-old stalwarts to the modern comforts of places like Le Meridien. A couple of good places can be found inside El Raval too. The area also hides some fine eating options. Avoid La Rambla itself, though, as restaurants tend to be tourist traps serving low-quality food.

HOTELS

🏨 LE MERIDIEN
$$$$$ ★★★★

LA RAMBLA 111, 08002

TEL 93 318 62 00

FAX 93 301 77 76

www.lemeridien-barcelona.com

Easily the best address along La Rambla, it was a favorite with celebrities until the Arts Barcelona (see pp. 251–52) opened in the wake of the 1992 Olympics. The rooms (not to mention the suites) are luxurious, and the restaurant serves fine food.

🚪 210 🚇 Metro: Línia 3 (Catalunya or Liceu) 🅿 ⬛ ⬛ ⬛ ⬛ All major cards

🏨 GAUDÍ
$$$ ★★★

CARRER NOU DE LA RAMBLA 12, 08001

TEL 93 317 90 32

FAX 93 412 26 36

www.hotelgaudi.es

A Gaudiesque entrance leads into this perfectly acceptable mid-range hotel, whose rooms are comfortable and well equipped. The hotel stands directly opposite the Palau Güell.

🚪 73 🚇 Metro: Línia 3 (Liceu or Drassanes) 🅿 ⬛ ⬛ All major cards

🏨 CONTINENTAL
$$ ★★★

LA RAMBLA 138, 08002

TEL 93 301 25 70

FAX 93 302 73 60

www.hotelcontinental.com

One of Barcelona's once grand hotels, the Continental offers a touch of old-world charm at low rates. Try for rooms overlooking La Rambla. All come with cable, safe, refrigerator, and microwave.

🚪 35 🚇 Metro: Línies 1, 2, & 3 (Catalunya) ⬛ ⬛ ⬛ All major cards

🏨 CUATRO NACIONES
$$ ★★

LA RAMBLA 40, 08002

TEL 93 317 36 24

FAX 93 302 69 85

www.h4n.com

A little more than 150 years after it first opened, the "Four Nations" is looking a little worn around the edges but it is in a prime location. The most appealing rooms look out over La Rambla, and all are comfortable.

🚪 34 🚇 Metro: Línia 3 (Liceu) 🅿 ⬛ ⬛ ⬛ All major cards

🏨 MESÓN CASTILLA
$$ ★★

CARRER DE VALLDONZELLA 5, 08001

TEL 93 318 21 82

FAX 93 412 40 20

www.husa.es

Modernisme creeps into the interior decoration in this hotel, particularly the stained glass and murals in the public areas. The rooms are cozily decorated, and the location is comparatively quiet. The breakfast room looks out on an interior courtyard.

🚪 56 🚇 Metro: Línies 1 & 2 (Universitat) 🅿 ⬛ ⬛ All major cards

🏨 ORIENTE
$$ ★★★

LA RAMBLA 45-47, 08002

TEL 93 302 25 58

FAX 93 412 38 19

www.husa.es

A little long in the tooth but strong in atmosphere is this mid-19th-century hotel, built around what was the cloister of a Franciscan monastery. The foyer and sky-lit restaurant are a high point. The rooms, with tiled floors, are bare but comfortable.

🛏 142 🚇 Metro: Línia 3 (Liceu or Drassanes) 🔁 🚫 All major cards

🏨 SANT AGUSTÍ
$$$ ★★★
PLAÇA DE SANT AGUSTÍ 3, 08001
TEL 93 318 16 58
FAX 93 317 29 28
www.hotelsa.com
Located just off La Rambla on a pleasant square, the hotel has been refurbished a couple of times and offers comfortable, understated but modernized rooms, most with views across the square.

🛏 75 🚇 Metro: Línia 3 (Liceu) 🔁 🗾 🚫 All major cards

RESTAURANTS

SOMETHING SPECIAL

🍴 CA L'ISIDRE
Since it was renovated in the late 1990s, this Catalan classic has become a highlight of Barcelona's culinary experience for many people. Traditional cooking mingled with a little innovation makes for tempting dishes, such as the little octopuses sautéed with parsley and garlic.

$$$
CARRER DE LES FLORS 12, 08001
TEL 93 441 11 39
🍴 140 🚇 Metro: Línia 3 (Drassanes) 🕐 Closed D Sun., Mon., Easter week, & Aug. 🚫 All major cards

🍴 CASA LEOPOLDO
$$$
CARRER DE SANT RAFAEL 24, 08001
TEL 93 441 30 14
Before they carved out the

Rambla del Raval boulevard in 2000, this must have been hard to find, deep in the heart of the dingiest Raval. A timber-beamed ceiling hovers above the well-spaced tables. The fish hot pot (cazuela de pescado) is tempting.

🍴 140 🚇 Metro: Línies 2 (Sant Antoni) & 3 (Liceu) 🕐 Closed D Sun., Mon., & Aug. 🚫 All major cards

🍴 RITA BLUE
$$
PLAÇA DE SANT AGUSTÍ 3, 08001
TEL 93 412 34 38
A hip spot with tables spread around the sides and back of the bar, where you will almost certainly spend some time over an aperitif before you are seated. The mix of cuisine is eccentric, ranging from adulterated Moroccan to Tandoori chicken wrapped in Mexican fajitas.

🍴 108 🚇 Metro: Línia 3 (Liceu) 🕐 Closed L on weekdays 🚫 All major cards

🍴 EL CONVENT
$
CARRER DE JERUSALEM 3, 08001
TEL 93 317 10 52
Spread out across four floors in a charming old building laden with antiques and atmosphere, this is a convivial restaurant where a range of good Catalan cooking can be cheaply. A good first course is the rice salad with shrimps.

🍴 370 🚇 Metro: Línia 3 (Liceu) 🕐 Closed Sun. & holidays 🚫 All major cards

THE WATERFRONT

Surprisingly, and with one outstanding exception, there is virtually nowhere to stay right along the waterfront in Barcelona. There is no shortage of places to eat, however, ranging from simple lunchtime stops through to higher quality locations for fine seafood.

HOTELS

🏨 GRAND MARINA
$$$$$ ★★★★
MOLL DE BARCELONA S/N, 08039
TEL 93 603 90 00
FAX 93 603 90 90
www.grandmarinahotel.com
Occupying the landward flank of the portside World Trade Center, the hotel is in a splendid part of the city. Rooms are all generous in size, but the best are those on the wings with sea views. Timber with a definite seaside flavor dominates the decoration in the rooms and sunny public areas.

🛏 235 🚇 Metro: Línia 3 (Drassanes) 🅿 🔁 🗾 🏊 🍸 🚫 All major cards

🏨 HOTEL ARTS BARCELONA
$$$$$ ★★★★★
CARRER DE LA MARINA 19-21, 08005
TEL 93 221 10 00
FAX 93 221 10 70
www.ritzcarlton.com
For the international jetset, this is the address. Occupying 44 floors in one of the twin towers overlooking the Port Olímpic, the hotel oozes both luxury and stunning views. Sculpture, paintings, and palms are part of the interior decor.

🛏 455 🚇 Metro: Línia 4 (Ciutadella–Vila Olímpica) 🅿 🔁 🗾 🏊 🍸 🚫 All major cards

RESTAURANTS

SOMETHING SPECIAL

🍴 TORRE D'ALTA MAR
Of one thing you can be sure: Nowhere in Barcelona will you be able to match the views you'll get from atop this steel giant of a tower while treating yourself to a taste festival. Seafood dominates the menu, a fine wine list accompanies it, and the evening mood is perfect for romantics.

$$$$
TORRE DE SANT SEBASTIÀ,

HOTELS & RESTAURANTS

PASSEIG DE JOAN BORBÒ 88,
08003
TEL 93 221 00 07
🛌 120 🚇 Metro: Línia 4
(Barceloneta) bus 17, 39, &
64 🕐 Closed Sun. & D Mon.
💳 All major cards

🍴 CAN SOLÉ
$$$
CARRER DE SANT CARLES 4,
08003
TEL 93 221 50 12
Various hoteliers direct their
out-of-town guests to this
comparatively unsung seafood
establishment in the heart of
Barceloneta. Many people will
find a first or second course
sufficient, but in a sense that
would be a shame.
🛌 110 🚇 Metro: Línia 4
(Barceloneta); Bus: 17, 39, 45,
57, 59, & 64 🕐 Closed D
Sun., Mon., & 2 weeks in Aug.
💳 All major cards

🍴 SET PORTES
$$$
PASSEIG D'ISABEL II 14, 08003
TEL 93 319 30 33
It seems remarkable that after
so many years (since 1836) a
restaurant can continue to
maintain a good name. This
is one of those cases, and,
as a mid-range option serving
traditional Catalan dishes
accompanied by a broad
range of wines, it is a sure
bet. It was long run by Paco
Parellada, one of the leading
lights in Catalan cuisine, and it
remains in the family.
🛌 300 🚇 Metro: Línia 4
(Barceloneta) 💳 All major
cards

🍴 AGUA
$$
PASSEIG MARÍTIM DE LA
BARCELONETA 30, 08005
TEL 93 225 12 72
Looking out to the sea, this
no-nonsense seafood haven
in Port Olímpic is a cut above
some of the surrounding
locales. The products, whether
you decide to indulge in tapas
or sit down to a full meal, are

fresh and the results delightful.
🛌 170 🚇 Metro: Línia 4
(Barceloneta); Bus: 45 & 59
🕐 Closed Christmas Day
💳 AE, MC, V

🍴 ELS PESCADORS
$$
PLAÇA DE PRIM 1, 08005
TEL 93 225 20 18
A combination of earthy local
fish eatery and upmarket
restaurant far from the tourist
spots, this is like a bright light
in an otherwise unremarkable
former fishing and industrial
zone. The seafood options are
good, and the place attracts
people from all over town.
🛌 130 🚇 Metro: Línia 4
(Poble Nou); Bus: 403
🕐 Closed Easter week,
Christmas, & New Year's Day
💳 All major cards

🍴 SUQUET DE
L'ALMIRALL
$$$
PASSEIG DE JOAN BORBÓ 65,
08003
TEL 93 221 62 33
Although some will tell you
it's not as good as it was,
this seafood establishment
remains outstanding. The
rice dishes and fish stews
(cazuelas) are hard to resist.
🛌 80 🚇 Metro: Línia 4
(Barceloneta); Bus: 17, 39, 45,
57, 59, & 64 🕐 Closed D
Sun. & holidays, & all Mon.
💳 DC, MC, V

LA RIBERA

In the course of the 1990s
the area around the Born was
rejuvenated. Here more than
anywhere else in La Ribera,
restaurants, bars, and cafés
continue to spring up like mush-
rooms after a fall shower. It is a
little surprising, given all this
activity, that only a handful
of small hostales and one or
two modest hotels offer
accommodations options.

HOTELS

🏨 PARK HOTEL
$$$ ★★★
AVINGUDA DEL MARQUÈS DE
L'ARGENTERA 11, 08003
TEL 93 319 60 00
FAX 93 319 45 19
www.parkhotelbarcelona.com
Resurrected from the austere
1950s, the Park has rediscovered itself as a minor local
design icon. Rooms are
roughly divided into two
types, in terms of decor.
The higher are charged with
various tones of brown, while
those on the lower floors are
dominated by timber and
subtle greens.
🛏 91 🚇 Metro: Línia 4
(Barceloneta) 🅿 🔼 🔽
💳 All major cards

SOMETHING SPECIAL

🏨 BANYS ORIENTALS
The best things come in small
packages. Dominated by
cool colors (sky and steel blue),
timber details, and clean lines,
this is a fine boutique option on
a busy pedestrian street that's a
two-minute walk away from the
Església de Santa Maria del Mar.
Rooms are smallish, but ooze a
stylish charm.
$$ ★★★
CARRER DE L'ARGENTERIA 37,
TEL 93 268 84 60
FAX 93-268 84 61
www.hotelbanysorientals.com
🛏 43 🚇 Metro: Línia 4
(Jaume I) 🔽 🔼 💳 All
major cards

RESTAURANTS

SOMETHING SPECIAL

🍴 ÀBAC
One of the great lights of
the new millennium in
Barcelona's gastronomic universe
is this avant-garde locale. Àbac is
a veritable gourmet dream
factory. Expect the unexpected,
combinations like suckling pig
with mango fries.
$$$$$
CARRER DEL REC 79-89, 08003

TEL 93 319 66 00
🚭 40 🚇 Metro: Línia 4
(Barceloneta) 🕐 Closed
Sun., L Mon., & Aug. 🚫 All
major cards

🍴 EL PASSADÍS DEL PEP
$$$$
PLA DEL PALAU 2, 08003
TEL 93 310 10 21
One of the secret addresses
that everyone should know
about, the *passadís* (corridor)
is more like a paradise for fish
lovers. Fresh fish is shipped in
from up and down the coast
to provide the raw materials
for a marine feast.
🚭 100 🚇 Metro: Línia 4
(Barceloneta) 🕐 Closed
Sun. & two weeks in Aug.
🚫 All major cards

🍴 HOFMANN
$$$$
CARRER DE L'ARGENTERIA 74,
08003
TEL 93 319 58 89
Welcome to cooking school.
Never fear; the students here
are at the top of the class, and
the Med.-International cuisine
keeps high-flying business
people happy at lunch.
🚭 60 🚇 Metro: Línia 4
(Jaume I) 🕐 Closed Sat. &
Sun. 🚫 All major cards

🍴 CAL PEP
$$$
PLAÇA DE LES OLLES 8, 08003
TEL 93 310 79 61
Known across the city, the bar
is almost always bursting with
diners eager to feast on Pep's
tapas, a cut way above the
average. For most, a selection
of these tasty little morsels
accompanied by wine makes a
perfect meal, but you can also
sit down to a full meal in a
diminutive dining area.
🚭 44 🚇 Metro: Línia 4
(Barceloneta) 🕐 Closed
Sun., holidays, L Mon., & Aug.
🚫 All major cards

🍴 LA CARASSA
$$
CARRER DE BROSOLI 1, 08003

TEL 93 310 33 06
For fondue in a different
atmosphere, try La Carassa, a
cramped, rambling stone
house where you can be
guaranteed of not finding a
table (open for dinner only
from 9 to 11 p.m.) without a
booking. The fondue may be
the best in town.
🚭 55 🚇 Metro: Línia 4
(Jaume I) 🕐 Closed Sun. & 3
weeks in Aug. 🚫 MC, V

🍴 L'OU COM BALLA
$$
CARRER DELS BANYS VELLS 20,
08003
TEL 93 310 53 78
Enter this dimly lit space and
allow the rhythms of mixed
North African and Spanish
world music to waft you off
into a reverie, where you can
enjoy a Med-mix of French-
Moroccan-Catalan cooking. If
they have no space, the same
people with the same menu
and music run El Pebre Blau
across the road.
🚭 32 🚇 Metro: Línia 4
(Jaume I) 🕐 Closed
Christmas Eve, Christmas
Day, New Year's Eve, & June
23 🚫 All major cards

🍴 TANTARANTANA
$$
CARRER DE TANTARANTANA
24, 08003
TEL 93 268 24 10
Collecting accolades from
many a satisfied customer, this
cheerful locale with a vaguely
traditional decor turns out a
range of Catalan and Mediterranean dishes, presented
with deceptive simplicity. A
few Asian spices are thrown
in just to titillate the taste-
buds further.
🚭 45 🚇 Metro: Línies 1
(Arc de Triomf) & 4 (Jaume I)
🕐 Closed L daily & Sun.
🚫 All major cards

PASSEIG DE GRÀCIA

Not surprisingly, for this, the chic
heart of central Barcelona, there

is no shortage of quality hotels
and a reasonable sprinkling of
eateries to suit most budgets.
Some wonderful little surprises
await discovery in the narrow
streets of Gràcia too.

HOTELS

🏨 RITZ
$$$$$ ★★★★★
GRAN VIA DE LES CORTS
CATALANES 668, 08007
TEL 93 510 11 30
FAX 93 318 01 48
www.ritzbcn.com
The name alone attracts high-
flyers to what is probably the
classiest old-world hotel in
Barcelona. Some of the suites
are equipped with tiled
"Roman baths" that you step
down into. The staff provides
service second to none.
🛏 125 🚇 Metro: Línia 4
(Girona) 🅿 🔄 📶 🔟
🚫 All major cards

🏨 CASA FUSTER
$$$$$ ★★★★★
PASSEIG DE GRÀCIA 132, 08008
TEL 93 255 30 00
FAX 93 255 30 02
www.hotelescenter.es
Hard to believe that this
remarkable *modernista* edifice
was long home to a bank.
Renovated and converted
into a luxury hotel in 2004, it
occupies a privileged spot at
the top end of Passeig de
Gràcia. Take in the views from
the roof. Modern, comfortable
rooms are complemented by
sumptuous public spaces.
🛏 96 🚇 Metro: Línies 3 & 5
(Diagonal) 🅿 🔄 📶 🔟
🚫 All major cards

🏨 CLARIS
$$$$$ ★★★★★
CARRER DE PAU CLARIS 150,
08009
TEL 93 487 62 62
FAX 93 215 79 70
www.derbyhotels.es
One of the city's top hotels,
the Claris is known for its
innovative modern design. It
has been hailed as one of the
best hotels in Europe, and the

rooms cover a range of decoration from angular modern to classic. Some of the etchings on the walls were ordered by Napoleon.

ⓘ 124 🚇 Metro: Línies 2, 3, & 4 (Passeig de Gràcia) 🅿 🛗 🛍 ♨ 🔺 🌀 All major cards

🏨 MAJÈSTIC
$$$$$ ★★★★★
PASSEIG DE GRÀCIA 70, 08007
TEL 93 488 17 17
FAX 93 488 18 80
A labyrinthine establishment, the hotel's plush, elegantly appointed rooms are huge A bright modern design combines with ageless style. Discreetly placed items of statuary and works of art throughout public areas heighten the sense of class.

ⓘ 329 🚇 Metro: Línies 2, 3, & 4 (Passeig de Gràcia) 🅿 🛗 🛍 ♨ 🌀 All major cards

---

SOMETHING SPECIAL

🏨 OMM
One of the most self-conscious design additions to the Barcelona hotel firmament, Omm is easily one of the most exciting options in town. Found in the heart of the city, it is a feast of modern style.

$$$$$ ★★★★★
CARRER DE ROSELLÓ 265, 08008
TEL 93 445 40 00
FAX 93 445 40 04
www.hotelomm.es
ⓘ 59 🚇 Metro: Línies 3 & 5 (Diagonal) 🛗 🛍 ♨ 🌀 All major cards

🏨 PRESTIGE
$$$$$ ★★★★
PASSEIG DE GRÀCIA 62, 08007
TEL 93 272 41 80
FAX 93 272 41 81
www.prestigepaseodegracia.com
The steel-framed entrance is inserted into the 1930s facade, which is about all that remains of the original build-

ing. Inside is a stylish 21st-century lodging option. Relax in the Zeroom with its library or in the Oriental garden out back. Rooms are sober and clean-lined with touches like Bang & Olufsen TVs.

ⓘ 45 🚇 Metro: Línies 2, 3 & 4 (Passeig de Gràcia) 🅿 🛗 🛍 ♨ 🌀 All major cards

🏨 AXEL
$$$$ ★★★★
CARRER D'ARIBAU 33, 08011
TEL 93 323 93 93
FAX 93 323 93 94
www.hotelaxel.com
The top-of-the-line gay-friendly hotel in the heart of the gay quarter, the Axel is an mix of stylish, century-old architecture and modern touches. The best rooms boast charming, sunny galleries. After sight-seeing, chill in the rooftop Skybar.

ⓘ 66 🚇 Metro: Línies 1 & 2 (Universitat) 🛗 🛍 ♨ 🍸 🌀 All major cards

🏨 CATALONIA DUQUES DE BERGARA
$$$$ ★★★★
CARRER DE BERGARA 11, 08002
TEL 93 301 51 51
FAX 93 317 34 42
www.hoteles-catalonia.es
The refurbished modernista building has some classy touches, including the masterly crafted ceiling in the main foyer and some art deco details. The rooms themselves are generous and modern.

ⓘ 148 🚇 Metro: Línies 1, 2, & 3 (Catalunya) 🅿 🛗 🛍 ♨ 🌀 All major cards

🏨 CRAM
$$$$ ★★★★
CARRER D'ARIBAU 54, 08011
TEL 93 216 77 00
FAX 93 216 77 07B
www.hotelcram.com
Beneath the beautifully restored 1893 facade beats the heart of a slick, urban-design hotel. A combination of muted lighting, soothing soft browns

and oranges, and the latest technology makes this an excellent, if noisy, choice. A trump card is the hotel's Michelin-rated restaurant.

ⓘ 67 🚇 Metro: Línies 1 & 2 (Universitat) 🅿 🛗 🛍 ♨ 🌀 All major cards

🏨 CRISTAL PALACE
$$$$ ★★★★
CARRER DE LA DIPUTACIÓ 257, 08011
TEL 93 487 87 78
FAX 93 487 90 30
www.hotel-cristalpalace.com
Marble floors, primary colors, and attractive modern design mark this centrally located hotel. Most rooms, completely refurbished in late 2000, have balconies. In room internet connections, and buffet breakfast.

ⓘ 149 🚇 Metro: Línies 1 & 2 (Universitat) 🅿 🛗 🛍 🌀 All major cards

🏨 HOTEL CONDES DE BARCELONA
$$$$ ★★★★
PASSEIG DE GRÀCIA 73-75, 08008
TEL 93 445 00 00
FAX 93 445 32 32
www.condesdebarcelona.com
Occupying two buildings facing opposite each other across Carrer de Mallorca, this is an elegant option. If you can, try for a room in the older of the two buildings, the stylishly remodeled Casa Enric Batlló. In either you will bathe in marble luxury.

ⓘ 109 🚇 Metro: Línies 2, 3, & 4 (Passeig de Gràcia) 🅿 🛗 🛍 ♨ 🌀 All major cards

🏨 ST MORITZ
$$$$ ★★★★
CARRER DE LA DIPUTACIÓ 262 BIS, 08002
TEL 93 412 15 00
FAX 93 412 12 36
www.hcchotels.com
The spacious rooms (each with mini-gym and marble bath) in this fine Eixample building are a pleasure to stay

---

in. A relaxing place for a drink is the terrace-garden bar.

ⓘ 91 Metro: Línies 2, 3 & 4 (Passeig de Gràcia) 🅿
⬄ 🚇 All major cards

ASTORIA
$$$ ★★★
CARRER DE PARÍS 203, 08036
TEL 93 209 83 11
FAX 93 202 30 08
www.derbyhotels.es
Located in a classic pre-Civil War building and a short walk from the top end of Passeig de Gràcia, this nicely renovated hotel has good sized, comfortable rooms. There is also a sauna.

ⓘ 117 Metro: Línia 3 (Diagonal) 🅿 ⬄ 🖫 🏊
🖫 All major cards

BALMES
$$$ ★★★
CARRER DE MALLORCA 216, 08002
TEL 93 451 19 14
FAX 93 451 00 49
www.derbyhotels.es
The crisp white brick of this modern and pleasing hotel sets the tone. Rooms are of average size with agreeable tiled bathrooms, and you have the option of lounging at the peaceful internal courtyard pool or in the cozy garden.

ⓘ 100 Metro: Línia 3 (Diagonal); FGC: Provença
🅿 ⬄ 🖫 🏊 🖫 All major cards

GRAN VIA
$$$ ★★★
GRAN VIA DE LES CORTS CATALANES 642, 08002
TEL 93 318 19 00
FAX 93 318 99 97
www.nnhotels.es
A modest establishment with just a hint of old-world elegance, this hotel is good value for money. An expansive lounge area opens out on to a roof terrace. Rooms are spacious and comfortable without being luxurious.

ⓘ 53 Metro: Línies 1, 2, & 3 (Catalunya) ⬄ 🖫 All major cards

GOYA
$$ ★
CARRER DE PAU CLARIS 74, 08010
TEL 93 302 25 65
FAX 93 412 04 35
www.hostalgoya.com
This quiet, family-run *hostal* is located on one of the most stylish streets in central Barcelona. From here, it's a quick walk to the Barri Gòtic and La Pedrera,. Try to reserve one of the renovated rooms, decorated with warm parquet floors. Some have balconies.

ⓘ 19 Metro: Línies 2, 3, & 4 (Universitat) ⬄ 🖫 All major cards

RESTAURANTS

BOTAFUMEIRO
$$$$
CARRER GRAN DE GRÀCIA 81, 08012
TEL 93 218 42 30
Long one of the best *locales* for seafood in the best maritime style of Galicia (northwestern Spain), the infinite variety of watery critters is impressive. They wash down with almost excessive ease with some fine Ribeiro whites.

🪑 300 Metro: Línia 3 (Fontana) 🕐 Closed Aug.
🖫 All major cards

SOMETHING SPECIAL

LA DAMA
Housed in a fine *modernista* mansion, the Gaudí-inspired Casa Sayrach, this is a luxury establishment with a penchant for Catalan-French cuisine and an extensive wine list. Michelin has awarded the restaurant a star.
$$$$
AVINGUDA DIAGONAL 423, 08036
TEL 93 202 06 86
🪑 50 Metro: Línia 3 (Diagonal); Bus: 6, 7, 15, 27, 33, 34, & 68 🖫 All major cards

JAUME DE PROVENÇA
$$$$
CARRER DE PROVENÇA 88, 08029
TEL 93 430 00 29
Once a star in Barcelona's gastronomical firmament, this classic dining hall with old-fashioned waiters is nevertheless one of the best places in town for excellent Spanish cooking. If you need more proof, it is one of seven in the city to get a Michelin star.

🪑 70 Metro: Línia 1 (Rocafort) 🕐 Closed D Sun., Mon., Easter, Aug., & Christmas & Boxing Days
🖫 All major cards

JEAN LUC FIGUERAS
$$$$
CARRER DE SANTA TERESA 10, 08012
TEL 93 415 28 77
Try the crayfish cannelloni and you'll soon want to taste other dishes on the imaginative menu of this comfortable little restaurant. You'll hit further high notes for dessert, and the wine list is strong. Michelin thinks it worth a star.

🪑 50 Metro: Línia 3 (Diagonal) 🕐 Closed L Sat., Sun., 1 week in Jan., Easter week, & 2 weeks in Aug.
🖫 All major cards

ROIG ROBÍ
$$$$
CARRER DE SÉNECA 20, 08006
TEL 93 218 92 22
A table by the quaint internal courtyard for some of Barcelona's rice dishes is just what the doctor ordered. Not that rice is the only item on the menu. How about delicate meatballs of cod with mushrooms and cuttlefish?

🪑 50 Metro: Línia 3 (Diagonal or Fontana) 🕐 Closed L Sat., Sun., & half of Aug. 🖫 All major cards

CINC SENTITS
$$$
CARRER D'ARIBAU 58, 08036
TEL 93 323 94 90
It's as though they wanted

🚭 Nonsmoking 🅰 Air-conditioning 🏊 Indoor/🏊 Outdoor swimming pool 🖫 Health club 🖫 Credit cards   **KEY**

to strip away all the fluff that sometimes accompanies New Wave eateries. In a stripped-back, well-lit setting, you treat your five senses (hence the place's name) to an international culinary adventure. Take a punt on the omakase tasting menu, in which the best daily ingredients are used to create surprise dishes.

🍴 38 🚇 Metro: Línies 1 & 2 (Universitat) ⊕ Closed Sun. & D Mon. 🅰 All major cards

🍴 OROTAVA
$$$
CARRER DEL CONSELL DE CENT 335, 08007
TEL 93 487 73 74
Meat, venison in particular, features strongly at this long-lived family temple to good eating. Sybarites will also be spoiled for choice when it comes to selecting wines, and while waiting for it all to arrive you can admire changing exhibitions of local artists' work on the walls.

🍴 120 🚇 Metro: Línies 2, 3, & 4 (Passeig de Gràcia) ⊕ Closed Sun. 🅰 All major cards

🍴 THAI GARDENS
$$$
CARRER DE LA DIPUTACIÓ 273, 08007
TEL 93 487 98 98
For a change from European cooking, this is a stylish (and Barcelona's only) ambassador for Thai cooking. Tables are arranged amid jungles of greenery in a light, airy, and spacious interior. The dishes are of high quality.

🍴 200 🚇 Metro: Línies 2, 3, & 4 (Passeig de Gràcia) ⊕ Closed New Year's Day 🅰 All major cards

🍴 TRAGALUZ
$$$
PASSATGE DE LA CONCEPCIÓ 5, 08008
TEL 93 487 01 96
Here you can enjoy light dining in a lavish and stylish setting. Dishes range from

vaguely Italian dishes to non-Mediterranean numbers such as chicken breasts and chutney. The apple pie with caramel ice cream is excellent. A good Japanese restaurant across the road is under the same management.

🍴 100 🚇 Metro: Línies 2, 3, & 4 (Passeig de Gràcia) 🅰 All major cards

🍴 CAN JUANITO
$$
CARRER DE RAMON I CAJAL 3, 08012
TEL 93 213 30 43
For its high-quality Catalan cooking with fresh market products, little pretense, and warm, cozy atmosphere, this is a longtime favorite with Barcelonians. The walls are covered with plates signed by visiting celebrities.

🍴 80 🚇 Metro: Línia 3 (Fontana) ⊕ Closed D Sun., Mon., Easter week, Christmas & Boxing Days 🅰 AE, MC, V

🍴 RESTAURANT DE L'ESCOLA DE RESTAURACIÓ I HOSTALATGE
$$
CARRER DE MUNTANER 70-72, 08011
TEL 93 453 29 03
The waiters and cooks learning their trade here may not always get everything spot on, but solid and frequently inventive cooking and enthusiastic staff make this place worth seeking out, especially for lunch.

🍴 50 🚇 Metro: Línies 1 & 2 (Universitat) ⊕ Closed weekends & mid-July–mid-Sept. 🅰 All major cards

🍴 L'HOSTAL DE RITA
$
CARRER D'ARAGÓ 279, 08007
TEL 93 487 23 76
An institution in Barcelona, you will almost always find lines outside for Rita's great home Catalan cooking. Across the road at No. 282 the same people run the

Restaurant Madrid Barcelona, where the lines are handled with little cardboard stools perched outside. In either case you will walk away (once you have managed to get inside—book ahead!) satisfied. So many Barcelonians can't be wrong!

🍴 120 🚇 Metro: Línies 2, 3, & 4 (Passeig de Gràcia) 🅰 MC, V

SAGRADA FAMÍLIA TO PARC GÜELL

Although there are few hotels of note in the area around the two Gaudí sensations, a handful of great dining experiences await.

HOTELS

🏨 HISPANOS SIETE SUIZA
$$$ ★★★
CARRER DE SICILIA 255, 08025
TEL 93 208 20 51
FAX 93 208 20 52
www.hispanos7suiza.com
The vintage cars that adorn the ground floor of this unique option set the scene. A brisk walk from the Sagrada Familia and with its own fine restaurant, this home away from home offers apartment-sized rooms with kitchens that can accommodate up to four guests.

🛏 19 🚇 Metro: Línies 2 & 5 (Sagrada Familia) 🅿 ⬍ ⊕ 🅰 All major cards

RESTAURANTS

SOMETHING SPECIAL

🍴 EL RACÓ D'EN FREIXA
A deserved Michelin star goes to this, one of Barcelona's finest restaurants. Inventive and exquisitely presented dishes (try the rice with almonds, zucchini, and Parmesan cheese) are brought to you with alacrity and considerable style.
$$$$
CARRER DE SANT ELIES 22-26, 08006
TEL 93 209 75 59

40 FGC: Sant Gervasi Closed D Sun. & holidays, Mon., Easter week, & Aug. All major cards

---

JAIZQUIBEL
$$$
CARRER DE SICÍLIA 180, 08013
TEL 93 231 32 62
Long before Basque tapas bars became hip, this place far from the tourist crowds was regaling its aficionados with fine seafood bar snacks and wonderful dining. The fish dishes are what the house does best.
35 Metro: Línia 1 (Arc de Triomf) Closed D Sun., Mon., & 2 weeks in Aug. All major cards

NORTHERN BARCELONA

Big, comfortable, but frequently characterless hotels dot the broad Avinguda Diagonal on its journey from the city outskirts and highways into the heart of the city. In the broad sweep of northern Barcelona, you can also find the occasional culinary gem, although at night most of this area is distinctly lacking in atmosphere.

HOTELS

REY JUAN CARLOS I
$$$$$ ★★★★★
AVINGUDA DIAGONAL 661-671, 08034
TEL 93 364 40 40
FAX 93 364 42 64
www.hrjuancarlos.com
Out on the edge of the city, this place is a businessman's high-rise luxury establishment. Rooms are gathered around open glass galleries that look out over the city or into the foyer.
419 Metro: Línia 3 (Zona Universitària); Bus: 67 & 68 P All major cards

COVADONGA
$$$ ★★★
AVINGUDA DIAGONAL 596, 08021
TEL 93 209 55 11
FAX 93 209 58 33
www.hcchotels.es
Set in a classic, early 1900 building, this fine mid-range hotel is in one of the most sought-after parts of uptown Barcelona. The rooms were overhauled in 2003.
101 Bus: 6, 7, 15, 33, 34, 63, 67, & 68 All major cards

RESTAURANTS

NEICHEL
$$$$
CARRER DE BELTRÁN 1 RÓZPIDE 16 BIS, 08034
TEL 93 203 84 08
This is the only restaurant in town that can boast two Michelin stars. Try the cheese trolley, loaded with local and French varieties, or the specialty dish, filleted pigeon.
55 Metro: Línia 3 (Palau Reial); Bus: 63 & 114 Closed Sun., Mon., holidays, Easter, & Aug. All major cards

VIA VENETO
$$$$
CARRER DE GANDUXER 10, 08021
TEL 93 200 72 44
If you asked some local gourmets where to go if you only had one night in the city, many would select the Via Veneto. Refined Catalan cuisine has been the mainstay here for more than 30 years. Service is impeccable, the wine selection top-notch, and the desserts sublime.
200 Bus: 6, 7, 15, 27, 33, 34, & 68 Closed L Sat., Sun., & Aug. 1–20 All major cards

SOMETHING SPECIAL

LA BALSA
The views and atmosphere of La Balsa alone, set in a splen-

did building amid dense vegetation, make this an attractive stop. Dishes vary regularly and the cuisines inspiring the chefs range from the Basque country to Italy, via Catalunya and France.
$$$
CARRER DE L'INFANTA ISABEL 4, 08022
TEL 93 211 50 48
76 (110 in summer) FGC: Tibidabo Closed Sun., L Mon., & Easter (buffet only in Aug.) AE, MC, V

PEIXEROT
$$$
CARRER DE TARRAGONA 177, 08014
TEL 93 424 69 69
For genuine catch-of-the day fish and seafood prepared in the most succulent manner, this place is one of the best addresses in town. The location may not excite, but the palate will definitely be gratified.
240 Metro: Línies 3 & 5 (Sants Estació) Closed D Sun. & Mon. (D Sat. & Sun. in Aug.) All major cards

MONTJUÏC

One of the city's green lungs, the parklands of Montjuïc clearly offer few options for sleeping or eating, but one or two alternatives suggest themselves lower down the slopes, especially in the area known as Poble Sec.

RESTAURANTS

ELCHE
$$
CARRER DE VILA I VILÀ 71, 08004
TEL 93 441 30 89
Named after a town in the region of Valencia, the home of paella, the Elche continues to live up to a long-established reputation for being one of the best places for paella and other rice-based dishes.
70 Metro: Línia 3 (Paral.lel) AE, MC, V

SHOPPING IN BARCELONA

Barcelona thinks of itself as the style capital of Spain, much in the way Milan is the fashion capital of Italy. You'll find just about every conceivable kind of store, ranging from local junk markets to cutting-edge design, from traditional foods to African crafts. A great deal of the big-name stores, especially in Spanish and foreign fashion and design, line a long, two-pronged axis that stretches up Passeig de Gràcia from Plaça de Catalunya and turns left along Avinguda Diagonal, along which it continues (with some interruptions) as far as Plaça de la Reina Maria Cristina. Most shops accept credit cards. Non-EU citizens can claim back the sales tax (IVA) on personal purchases more than 90.15 euros made at shops displaying the Europe Tax Free Shopping sticker. You need to keep the till receipt and, where possible, obtain a tax refund form for presentation to customs at the airport before you leave Spain.

OPENING HOURS & SERVICE

Shop opening hours vary enormously. Big department stores are generally open all day from about 10 a.m.–9 p.m. Most other shops tend to open from around 8 a.m.–8 p.m., with a two- or three-hour break from 1:30 p.m. or 2 p.m. Nearly all stores open on Saturday morning but relatively few in the afternoon. Sunday trading is still unusual.

If you are used to the sunny standards of service common in North America, the situation in Barcelona can at times seem a little dire. In much the same way as waiting staff in many restaurants, shop assistants in some instances do not see the customer as coming first. Don't take it personally though; it's just the way it is here sometimes. That said, in many stores the staff is helpful and obliging, so it can all be a bit hit-and-miss.

ANTIQUE SHOPS & MARKETS

As a rule, picking up a bargain in antiques in Barcelona is a tough assignment. There are two main areas to look around. In the Barri Gòtic, Carrer dels Banys Nous is the obvious starting point. It is lined with antique shops. A couple of nearby streets, like Carrer de la Palla, are also home to a few interesting stores. Metro: Línia 3 (Liceu).

The other concentration of around 70 antiques shops is the **Bulevard des Antiquaris,** located in the Bulevard Rosa shopping center on Passeig de Gràcia. Some stores specialize in antique jewelry, crystal, porcelain, and so on, while others are more general.

If you want to spend a morning trawling through junk (of varying quality) then the **Els Encants** market on the northern side of the huge traffic circle Plaça de les Glòries Catalanes is the place to go. Metro: Línia 1 (Glòries). For more on markets around Barcelona, see pages 136–37.

ART GALLERIES

Three general areas suggest themselves for browsing.

The first is **Carrer de Montcada** (see pp. 124–29), where interspersed between the Picasso gallery and other museums you will find several private collections and commercial galleries. Because so much tourist traffic gets down here you should be circumspect about any purchases

Around the **MACBA,** especially in Carrer del Doctor Dou, Carrer d'Elisabets, and Carrer dels Àngels, are several contemporary art galleries. Another concentration is on and near the strip of **Carrer del Consell de Cent** between Rambla de Catalunya and Carrer de Balmes.

BOOKS

Altaïr Gran Via de les Corts Catalanes 616, 08007, tel 93 324 71 71, metro: Línies 1 & 2 (Universitat).
This is easily the city's most complete travel book store. If hanging around Barcelona has given you an appetite to travel more, this is the place to whet your interest with guides and other material in English.

Casa del Libro Passeig de Gràcia 62, 08007, tel 93 272 34 80, metro: Línies 2, 3, & 4 (Passeig de Gràcia)
This is one of the best-stocked general bookstores in town, with reasonable foreign language sections, a plethora of material on Barcelona, and plenty of general literature.

Come In Carrer de Provença 203, 08008, tel 93 453 12 04, metro: Línies 3 & 5 (Diagonal); FGC: Provença.
Plenty of books on Spain, as well as a selection of fiction, mainly in English and French.

Elephant Carrer de la Creu dels Molers 12, 08004, tel 93 443 05 94, metro: Línia 3 (Poble Sec)
A knock-about sort of place where you can buy and unload books predominantly in English, Elephant is tucked away on a side street of Rumbling Avinguda del Para.lel.

Laie Carrer de Pau Claris 85, 08010, tel 93 302 73 10, metro: Línies 1, 2, & 3 (Catalunya).
Novels and books on architecture, art, and film in English, French, Spanish, and Catalan. Upstairs is a cozy café where you can sip hot chocolate over the paper or look through your latest book purchases.

Llibreria de la Virreina Palau de la Virreina, La Rambla de Sant Josep 99, 08002, tel 93 301 77 75, metro: Línia 3 (Liceu).
Selection of architecture and art history books, many with Barcelona or Catalan themes.

Quera Carrer de Petritxol 2, 08002, tel 93 318 07 43, metro: Línia 3 (Liceu).
This is one of Barcelona's top specialists in maps and guides,

including hiking in Catalunya and beyond its borders.

CLOTHING

If you came to Barcelona but your shopping soul really wanted to be in Italy, never fear, for several of the big names in Italian fashion are represented here. Armani, Versace, Gucci, and Benetton are all scattered about town, especially along Avinguda Diagonal. They mix with other international names such as Calvin Klein and Jean Paul Gaultier. There's plenty of tempting local fashion too. Check out some of these below:

Adolfo Domínguez Passeig de Gràcia 32, 08007, tel 93 487 41 70, metro: Línies 3 & 5 (Diagonal).

Since the 1980s, this store, which took off in Galicia in Spain's northwest, has maintained a prominent international profile as a purveyor of fine men's and women's clothing. The materials used are high quality and the designs contemporary but restrained.

Antonio Miró Carrer del Consell de Cent 349, 08007, tel 93 487 06 70, metro: Línies 2, 3, & 4 (Passeig de Gràcia).

One of Catalunya's leading fashion designers, Miró combines a certain stylish conservatism with a light Mediterranean touch. The store offers a range of men's and women's clothing along with shoes and accessories.

Custo Barcelona Plaça de les Olles 7, tel 93 268 78 93, metro: Línia 4 (Jaume I).

A local fashion label aimed mostly at a young, uninhibited set with a love of splashy color, Custo Barcelona has taken world catwalks by storm and is opening stores around the globe. This is home base.

Mango Passeig de Gràcia 21, 08007, tel 93 215 75 30, metro: Línies 2, 3, & 4 (Passeig de Gràcia).

Another home-grown fashion success story that has become

an international household name in smart gear. This flagship store (there are many around town) is in a *modernista* building and has a wide range of clothing and leather accessories on display.

Purificación García Passeig de Gràcia 21, 08007, tel 93 487 72 92, metro: Línies 2, 3, & 4 (Passeig de Gràcia).

Concentrating on attractive, mid-range women's fashions, Purificación García offers plenty of seasonal inspiration. Casual but dressy slacks, jackets, and somewhat more adventurous dresses are the mainstay. She does a growing range of accessories too.

Roser-Francesc Carrer de València 285, 08009, tel 93 459 14 53, metro: Línies 2, 3, & 4 (Passeig de Gràcia).

The owners of this store go to bat for established and rising names in the Spanish fashion industry.

Zara Passeig de Gràcia 16, 08007, tel 93 301 74 43, metro: Línies 2, 3, & 4 (Passeig de Gràcia).

This popular fashion chain for men, women, and children is one of Spain's international success stories. A big range of quality, if middle-of-the-road, clothing is available at reasonable prices. Other branches are scattered about the city.

CRAFTS

Casa Oliveras Carrer de la Dagueria 11, 08002, tel 93 315 19 05, metro: Línia 4 (Jaume I).

If you walk by here on a sunny summer's day, you may see the ladies out on the street busy making some lace. This place has been the shopping spot for lace since the 19th century.

Cereria Subirà Baixada de la Llibreteria 7, 08002, tel 93 315 26 06, metro: Línia 4 (Jaume I).

It's all a load of old wax to some, but to others the candle creations here are a marvel. This is one of the oldest businesses in the city, with roots in the 18th century.

DEPARTMENT STORES & SHOPPING CENTERS

Huge department stores and shopping malls are not as popular a phenomenon in Barcelona as in North America, although for better or worse the idea is catching on fast. The biggest national chain of such stores is **El Corte Inglés,** which has branches in several locations around town. The most central branch takes up a whole block on the east side of Plaça de Catalunya (Metro: Catalunya, tel 93 306 38 00). Since they couldn't fit all its departments into the one store, some (such as CDs, videos, electronics, and so on) are located in another branch at Avinguda del Portal del Àngel 19-21.

Another shopping emporium on this central square is **El Triangle,** which plays host to several stores such as Habitat (tel 93 301 74 84) and a branch of the French mega-store **FNAC** (tel 93 344 18 00), which sells books, CDs, and multimedia products.

The same competition between these stores is played out again along Avinguda Diagonal, where El Corte Inglés has two mega-stores, one at No. 471, near Plaça de Francesc Macià, and another at No. 617, off Plaça de la Reina Maria Cristina. FNAC is at No. 549, part of the immense **L'Illa del Diagonal** shopping complex, probably the most attractive of a handful of such shopping centers in the city. Metro: Línia 3 (Maria Cristina); bus: 6, 7, 27, 33, 34, & 127. A more discreet shopping arcade is **Bulevard Rosa,** Passeig de Gràcia 55, metro: Línies 2, 3, & 4 (Passeig de Gràcia).

HOUSEWARES & INTERIOR DESIGN

Vinçon Passeig de Gràcia 96, 08008, tel 93 215 60 50, metro: Línies 3 & 5 (Diagonal).

In this deceptively extensive store you'll find everything from stylish candles to designer kitchenware, from furniture items to lamps. The building once belonged to the painter Ramon Casas, one of the leading lights of the *modernista* movement in the late 19th and early 20th centuries.

When you're through with the shopping, head upstairs to the rear terrace area, from where you can get an unusual view of La Pedrera (see p. 145).

ArtQuitect Carrer de Çomerç 31, 08003, tel 93 268 30 96, metro: Línia 4 (Barceloneta).

If you are looking for some fresh ideas on bathroom beauty, this is the place to come. At ArcQuitect they have made the humble bathroom an object of imaginative, artistic creation.

Bd Ediciones de Diseño Carrer de Mallorca 291, 08037, tel 93 458 69 09, metro: Línies 3 & 5 (Diagonal); Línies 4 & 5 (Verdaguer).

Some of the city's top interior designers have contributed pieces to this extensive furniture and home accessories store. You may not wish to buy anything but anyone interested in home-making with style will want to browse here. The shop is in a *modernista* house built by Domènech i Montaner and restored in 1979.

JEWELRY

Forum Ferlandina Carrer de Ferlandina 31, 08001, tel 93 441 80 18, metro: Línies 1 & 2 (Universitat).

An intriguing den of contemporary jewelry design, this place doubles as a store and platform for artists working in decoration for the hands.

Joyería Bagués Passeig de Gràcia 41, 08007, tel 93 216 01 74, metro: Línies 2, 3, & 4 (Passeig de Gràcia).

This is one of Barcelona's prestige names in high-priced rocks. This branch is housed in the ground floor of the Casa Amatller, but others are scattered about the city

LEATHER

Loewe Avinguda Diagonal 570, 08021, tel 93 216 04 00, metro: Línia 3 (Diagonal); bus: 6, 7, 27, 33, 34, & 127.

One of Spain's leading and oldest fashion stores, this chain was founded in 1846. There's another branch, opened in 1943, in the *modernista* Casa Lleo Morera, Passeig de Gràcia 35. Loewe is especially known for its quality leather goods, in particular bags and jackets.

MUSIC

Sometimes you could almost be forgiven for thinking that medieval guild norms are still in force today. **Carrer dels Tallers** in El Raval should be renamed Carrer dels Discos (Records Street) for the concentration along most of its length of a dozen or so record stores. You can find anything from rare vinyl items to classical to hip-hop hits. Metro: Línies 1, 2, & 3 (Catalunya).

FNAC and **El Corte Inglés** (see Department Stores) have substantial CD collections.

PERFUME

Perfumería Coderch Carrer d'Aribau 114, 08036, tel 93 454 89 83, metro: Línia 5 (Hospital Clínic).

One of the city's long-established firms specializing in perfume distribution, Coderch has a broad selection of local and imported perfumes.

Regia Passeig de Gràcia 39, 08007, tel 93 216 01 21, metro: Línies 2, 3, & 4 (Passeig de Gràcia).

The top name in perfume in Barcelona, this branch of the store also houses a small perfume museum (see p. 154)

SHOES

Camper Carrer de València 249, 08007, tel 93 215 63 90, metro: Línies 2, 3, & 4 (Passeig de Gràcia).

One of the most successful shoe companies to come out of Spain, Camper started out decades ago as a family affair on Mallorca.

Farrutx Carrer de Rosselló 218, 08008, tel 93 215 06 85, metro: Línies 3 & 5 (Diagonal). Another Mallorcan success story, Farrutx concentrates on a more up-market base.

SOUVENIRS

High-quality and original souvenirs are on sale at shops in various museums and sights around town. Among those worth keeping an eye out for are Museu de Picasso, Fundació Joan Miró, MACBA, and La Pedrera.

STATIONERY

Papirum Baixada de la Llibreteria 2, 08002, tel 93 310 52 42, metro: Línia 4 (Jaume I).

An exquisite array of handmade stationery, picture frames, and decorative items made of paper.

Raima Carrer Comtal 27, 08002, tel 93 317 49 66, metro: Línies 1, 2, & 3 (Catalunya)

Another high-quality stationery shop, with items ranging from parchment to albums and notebooks of all sorts.

TASTE TREATS

El Celler-Gran Bodega del Maestrazgo Carrer de Sant Pere més Baix 90, 08003, tel 93 310 26 73, metro: Línies 1 & 4 (Urquinaona).

In this extensive wine cellar are stocked hundreds of types of Spanish wine, as well as several imported labels.

El Magnífico Carrer de l'Argentería 64, 08003, tel 93 319 60 81.

For about a century fine coffees have been roasted here.

Mas Saloni Carrer d'Enric Granados 68, 08008, tel 93 453 43 58, metro: Línies 3 & 5 (Diagonal).

Specialists in Catalan wines and *cava*, although the products of other Spanish regions and even a few French wines are stocked.

ENTERTAINMENT

Barcelonians may have a reputation in Spain for keeping their noses to the grindstone and even being a little dour, but compared with many European cities, Barcelona hops. Busy theater, dance, and concert calendars, with frequent appearances by international performers and companies, are counterbalanced by a frenetic nightlife, especially from Thursday to Saturday nights. It is not difficult to stay out for the entire evening. Although not as wild as Madrid or one or two other Spanish cities, Barcelona offers more than enough to keep all but the most demanding partyers content.

Details of what's on are available from several sources. The weekly *Guía del Ocio* is the city's main entertainment guide, although it is far from complete. For the day's theater and cinema listings you can check the daily papers; the best and clearest listings pages *(cartelera)* are those in *El País*. For the latest news on what's cool in bars, clubs, and the like, you need to track down a couple of hard-to-find free listings publications. *Micro* and *Go Mag* are just two. They are distributed among bars and clubs, especially in the Born and El Raval, but stumbling across them is hit-and-miss.

Barcelona's theater and concert season gets under way in late September to early October and stretches into May and June. This period is marked by several highlight moments, such as **BAM** (Barcelona Acció Musical), a series of concerts (many free) staged across the city for the Festes de la Mercè in the second half of September (for more on Barcelona's festivals see pp. 50–53.) From late October to late November, the city stages the **Festival Internacional de Jazz de Barcelona**, when the city's bars and other venues hum to the sounds of jazz musicians from around the country and abroad. In June, Europe's biggest electronic music fest, **Sonar**, is staged in Barcelona.

Even in the hot months of summer all is not over, for between June and August a dense program of theater, dance, and music comes to town in the shape of the **Festival del Grec**, named after the amphitheater on Montjuïc where some of the performances are held.

Year-round the cinema offerings in Barcelona are top notch. What's more, Barcelonians *like* seeing movies in the original language with subtitles. Several cinemas cater to this taste, and lines of locals and foreigners alike are not uncommon.

Live music and dance venues, bars and taverns of all descriptions, and plenty of clubs cater to the nocturnal needs of just about everyone.

Tickets *(entradas)* for theater, concerts, and so on can be bought at the theaters concerned, but it is frequently easier to use ticket sales services. Tickets can be purchased at the main tourist office at Plaça de Catalunya 17-S (where half-price tickets are available for some shows), as well as the municipal information office in the Palau de la Virreina, La Rambla de Sant Josep 99, tel 93 301 77 75. Branches of the FNAC store also sell tickets, as does El Corte Inglés on Plaça de Catalunya.

Finally, the most common service used is the Caixa de Catalunya bank's Tel-Entrada service at tel 90 210 12 12, or on the Internet at www.telentrada.com. You make a booking with a credit card and pick up the tickets from the theater up to an hour before the show. Some theaters use an alternative service, the Servicaixa, tel 90 233 22 11.

BARS

The city is crawling with bars, from the grungy daytime spit-and-sawdust variety to trendy late-night cocktail joints. What follows is a brief selection.

Bar Marsella Carrer de Sant Pau 65, 08001, tel 93 442 72 63, metro: Línia 3 (Liceu).
A Frenchman from Marseille opened this place in 1820 and introduced the drinking of absinthe to Barcelona. Nothing seems to have changed since.

Bar Pastís Carrer de Santa Mònica 4, 08001, tel 93 318 79 80, metro: Línia 3 (Drassanes).
The theme of this conspiratorial little drinking corner is French singer Edith Piaf and the music French cabaret (except for tango nights on Tuesday)

Casa Almirall Carrer de Joaquim Costa 33, 08001, metro: Línies 1 & 2 (Universitat).
With its dark *modernista* décor, this old bar has been a haunt of locals since the 1860s.

CDLC Passeig Maritim 32, 08003, tel 93 224 04 70, metro: Línia 4 (Ciutadella-Villa Olímpica).
One of several chill-out lounge bars and clubs stacked up together on the waterfront on the Barceloneta side of Port Olímpic, this is a hip spot for sundown drinks.

Gimlet Carrer del Rec 24, 08003, tel 93 310 10 27, metro: Línia 4 (Barceloneta).
Born in the 1970s, this is a classic, melancholy cocktail bar. One might almost expect Humphrey Bogart to sidle up to the bar.

La Vinya del Senyor Plaça de Santa Maria del Mar 5, 08003, tel 93 310 33 79, metro: Línia 4 (Jaume I).
An enormous wine list to savor either inside or outside in the shadow of the grand Santa Maria del Mar church.

Michael Collins Pub Plaça de la Sagrada Família 4, 08013, tel 93 459 19 64, metro: Línies 2 & 5 (Sagrada Família).
Of the swelling ranks of Irish and Anglo-style pubs in town, this is one of the best. In the shadows of the towers of the city's most emblematic buildings, it is far from the madding crowds of the city center and attracts a busy mix of locals and expats.

ENTERTAINMENT

Schilling Carrer de Ferran 23, 08002, tel 93 317 67 87, metro: Línia 3 (Liceu).
Prominently located and lively with a mixed 30-something androgynous crowd.
Va de Vi Carrer dels Banys Vells 16, 08003, tel 93 319 29 00, metro: Línia 4 (Jaume I).
For a spot of wine tasting in a medieval setting, wander into this cavernous Gothic space. All dark stone and broad arches, it is perfect for a quiet, romantic drink over candlelight.
Vaixell Luz de Gas Port Vell, 08002, tel 93 209 77 11, metro: Línia 4 (Barceloneta).
On a summer evening, there is nowhere better for sipping a beer or cool white wine than this boat tied up in the Old Port near the Museu d'Història de Catalunya (see p. 113).

CLUBS

There is no shortage of dance clubs that go on until the sun comes up. A number of the live music places listed on page 263 double as clubs too. The Maremàgnum and Port Olímpic areas are crammed with late-night bars and dance clubs—a little tacky but they will keep you going for most of the night. A few more are listed here.

Arena Carrer de Balmes 32, 08007, tel 93 487 83 42, metro: Línies 1 & 2 (Universitat).
This is a popular gay club with a dark room, and is one of three Arena clubs within a couple of minutes' walk of one another. The others attract a more mixed clientele.
Discothèque Poble Espanyol, Avinguda del Marquès de Comillas, 08037, tel 93 423 12 85, metro: Línia 3 (Espanya).
One of the city's top clubs, this place draws a dance-eager posse from all over the city. In summer the outdoor version, Terrazza, opens up to equal acclaim.
Mirablau Plaça del Doctor Andreu, 08035, tel 93 418 58 79, taxi.
Dancing with the spectacular

view of nocturnal Barcelona laid out at your feet.
Otto Zutz Carrer de Lincoln 15, 08006, tel 93 238 07 22, FGC: Gràcia.
The beautiful people's club and possibly the best known club name in Barcelona.
Paloma Carrer del Tigre 27, 08001, tel 93 301 68 97, metro: Línies 1 & 2 (Universitat).
In the afternoons older folk still come here for old-time dancing, but late on Thursday to Saturday nights, it explodes with the latest club sounds, hosted by the Bongo Lounge team of DJs.
Sala Cibeles Carrer de Còrsega 363, 08037, tel 93 457 38 77, metro: Línies 3 & 5 (Diagonal).
This may look like an old-fashioned ballroom, but it has morphed into a top club stop on the Barcelona night circuit, especially on Friday nights.
The Sutton Club Carrer de Tusset 13, 08006, tel 93 414 42 17, metro: Línies 3 & 5 (Diagonal).
In this busy weekend nightlife area, the Sutton is one of the best club options. Bars ring the main dance area, a kind of pit of beautiful people.

FLAMENCO

Although more readily associated with Madrid and southern Spain, there is some tradition of flamenco among *Gitanos* (Gypsies) and Andalusian migrants long settled in and around Barcelona. Some of the great singers, guitarists, and dancers of flamenco were indeed born in Catalunya. The regular acts in the handful of flamenco places in town are often of indifferent to poor quality but occasionally quality performers come to town.
Cordobés La Rambla 35, 08002, tel 93 317 57 11, metro: Línia 3 (Liceu).
This place is more given to cheesy performances with a meal thrown in. Nevertheless, even here decent acts sometimes appear.

El Tablao de Carmen Carrer dels Arcs 9, 08038, tel 93 325 68 95, metro: Línies 1 & 3 (Espanya); bus 61.
In much the same vein as Cordobés, although don't expect to see anything but a tourist version of flamenco.
Sala Tarantos Plaça Reial 17, 08002, tel 93 318 30 67, metro: Línia 3 (Liceu).
Every now and then, serious flamenco musicians perform here. So of the readily available options, this place is probably the best bet. Usually shows are held on Friday and Saturday nights beginning about 11 p.m. The place later reverts to a dance club that goes on into the early hours.

MOVIE THEATERS

Several movie theater complexes offer eager local viewers the opportunity to see many mainstream and art house movies from abroad in the original language. Consequently, out-of-towners can catch recent movies in their own language too! In listings, movies shown in the original are identified with *v.o. (version original)*. During the week the last session tends to start around 10:30 p.m. On Friday and Saturday nights most movie theaters stage an extra late-night session, starting around 1 a.m. All of the following put on some movies with subtitles:
Casablanca Passeig de Gràcia 115, 08008, tel 93 218 43 45, metro: Línies 3 & 5 (Diagonal).
Filmoteca Avinguda de Sarrià 31-33, 08029, tel 93 410 75 90, metro: Línia 5 (Hospital Clinic).
This movie theater stages seasons that concentrate on particular directors, styles, and eras of film.
Icària-Yelmo Carrer de Salvador Espriu 61, 08005, tel 93 221 75 85, metro: Línia 4 (Ciutadella Vila Olímpica).
A major movie theater complex-mall striking for its lack of personality, it has plenty of movie options with five screens!

Méliès Cinemes Carrer de Villarroel 102, 08011, tel 93 451 00 51, metro: Línia 1 (Urgell). Old classics (subtitled), often from the halcyon days of black and white, are standard here.

Verdi Carrer de Verdi 32, 08012, tel 93 238 79 90, metro: Línia 3 (Fontana).

A handy location for post-movie eating and drinking in the surrounding streets and squares of Gràcia.

OPERA/DANCE/ CLASSICAL MUSIC

In addition to the venues listed here, performances are occasionally held in churches and other onetime locations. The acoustics of the Església de Santa Maria del Mar, for example, are nothing great, but such a setting for music recitals is inspirational!

Gran Teatre del Liceu La Rambla 51-59, 08002, tel 93 485 99 13, metro: Línia 3 (Liceu). Barcelona's grand establishment lyric theater. This is where the main opera season is staged, but classical music recitals and dance are also on the menu. Book well in advance for big-name companies, local or from abroad. (www.liceubarcelona.com)

L'Auditori Carrer de Lepant 150, 08018, tel 93 247 93 00, metro: Línia 1 (Glòries) or Línia 2 (Monumental).

Opened in the late 1990s, this is the city's main stage for fine listening, with a busy program of classical, chamber, religious, and other music. (www.auditori.org)

Palau de la Música Catalana Carrer Sant Francesc de Paula 2, 08003, tel 93 295 72 00, metro: Línies 1 & 4 (Urquinaona).

The acoustics have never been the best here, but the luxuriant *modernista* setting makes an evening of music unforgettable. (www.palaumusica.org)

POP/ROCK/JAZZ

Big local and international rock and pop acts tend to play in places like the **Palau Jordi**

sports arena (on Montjuïc), the **Mercat de les Flors** theater, and one or two other larger venues. Tickets are generally available at the ticketing agencies and centers that are named at the beginning of this section. Otherwise, you can hear live music on a more modest scale in locations around town, a few of which are listed below. Acts rarely come on stage much before 11 p.m.

Bikini Carrer de Deu i Mata 105, 08029, tel 93 322 08 00, metro: Línia 5 (Enteça) bus: 6, 7, 33, 34, 63, 67, & 68.

A multi-hall dance club that puts on concerts ranging from rock to blues.

Harlem Jazz Club Carrer de la Comtessa de Sobradiel 8, 08002, tel 93 310 07 55, metro: Línia 4 (Jaume I).

An old favorite with jazz hounds where you can be sure of good music, plenty of people, and the smoky atmosphere all jazz bars should have!

Jamboree Plaça Reial 17, 08002, tel 93 301 75 64, metro: Línia 3 (Liceu).

Before giving itself over to club music to carry on into the wee hours of the morning, this underground club stages a range of jazz and funk most nights.

Luz de Gas Carrer de Muntaner 246, 08021, tel 93 209 77 11, bus: 6, 7, 15, 33, 34, 63, 67, & 68.

Live soul, country, salsa, and rock most nights, followed by club sounds and dancing into the early hours.

Sala Apolo Carrer Nou de la Rambla 113, 08004, tel 93 301 00 90, metro: Línia 3 (Paral.lel). World music leads the way, which can mean everything from Latin to African beats. On weekends there is live salsa before this former old-time dance hall becomes a full-on club.

THEATER

The majority of theater in Barcelona is, quite naturally, either in Catalan or Spanish— which is great if you are looking

to practice one or the other of these languages. Occasionally, international acts come to town and perform in their native tongue (in which case simultaneous interpreting headsets may be distributed).

Mercat de les Flors Carrer de Lleida 59, 08004, tel 93 426 18 75, metro: Línia 3 (Poble Sec) bus 55.

A pleasing modern stage where everything from theater to dance and rock concerts are held. The theater has been expanded with a couple of smaller stages. (www.mercatflors.org)

Teatre Lliure Plaça de Margarida Xirgu s/n, 08004, tel 93 289 27 70, metro: Línia 3 (Poble Sec) bus: 55

Dedicated to theater in Catalan, it puts on classics, avant-garde, and everything in between. If you want to see theater in this language, this is the place to be. (www.teatrelliure.com)

Teatre Nacional de Catalunya Plaça de les Arts 1, 08018, tel 93 306 57 00, metro: Línies 1 (Glòries) or 2 (Monumental).

Ricard Bofill's grand national theater opened in 1997 and puts on a broad range of mainstream drama and occasionally dance performances on the smaller of its two stages. (www.tnc.es)

Teatre Tantarantana Carrer de les Flors 22, 08001, tel 93 441 70 22, metro: Línia 3 (Paral.lel). Although it indulges in much contemporary theater, this place is also worth watching for kids' shows, puppet shows, and similar events, which usually begin around 6 p.m. (www.tantarantana.com)

Teatre Victòria Avinguda del Paral.lel 67-69, 08004, tel 93 443 29 29, metro: Línia 3 (Paral.lel). Frequently a stage for ballet and dance, the theater regularly hosts such Barcelona favorites as Tricicle, a trio of comic mimes who transcend all linguistic barriers. (www.teatrevictoria.com)

LANGUAGE GUIDE

Barcelona is a bilingual city. Visitors with a reasonable grasp of Spanish will soon learn to distinguish it from the local tongue, Catalan (although some words are the same). Signs, menus, and so on increasingly appear exclusively in Catalan, so the following language guide and menu reader are given in Catalan/Spanish. See page 244.

USEFUL WORDS & PHRASES

Yes *si/sí*
No *no*
Excuse me *perdoni/perdone*
Hello (before lunch) *bon dia!/¡buenos días!*, (after lunch) *¡bona tarda!/¡buenas tardes!*
Hi *Hola!/¡hola!*
Please *si us plau/por favor*
Thank you *gracies/gracias*
You're welcome *de res/de nada*
OK *d'acord/de acuerdo*
Goodbye *adéu/adiós*
Good night *bona nit/buenas noches*
Sorry *ho sento/lo siento*
Here *aquí/aquí*
There *allà/allí*
Today *avui/hoy*
Yesterday *ahir/ayer*
Tomorrow *demà/mañana*
Now *ara/ahora*
Later *més tard/más tarde*
This morning *aquest matí/esta mañana*
This afternoon *aquesta tarda/esta tarde*
This evening *aquest vespre or aquesta nit/esta noche*
Open *obert/abierto*
Closed *tancat/cerrado*
Do you have? *¿Té?/¿Tiene?*
Do you speak English? *¿Parla anglès?/¿Habla inglés?*
I don't understand *No entenc/No entiendo*
Please speak more slowly *Si us plau, parli més a poc a poc/Por favor, hable más despacio*
Where is? *¿On és?/¿Donde está?*
I don't know *No ho sé/No lo sé*
That's it *Això mateix/Eso es*
What is your name? *¿Com es diu?/¿Como se llama?*
My name is… *Em dic…/Me llamo…*
At what time? *¿A quina hora?/¿A qué hora?*
When? *¿Quan?/¿Cuándo?*
What time is it? *¿Quina hora és?/¿Qué hora es?*
Can you help me? *¿Em pot ajudar?/¿Me puede ayudar?*
I'd like… *Voldria…/Quisiera…*
How much is it? *¿Quant costa?/¿Cuánto vale?*

MENU READER

breakfast *el esmorzar/el desayuno*
lunch *el dinar (el menjar)/el almuerzo (la comida)*
dinner *el sopar/la cena*
appetizer *l'entrant/el entrante*
first course *el primer/el primero*
main course *el segon/el segundo*
vegetable, side dish *la guarnició/la guarnición*
dessert *les postres/el postre*
menu *la carta*
wine list *la carta de vins/la carta de vinos*
the check *el compte/la cuenta*
I'd like to order *Ja pot prendre nota/Ya puede tomar nota*

DRINKS BEGUDES/BEBIDAS

water *aigua/agua*
orange juice *suc de taronja/zumo de naranja*
beer *cervesa/cerveza*
white wine *vi blanc/vino blanco*
red wine *vi negre/vino tinto*
coffee *cafè/café*
short black coffee *cafè sol*
tea *tè/té*
with milk *amb llet/con leche*
with lemon *amb llimona/con limón*

SAUCES SALSES/SALSAS

allioli pounded garlic with olive oil, often with egg yolk added
picada ground almonds, with garlic, parsley, pine, or hazel nuts
romesco almond, tomato, olive oil, garlic, and vinegar sauce
sofregit onion, tomato, and garlic

CLASSICS CLÀSSICS/CLÁSICOS

Fideuà vermicelli noodle-based dish with seafood or cooked in the black ink of cuttlefish
Paella originally from Valencia but now a national dish. The original version mixed seafood with saffron rice. In Catalunya, variations include different combinations of seafood and/or meat. The Catalan dishes go by the name of *arròs a la…*(whatever it may be)
Truita/tortilla omelette (with potatoes it is *tortilla española*)

MEAT CARN/CARNE

anyell/cordero lamb
ànec/pato duck
bistec beefsteak
bou/buey bull (beef)
conill/conejo rabbit
fetge/higado liver
guatlle/codorniz quail
perdiu/perdiz partridge
pernil/jamón ham
ronyons/riñones kidneys
vedella/ternera veal
porc/cerdo pork
pollastre/pollo chicken
salxitxa/salsicha sausage (of which there are many types!)

SEAFOOD MARISCOS

bacallà/bacalao salted cod
cloïsses/almejas clams
cranc/cangrejo crab
gambes/gambas prawns
llagosta/langosta lobster
lluç/merluza cod
musclos/mejillones mussels
ostres/ostras oysters
pop/pulpo octopus
tonyina/atún or bonito tuna

VEGETABLES VERDURES/VERDURAS

albergínia/berenjena eggplant
all/ajo garlic
amanida/ensalada salad
arròs/arroz rice
bolets/setas mushrooms
carxofa/alcachofa artichoke
ceba/cebolla onion
pastanaga/zanahoria carrot
pèsols/guisantes peas

FRUIT FRUITES/FRUTAS

cireres/cerezas cherries
maduixes/fresas strawberries
pinya/piña pineapple
poma/manzana apple
préssec/melocotón peach
raïm/uva grapes
taronja/naranja orange

IILLUSTRATIONS CREDITS

Illustrations credits
Abbreviations for terms appearing below: (t) top; (b) bottom; (l) left; (r) right; (c) center

Cover (l), Art Directors and Trip/M. Feeney. (c), David Alan Harvey/National Geographic Society. (r), Pictures Colour Library.

1, S. L. Day/AA Photo Library. 2/3, Victor Sarto. 4, Tino Soriano/Victor Sarto. 9, Index. 11, Victor Sarto. 12/13, M. Feeney/Trip & Art Directors Photo Library. 14/15, Rosmi Duaso/Fototext. 16/17, Rosmi Duaso/Fototext. 18/19, Nik Wheeler/Corbis. 20/21, Mike Hewitt/Allsport/Firofoto. 22/23, Index. 24, Rosmi Duaso/Fototext. 25, Index. 26/27, Index. 27, Rosmi Duaso/Fototext. 28, Rosmi Duaso/Fototext. 29, Index. 30/31, A. Guinart/Victor Sarto. 32/33, Index. 34/35, Index. 35, Index. 36, Index. 36/37, Rosmi Duaso/Fototext. 39, Rosmi Duaso/Fototext. 40/41, Rosmi Duaso/Fototext. 42, S. L. Day/AA Photo Library. 44/45, David Campos/Museu d'Art Contemporani de Barcelona (MACBA). 46/47, B. Cruells/Firofoto. 48, Philippe Halsman/Magnum Photos. 49, Hulton-Deutsch Collection/Corbis. 50/51, Rosami Duaso/Fototext. 52, Rosami Duaso/Fototext. 53, Xavier Marti Alavedra/Fototext. 54, M. Chaplow/AA Photo Library. 55, Michelle Chaplow/Andalucia Slide Library. 56, Rosmi Duaso/Fototext. 57, S. L. Day/AA Photo Library. 58, Ulrike Welsch. 60, A. Guinart/Victor Sarto. 61, S. L. Day/AA Photo Library. 62, Jaume Balanya/Victor Sarto. 64, S. L. Day/AA Photo Library. 65, Jeffrey Aaronson/Network Aspen. 66, Barcelona City Council. 67, A. Guinart/Victor Sarto. 68/69, A. Guinart/Victor Sarto. 70, P. Kenward/AA Photo Library. 70/71, Tino Soriano/Victor Sarto. 71, Rosmi Duaso/Fototext. 72, Index. 73, A. Guinart/Victor Sarto. 74, M. Jourdan/AA Photo Library. 75tl, A. Guinart/Victor Sarto. 75tr, Rosmai Duaso/Fototext. 75b, Saray Lozano/Victor Sarto. 76, A. Guinart/Victor Sarto. 77, S. L. Day/AA Photo Library. 78, S. L. Day/AA Photo Library. 79, S. L. Day/AA Photo Library. 80t, S. L. Day/AA Photo Library. 80b, Mecky Fögeling. 81, A. Guinart/Victor Sarto. 82, Dani Codina/Fototext. 83, Dani Codina/Fototext. 85, S. L. Day/AA Photo Library. 86, M. Jourdan/AA Photo Library. 88, Robert Frerck/Odyssey

Productions, Inc. 89, S. L. Day/AA Photo Library. 90/91, Rosami Duaso/Fototext. 91, Martin Hughes/Lonely Planet Images. 92, Index. 93, M. Jourdan/AA Photo Library. 94, Tino Soriano/Victor Sarto. 95t, Gregor M. Schmid/Corbis. 95b, Miguel Raurich/Iberimage. 96, A. Guinart/Victor Sarto. 97, Heinz Hebeisen/Iberimage. 98, Rosmi Duaso/Fototext. 99, Tino Soriano/Victor Sarto. 101, H.G. Schmidt/Travel Library. 102, Museum Maritim. 103, Museu Maritim. 104t, Museu Maritim Atarazanas, Barcelona, Catalunya, Spain/Bridgeman Art Library. 104b, Hulton Getty Picture Collection Ltd. 105, Francisco Ontanon/Getty Images. 106, M. Jourdan/AA Photo Library. 107, Terry Harris. 108/109, S. L. Day/AA Photo Library. 109t, M. Jourdan/AA Photo Library. 109b, M. Jourdan/AA Photo Library. 110, Biblioteca Nazionale, Turin, Italy/Bridgeman Art Library. 110/111, Library of Congress, Washington D.C., USA/Bridgeman Art Library. 111, Bernd Ducke/ Superbild Bildagentur. 112, M. Jourdan/AA Photo Library. 113t, Tino Soriano/Victor Sarto. 113b, S. L. Day/AA Photo Library. 114/115, Paul Murphy. 115, Grant Pritchard/Travel Library. 116, M. Jourdan/AA Photo Library. 117, A. Guinart/Victor Sarto. 119, Rosmi Duaso/Fototext. 120/121, P. Krisan/Firofoto. 121, Dani Codina/Fototext. 122, Index. 123t, Institut Amatiller d'Art Hispanic (MAS). 123b, Erich Lessing/Art Resource, NY. 124/125, Dani Codina/ Fototext. 125, Francis G. Mayer/ Corbis. 126, Miguel Raurich/ Iberimage. 127, Grant Pritchard/ Travel Library. 128, Rosmi Duaso/ Fototext. 129t, Textile Museum, Barcelona, Spain/Bridgeman Art Library. 129b, Rosmi Duaso/Fototext. 130, M Jourdan/AA Photo Library. 131, Rosmi Duaso/Fototext. 132t, M. Jourdan/AA Photo Library. 132b, Rosmi Duaso/Fototext. 133, A. Guinart/Victor Sarto. 134 Rosmi Duaso/Fototext. 135, Paul Murphy. 136, Rosmi Duaso/Fototext. 137tl, Rosmi Duaso/Fototext. 137tr, Ulrike Welsch. 137b, Rosmi Duaso/Fototext. 138, Rosmi Duaso/Fototext. 139, Victor Sarto. 140, Mecky Fögeling. 142, Hugh Rooney/Eye Ubiquitous. 143t, Jeremy Bright/Robert Harding Picture Library. 143b, Victor Sarto. 144, Firofoto. 145, R. Campillo/Victor Sarto. 146, Keith Russell. 147, S. L. Day/AA Photo Library. 148, H. Spichtinger/zefa/Corbis. 149t, Tino Soriano/Victor Sarto. 149b, Firofoto. 150, A. Guinart/Victor Sarto. 150/ 151, A.

Guinart/Victor Sarto. 152/153, David Alan Harvey/ Magnum Photos. 153, Rosmi Duaso/ Fototext. 154, Tino Soriano/Victor Sarto. 155, S. L. Day/AA Photo Library. 156, Rosmi Duaso/Fototext. 158, Grant Pritchard/Travel Library. 159, Rosmi Duaso/Fototext. 160t, P. Wilson/AA Photo Library. 160b, Getty Images. 161, Anders Blomqvist. 162, M. Jourdan/AA Photo Library. 163, S. L. Day/AA Photo Library. 164, Archivo Iconografico, S.A/Corbis UK Ltd.. 165t, S. L. Day/AA Photo Library. 165b, Rosmi Duaso/Fototext. 166, Michelle Chapman/Andalucia Slide Library. 166/167, Terry Harris. 168, John Dakers/Eye Ubiquitous. 169t, Victor Sarto. 169b, Rosmi Duaso/Fototext. 170, Dani Codina/Fototext. 171, S. L. Day/AA Photo Library. 174/175, Paul Murphy. 175, S. L. Day/AA Photo Library. 176t, S. L. Day/AA Photo Library. 176b, Rosmi Duaso/Fototext. 177, Firofoto. 178t, Index. 178b, Dani Codina/Fototext. 179, S. L. Day/AA Photo Library. 180, P. Wilson/AA Photo Library. 181, S. L. Day/AA Photo Library. 182, Paul Murphy. 183, S. L. Day/AA Photo Library. 184, Victor Sarto. 186, David Barnes/Stone. 187, Index. 188t, Museu de Arte de Catalunya, Barcelona, Spain/Bridgeman Art Library. 188b, Museo de Arte de Catalunya, Barcelona, Spain/Bridgeman Art Library. 189, Museu Nacional d' Art de Catalunya. 190, Miguel Raurich/Iberimage. 191t, S. L. Day/AA Photo Library. 191b, Paul Murphy. 192, Danita Delimont/Alamy. 193, A. Guinart/Victor Sarto. 194/195, Robert Frerck/ Odyssey Productions, Inc. 197, Nik Wheeler/Corbis. 198t, Heinz Hebeisen/Iberimage. 198b, S. L. Day/AA Photo Library. 199, A. Guinart/Victor Sarto. 200, S. L. Day/AA Photo Library. 201, A. Guinart/Victor Sarto. 203, Rosmi Duaso/Fototext. 204, Rosmi Duaso/Fototext. 205, A. Guinart/Victor Sarto. 206, Rosmi Duaso/Fototext. 207, Pictures Colour Library. 209t, Index. 209b, Marti Alaverda/Fototext. 211t, P. Wilson/AA Photo Library. 211b, Rosmi Duaso/Fototext. 212, Rosmi Duaso/Fototext. 212/213, Rosmi Duaso/Fototext. 214, A Guinart/ Victor Sarto. 215t, Index. 215b, Rosmi Duaso/Fototext. 216, P. Enticknap/AA Photo Library. 217, P. Wilson/AA Photo Library. 218t, Rosmi Duaso/ Fototext. 218b, Dani Codina/ Fototext. 219, Index. 221, Index. 222/223, Index. 224, P. Enticknap/AA Photo Library. 225, Museu del Cinema. 226t, M.

The world's largest nonprofit scientific and educational organization, the National Geographic Society was founded in 1888 "for the increase and diffusion of geographic knowledge." Since then it has supported scientific exploration and spread information to its more than nine million members worldwide.

The National Geographic Society educates and inspires millions every day through magazines, books, television programs, videos, maps and atlases, research grants, the National Geographic Bee, teacher workshops, and innovative classroom materials.

The Society is supported through membership dues, charitable gifts, and income from the sale of its educational products. Members receive NATIONAL GEOGRAPHIC magazine —the Society's official journal— discounts on Society products, and other benefits.

For more information about the National Geographic Society, its educational programs, publications, or how to support its work, call 1-800-NGS-LINE (647-5463), or write to: National Geographic Society, 1145 17th Street, N.W., Washington, D.C. 20036 U.S.A.

Published by the National Geographic Society

John M. Fahey, Jr., *President and Chief Executive Officer*

Gilbert M. Grosvenor, *Chairman of the Board*

Nina D. Hoffman, *Executive Vice President; President, Books and School Publishing*

Kevin Mulroy, *Senior Vice President and Publisher, Book Division*

Marianne Koszorus, *Design Director*

Kristin Hanneman, *Illustrations Director*

Elizabeth L. Newhouse, *Director of Travel Publishing*

Barbara A. Noe, *Series Editor*

Cinda Rose, *Art Director*

Carl Mehler, *Director of Maps*

Caroline Hickey, *Senior Researcher (2006 Ed. Coordinator)*

Gary Colbert, *Production Director*

Richard S. Wain, *Production Project Manager*

Rebecca Hinds, *Managing Editor*

Jennifer Davis, Steven D. Gardner, Robin Reid, Carol Stroud, Teresa Neva Tate, Ruth Thompson, Mapping Specialists, *Contributors to 2006 edition*

First edition edited and designed by AA Publishing (a trading name of Automobile Association Developments Limited, whose registered office is Millstream, Maidenhead Road, Windsor, England SL4 5GD. Registered number: 1878835).

Virginia Langer, *Project Manager*

David Austin, *Senior Art Editor*

Allen Stidwill, *Editor*

Keith Russell, *Designer*

Keith Brook, *Senior Cartographic Editor*

Cartography by AA Cartographic Production

Richard Firth, *Production Director*

Steve Gilchrist, *Prepress Production Controller*

Carol Walker, *Picture Research Manager*

Picture Research by Zooid Pictures Ltd.

Area and drive maps drawn by Chris Orr Associates, Southampton, England

Cutaway illustrations drawn by Maltings Partnership, Derby, England; pp. 62, 208–209, & 220–221

Second edition (2006)
ISBN: 0-7922-5365-5

ISSN 1538 5523 (1st edition)

Printed and bound by Cayfosa Quebecorp, Barcelona, Spain.
Color separations by Leo Reprographic Ltd., Hong Kong.
Cover separations by L.C. Repro, Aldermaston, U.K.

Visit the society's Web site at http://www.nationalgeographic.com

Printed in Spain

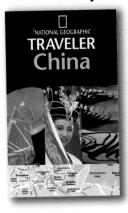

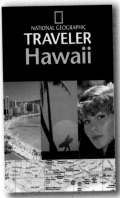